PORTLAND
HIKES

The Best Day-Hikes in Oregon and Washington Within 100 Miles of Portland

ART BERNSTEIN

AND

ANDREW JACKMAN

Mountain N' Air Books
P. O. . Box 12540
La Crescenta, CA 91224

Published in the United States of America by
Mountain N' Air Book—P. O. Box 12540, La Crescenta, CA 91224
Phones: (818) 951-4150, Fax (818) 951-4153
E-Mail address: mtn n air@aol.com

Cover photo: Corel Professional Photo CD-Rom Series 2000
Design: Cover and book layout by Gilberto d' Urso

Library of Congress Cataloging-in-Publication Data

Bernstein, Art .

   Portland Hikes: the best day-hikes in Oregon and Washington within 100 miles of
   Portland / Art Bernstein and Andrew Jackman. — 2nd ed.

      p.   cm.
   includes index.
   ISBN: 1-879415-22-4 (pbk.)
   1. Hiking — Oregon — Portland Metropolitan area — Guidebooks.
   2. Hiking Washington (State) — Guidebooks. 3. Portland Metropolitan Area (Or.)
   — Guidebooks. 4. Washington (State) — Guidebooks.

I. Jackman, Andrew. II. Title.

GV199.42.072P673   1997
917.95'490443—dc21   97-38136
                                                          CIP

ISBN: 1-879415-22-4

**MOUNTAIN
N'AIR BOOKS**

Portland Hikes

Washington

I.
Introduction

I. Why Portland?

People who choose to live in or near Portland, Oregon, do not do so for the same reasons one might reside, for example, in Detroit or Chicago. While these are fine places, most Portlanders would panic at the thought of trading places with their residents. A prime Portland allure is the overwhelming array of tongue dangling gorgeous scenery lapping at the doorstep of our blessed metropolis.

Within 100 miles of Portland, including southwest Washington, can be found ancient rain forests, three mountains over 10,000 feet high, an active volcano, the Pacific Ocean, the greatest concentration of high waterfalls outside Yosemite and 11 federally designated Wilderness Areas. This is not to mention a plethora of wild river canyons, alpine lakes, mountain streams and geological formations that would put many National Parks to shame.

II. Why day-hikes?

Although my passion for the outdoors remains undiminished as I approach middle-age, I find not only my free time waning, but my motivation to wander around in the woods for days lugging a 70 pound backpack. While I'm not above such excursions, they tend to be shorter and farther apart than 20 years ago.

Worse, I've developed a minor back problem that renders sleeping on boulders, or even air matresses, uncomfortable. I never was too good at sleeping in tents. I tend to dream about hydrophobic bears.

For the busy individual who hasn't the time and/or money for extended back country journeys but feels compelled to get away from time to time, for the sake of their physical and spiritual well being, day-hiking is ideal. Usually, you needn't carry anything heavier than a camera, although water is advisable on longer trails in mid-summer.

Day-hiking ranks among the least environmentally damaging back country uses, since there is no need to set up camp, build a fire or tether a horse. Not enough Portlanders realize that it's possible to hike, for example, to the heart of the Mount Jefferson Wilderness, spend a fabulous day exploring, and be home in time for dinner.

III. On co-authoring.

While the Introduction and chapters are written in the first person singular, this book lists two authors, Art Bernstein and Andrew Jackman. Art hiked and wrote up the Oregon trails while Andy was responsible for nearly all the Washington entries. Art wrote the Introduction and edited all chapters for consistency of tone, style and content. Since both authors are experienced naturalists, information and insights were shared on many chapters.

Actually, there's a third co-author, Art's daughter, Sara T. Bernstein. Sara is nineteen, and in the process of transferring from Portland's Lewis and Clark College to the University of Oregon. Chapter 8, on Tryon Creek Park, which is adjacent to the Lewis and Clark campus, is her expert journalistic handiwork.

Art Bernstein is a Naturalist and Forester who has lived in Oregon since 1970. He has an MS in Forestry from the University of Michigan. Aside from his present self-employment as a Forestry Consultant and writer, he has worked as a County Forester, a National Park Naturalist (Oregon Caves) and a Forestry Instructor at Rogue Community College in Grants Pass. This is Art's 10th hiking and natural history guide to the Pacific Northwest and Northern California.

Andy Jackman has an MS in Environmental Studies from California State University at Fullerton. After teaching in, then heading, Rogue Community College's Department of Natural Resource Management for 12 years, he moved on to the Oregon State University Forest Resources Department, in 1989, as an Instructor. He recently finished his PhD in Forest Resources at Oregon State.

Aside from 17 years teaching experience, Andy has led numerous naturalist trips throughout Oregon and Washington and served on many advisory committees. His previous book, "The Hip-Pocket Naturalist: A Guide to Oregon's Rogue River Basin," was co-authored with Art Bernstein.

IV. On writing hiking guides.

I've tried in my writing to capture each locale's essence (although, admittedly, there are only so many ways to describe a lake or an uphill climb). The goal is to provide not only a solid reference when you hit the dirt promenade, but readable fare if you don't. Even if you never poke your nose out the front door, you'll know what each trail feels like.

If you must carry a book on the trail, make it a wildflower or bird guide; although as with trail guides, I prefer to study such tomes at home, instead of hauling them around. The first time I ever encountered a foxtail pine, for example, I knew exactly what it was because I'd read about them.

V. On selecting trails.

The paths described herein don't even come close to presenting the full array of trails in northwest Oregon and southwest Washington. To write about every single path would require thousands of pages and several decades research. And most entries would barely justify leaving home. This book attempts to screen out the klunkers and offer what the authors feel are the region's very best.

In selecting trails, Andy and I tried to present a variety of destination types (lakes, waterfalls, etc.), degrees of difficulty, lengths, accessibility and levels of solitude. Some trailheads lie just off the freeway while others hide at the end of impossible jeep roads.

We both far prefer trails with a clear destination such as a mountaintop or waterfall. Routes which merely wander off through the woods are avoided, although such paths can certainly be uplifting and rejuvenating.

For the most part, we shied away from trails where the destination is more easily reached some other way. A prime rule was, "Why hike to a place if you can drive?" Save your legs for some place you can't drive. Similarly, we chose the shortest route to each destination, unless there was a compelling reason not to. Trails range in length from 1 to 6 miles, one way.

I (Art) hasten to add, and forewarn, the reader that my hiking habits tend to be compulsive and quirky. I collect trails the way some people collect stamps. Although hiking may be the most important thing in my life after my wife and daughters, once

I've reached an objective, the challenge ceases and I feel no urge to hang around, except to catch my breath and take a picture.

For this reason, I give no time estimates in the chapter head information. I've learned that visitors bring to the wilderness a diverse and enthralling array of personal styles, needs, interests and motivations. Mine aren't any more bizarre, or any more or less valid, than anybody else's.

I am reminded of a gentleman I met atop California's Mount Whitney, in 1967. Wearing sandals, dress slacks and a white shirt with, yes, a bow tie, he'd hiked the exhausting, ten mile trail carrying his lunch in a picnic basket. His reason for climbing America's highest mountain outside Alaska? He was collecting butterflies.

VI. Chapter Head Information.

The "nuts and bolts" information on each hike is condensed at the head of each chapter. It includes:

A. Map inset. Readers should reach most objectives using the maps insets and descriptions in this book. Insets include the trail itself and the last connecting road or two. All are oriented with north up and the scale varies with the trail length.

Insets are taken from the United States Geological Survey (USGS) 7.5 minute topographic maps listed at the chapter head. While USGS maps are considered public domain, we gladly acknowledge this invaluable source.

Supplementary maps are recommended. National Forest Wilderness maps cost a few dollars and show contour lines, all associated features, connecting trails and roads in the immediate vicinity. USGS topographic maps further detail steepness and minute twists and turns. Recreation maps of Mount Hood, Gifford Pinchot and Willamette National Forests lack contour lines but are invaluable for locating trailheads. State Park brochures show trails in fair detail but without contour lines.

Many book and outdoors stores sell Forest Service and USGS maps. Forest Service maps, predictably, can also be obtained at any Forest Service office.

B. Trail length. Each chapter head gives length as distance from the trailhead to the farthest objective or turnaround point. For loop trails, both the distance to the farthest point and the loop distance are given. Distances are rounded to the nearest half-mile.

Since flat maps show only horizontal distance, that is the length figure shown. Bear in mind that a trail rising 1000 feet over a horizontal mile (5280 feet), actually spans 5373 feet. Total distance is calculated with the old high school snoozer, "The square of the hypotenuse (total distance) equals the sum of the squares of the other two sides (horizontal and vertical distance)." Don't forget to square root your answer.

Hiking time, being highly variable, is not given. A level mile, without pack, takes me twenty minutes while an uphill mile can take half hour or more.

C. Difficulty. In general, an "easy" rating means the path rises at a grade of less than 5% (5 feet vertical per 100 feet horizontal). The "difficult" ratings begin at 10%, or 10 feet vertical per 100 horizontal. It may not seem much of a difference but a 5% grade translates to a rise of 264 feet per mile while a 10% grade climbs 528 feet in a mile. A slope of infinity would rise one foot vertical for every zero feet horizontal, or straight up and down.

The steepest trail herein (Chapter 20), rises 1000 feet per mile. Over a short pitch, a trail's gradient can exceed 100%, or one foot vertical for every foot horizontal, equalling a 45 degree angle (see Chapter 17, Castle Canyon).

Everything between 5% and 10% is considered "moderate." This is sometimes modified by the trail's overall length and the amount of level land between upgrades. A two-mile trail with a rise of 500 feet per mile obviously takes less out of you than a five mile trail with the same average rise.

D. Elevation. Elevations are given in feet and most are rounded to the nearest 100. Where there are two numbers, they represent the highest and lowest points, not necessarily the beginning and ending elevations.

E. Season. Although the Pacific Northwest is famous for rain, an occasional fabulous winter day, with sunshine and toasty weather, is not unusual. While most high trails do not open until June or July, lower areas, including the coast, the Willamette Valley and the Columbia Gorge, remain accessible year round.

Since Pacific Northwest weather varies greatly, the seasons indicated in the chapter head are based on elevation and should be considered extremely general. If it snowed down to 1000 feet a few days earlier, inquire before setting out on a 3000 foot elevation trail. Look for mud and high water from autumn through mid-July. Also, be aware that flash floods can be a problem on Mount Hood, Mount Jefferson and Mount Adams and that some old growth forest areas are prone to blowdown during winter storms.

The high country offers a wonderful respite from mid-summer valley heat, but be prepared for an occasional cold night. Also, summer thunderstorms, frequently born in these mountains, can be terrifying. Avoid ridgetops, flash flood-prone creeks (such as Newton Creek, Chapter 21), open areas and standing under the highest trees, if caught in a lightning storm.

F. Trailhead location. This heading gives the township, range and section of the trailhead, for quick map reference. A township contains 36 sections while a section consists of one square mile or 640 acres. Range designations refer to the Willamette Meridian, which runs north and south through the middle of Portland and forms the basis for all Oregon and Washington land surveys.

G. Water. If a trail is less than two or three miles long, it's below 70 degrees out and the path is rated "easy," you probably needn't worry about water. Consider leaving a canteen or cooler in the car, however.

As for drinking from creeks or lakes, my personal rule is not to if there's habitation, cattle or horse use between me and the stream source. Also, if I can't cross a creek in a step or two, or the water is stagnant, I won't drink from it. Icy springs in the deep woods or near a mountaintop, are probably safe.

Any water can make you sick, however, and the means through which disease is spread are myriad, especially in an area as heavily trod as the forests and mountains around Portland. Except in an emergency, it's never wise to drink unpurified water.

See the "About Hiking" section for suggested ways to avoid dehydration.

H. USGS 7.5" topo: This refers to the appropriate USGS map on which the trail appears. My only complaint about USGS maps is that while they contain the very best detail available over a small area, they aren't updated often enough.

I. Ownership. The proprietary agencies have devoted much time, money and expertise to designing, building and maintaining the routes under their jurisdiction. They are justifiably proud of their efforts and I am pleased to acknowledge them. I might add that the folks at the Forest Service have been uniformly patient, gracious and helpful in responding to my incessant barrage of questions.

Their kind assistance is available to you, as well. Pertinent addresses are as follows:

OREGON.

Mt. Hood National Forest
(Supervisor's Office)
2955 NW Division St.
Portland, OR 97030   *(503) 666-0771*

Bear Springs Ranger District
Route 1, Box 222
Maupin, OR 97037   *(503) 328-6211*

Clackamas Ranger District
61431 E. Highway 224
Estacada, OR 97023   *(503) 630-4256*

Estacada Ranger District
595 NW Industrial Way
Estacada, OR 97023   *(503) 630-6861*

Zig-Zag Visitor Center
65000 E. Highway 26
Welches, OR 96067   *(503) 622-5741*

Columbia Gorge National Scenic Area
902 Wasco Ave, Suite 200
Hood River, OR 97761   *(503) 386-2333*

Willamette National Forest (Supervisor's Office)
211 E. 7th Ave.
PO Box 10607
Eugene, OR 97401   *(503) 687-6521*

Detroit Ranger District
HC Box 320
Mill City, OR   *(503) 854-3366*

Salem District, Bureau of Land Management
1717 Fabry Road
Salem, OR 97306   *(503) 375-5646*

Oregon State Parks
525 Trade Street
Salem, OR 97310   *(503) 378-6305*

Portland Parks and Recreation
1120 SW Fifth Ave., Suite 1302
Portland, OR 97204   *(503) 823-5132*

WASHINGTON.

Gifford Pinchot National Forest (Supervisor's Office)
6926 E. Fourth Plain Blvd.
Vancouver, WA 98668   *(206) 750-5000*

Mt. Adams Ranger District
2455 Hwy 141
Trout Lake, WA 98650   *(509) 395-2501*

Packwood Ranger District
Packwood, WA 98361   *(206) 494-5515*

Randle Ranger District
10024 Highway 12
Randle, WA 98377   *(206) 497-7565*

Wind River Ranger District
Carson, WA 98610   *(509) 427-5645*

Mt. St. Helens National Volcanic Mon.
Amboy, WA 98601   *(206) 247-5473*

Washington State Parks
7150 Clearwater Lane
Olympia, WA 98504-5711   *(206) 753-2027*

J. Phone. The number given in the chapter head will get you the nearest Forest Service Ranger District to each trail rather than the Supervisor's Office. For state parks, you'll get the individual park. For the one BLM managed area (Chapter 46), you'll get their Salem District office.

Phone ahead if you plan to bring a dog, horse, large group, mountain bike or dirt bike. They are not permitted in many areas.

A free permit is required for entry to some Wilderness areas. Permits are available at trailhead sign-in boxes, in person at Forest Service offices or by mail if you write or phone. Ranger Station information offices near the most popular areas, such as Detroit Lake, Timberline, Zig-Zag and Ripplebrook, are open weekends in summer.

K. Camping. I realize not every reader of this book comes from Portland. I also realize that readers may combine several day-hikes with an overnight stay at one the countless fine (and not-so-fine) campgrounds dotting the National Forests and State Parks. Thus, the nearest developed and maintained campground with restroom facilities, is given. National Forests also contain many smaller campsites, often along the trail and marked only by a stone fire ring.

L. Directions. These are given in the chapter head instead of the narrative because my goal is to make each chapter interesting and readable, not bore the reader.

The directions presume you're starting from Portland and follow what I believe is the shortest and/or fastest route. Before leaving home, trace the route on the map to orient yourself and decide if it's best for you. If you live in Eugene, the Dalles, on the coast or 50 miles into Washington, you're probably better off figuring out your own route.

At Norway Pass (Chapter 50) and a few other places, two routes were nearly identical in time, distance, scenery and complexity. The described route thus represents little more than a coin toss.

VII. About hiking.

Before getting to the standard list of hiking do's and don'ts required in books of this nature, Andy and I would like to offer a few unscientific observations on a variety of subjects:

A. Since hiking offers a way of getting in shape, lack of previous conditioning shouldn't dissuade you. Start on easy or moderate paths and take your time. If you have a heart condition or other limitation, consult your physician first.

Physical stress is not confined to uphill tracks. The overweight or out of shape person is likely to be bothered by upgrades because they stress the cardiovascular system. Steep downgrades, on the other hand, stress the knees, ankles and feet. If you have arithritis or orthopedic problems, it's the downgrades that'll get you. Most blisters develop on downgrades, which can ruin a trip far more quickly than a little huffing and puffing.

B. As I settle into middle age, I've developed a paranoia about dehydration. Back in my 20's, when little tired me out, I didn't care if my mouth got a little dry. These days, I worry about fatigue, blood pressure, respiration and pulse rates, electrolytes, etc. I sip water constantly as I hike and have been known to slip a little Gatorade in my canteen.

Fluid retention can be increased by eating (and avoiding) certain foods. Grains (particularly wheat), milk and carbonated drinks should be kept to a minimum. Foods with high water content, such as celery or fruit, are most beneficial, as are foods rich in unsaturated oil, carbohydrates, acid and salt.

The objective is to get the nourishment out of your stomach and into your blood as quickly as possible. Difficult to digest meals should be avoided. Thus, several small, nibbly snacks are far better than a Bacchanalian binge. And foods cut into bite sized portions tend to get chewed more thoroughly. So bring apple slices rather than a whole apple. Slices also free you from having to carry the core home with you.

Peanut butter and jelly sandwiches, cookies, cheese sticks and the redoubtable trail mix are all dandy, provided you keep the portions down. Liquefied foods are marvelous. Try topping your meals with orange or V8 juice.

These days, you can buy school lunch boxes in the form of extremely light weight, soft sided coolers. I've taken to swiping my daughter's when I go backpacking. With a block of blue ice, it will keep a salad fresh and juice cold in a backpack for 24 hours or more.

C. The once popular heavy hiking boots, with non-skid, cleated soles, are somewhat out of vogue. They're environmentally damaging and necessary only when in snow, or off the trail in wet weather. I find cloth-top, lightweight, modern hiking boots much more comfortable, although I bruise an ankle in them occasionally.

D. Hiking can make you hot and sweaty no matter what the weather conditions. On cool days, especially if it's raining or breezy, this can lead to disaster in the form of hypothermia. Hypothermia is defined as the body's inability to regenerate body-heat necessary to sustain normal vital functions. Hypothermia can not only be fatal, it can occur with extreme suddenness.

The main way to prevent hypothermia is to wear a sweater or jacket in cool weather, no matter how sweaty you become. The recommended treatment is to replace the body heat through warmth and food. If you feel dizzy, queasy or shivery, stop immediately, get warm and eat something sugary if you can.

E. Never hike alone, inform someone of your destination, check the weather forecast, etc.

I've been lost only twice in my life. I once spent the night at 9000 feet with no food, jacket, water or matches. After that, I vowed never to leave home without a basic survival kit. I haven't forgotten my lunch since.

I've always carried a small first-aid kit, including a few Band-Aids, "blister adhesives", gauze pads, mosquito repellent and sun block. In addition to the above, my "absolute necessity" list includes toilet paper, water purification tablets, map and a few extra high energy snacks such as a candy bar or trail mix.

Andy thinks I'm asking for trouble by not carrying a more complete survival kit but I'm not convinced of it's necessity on a short day-hike, except if you're headed for Paradise Park (Chapter 19), Serene Lake (Chapter 32) or some other trail where you're really "out there."

Survival kits, according to Andy, should be carried by each individual in your party. In addition to the items described above, Andy would add a large plastic trash bag (for use as rain gear, blanket, ground tarp or water collector), matches, a long sleeve shirt and a knife. Matches should be kept in a waterproof jar with the striker.

Andy also carries a metal bandage box with tweezers, scissors, a fingernail clipper, a wire saw, signal-to-air mirror and air-to-ground signal card. He wraps a little tape, both duct and adhesive, around the outside of the box.

Other survivial items might include a fishing kit, compass, whistle, aspirins, wire, space blanket, your name and address, and the phone number of the nearest Forest Service office.

F. If you wish to take a break while hiking, it is a good idea to find a spot 10 to 15 yards away from the path. This provides a more isolated experience and allows other hikers to pass without having to step over you or your day pack.

G. Over the years, I've received phone calls and letters, some miffed, from readers unable to find trailheads, or who got lost on the trail, or who expressed some complaint or another (although people who spot the rare errors in my books are simply interested in passing the information along.)

While I love hearing from readers, and do my best to keep my information up-to-date, accurate and clear, I believe that they, not me, are responsible for the outcome of their journeys. Part of the adventure of the mountains is that things change. Roads may be gated without notice or become washed out or blocked, forests burn, boundaries get moved, things dry up or get muddy, bridges deteriorate or disappear, trails become overgrown, trailhead and road markers vanish, new roads and trails are built.

These uncertainties, to me, enhance the experience. If I'm unable to reach an objective, which happens from time to time, I simply go somewhere else or go home.

H. Finally, the Forest Service offers a list of camping guidelines far more important than mine. As part of "no trace" camping, they ask the following:

1. Pack out all litter.

2. For human waste, select a spot at least 200 feet from open water and dig a hole six to eight inches deep. Cover it with dirt when done.

3. If a fire is absolutely necessary, build it in a safe, previously used spot; preferably a fire ring at an established campsite. Wood collection can be environmentally damaging and portable stoves are recommended.

4. Pitch tents so no drainage ditch is required and replace rocks and other material removed from sleeping areas. Campsites should be at least 100 feet from open water and animals should be pastured at least 200 feet from open water.

VII. About the land.

The chapters herein include a trove of natural history. Since several trails may penetrate the same area, and since each description is written to stand on its own, some repetition was unavoidable. While natural history is often described in detail; to list the identifying traits of every rock type, tree species and flower at each mention; would take far too much space.

The following concepts, for the most part, failed to find their way into the chapters or are spread thinly among many:

A. Geology. Two major geological provinces are represented in Northwest Oregon and Southwest Washington, the Cascade Mountains and the Coastal Ranges, separated by the sedimentary deposits of the Willamette Valley. Most spectacular and best known are the Cascades, capped by 11,253 foot Mount Hood, Oregon's highest peak; and 12,326 foot Mount Adams, Washington's second loftiest summit.

The Cascades stretch from California's Mount Lassen to British Columbia's Mount Garibaldi and are characterized by extremely young volcanic peaks. Lava and ash blankets the landscape.

Geologists distinguish between the High Cascades and the Western Cascades. The more easterly High Cascades began forming four million years ago and are still very much under construction. The more obvious volcanic formations; high peaks, craters and fresh lava flows; belong to the High Cascades. Many High Cascades volcanoes, including Mount Hood, Mount Jefferson, Mount Adams and Mount Saint Helens, are considered dormant rather than extinct.

The Western Cascades, being much older and more eroded, do not boast spectacular cones and lava fields. They do boast many exposed volcanic necks, such as Table or Beacon Rocks (Chapters 46 and 47), where the surrounding mountain has eroded away.

The Pacific Northwest's other dominant system is the Coast Range. It is an area of steeply folded and faulted sandstone, along with other marine rocks, both sedimentary and volcanic. Along the northern Oregon and southern Washington coasts, few of its summits exceed 4000 feet.

𝘅𝘅 𝘅𝘅 𝘅𝘅

Many of the higher peaks around Portland have experienced glaciation. Glaciers form when annual snowfall exceeds melt and ice starts oozing down the mountain. While our area's glaciers have retreated considerably since the Ice Age ended 10,000 years ago, they are still very much in evidence on peaks Mount Hood, Mount Jefferson and Mount Adams.

Gouged out scars from former glaciers abound on the lower slopes. Glaciers not only carve out round-bottomed valleys as they move downward, they also chisel sharply backward into the peak. This headward cutting creates "cirque" basins with steep, amphitheater headwalls rising above a bowl. Many of the region's alpine lakes occupy glacial cirque basins. Typically, in the northern Oregon and southern Washington Cascades, the headwall is badly eroded and the lake is in a fairly late stage of silting in.

B. Botany. More important than memorizing long species lists, in understanding the botany of the Portland region, is the concept of "association." This refers to different plant species found predictably together in similar kinds of places. For example, you'll rarely find bigleaf maple and lodgepole pine in the same stand whereas bigleaf maple and Douglas-fir nearly always hang out together. Associations range from the broadly geographic to the highly site specific.

Northwest Oregon and southwest Washington are covered by a single geographic association: The Pacific Northwest forest region. Dominant species include Douglas-fir, Western hemlock and Western redcedar, plus red alder and bigleaf maple. Look also for Sitka spruce along the coast. At higher elevations, you'll find

Alaska cedar, mountain hemlock, lodgepole pine, noble fir and Western white pine, with whitebark pine on the highest ridges.

An astute observer will also distinguish riverbank associations, dry upland associations, bog associations, north slope associations (shady), south slope associations (sunny), elevational associations, etc. Component species are elaborated in the individual chapters.

While my main naturalist expertise is trees and shrubs, that is not why Andy and I devote more space to them than to herbaceous species. There are simply so many herbaceous species, they're difficult to list without lapsing into a boring litany. On trails hiked in August and September or later, the majority of wildflowers are no longer in bloom.

C. Wildlife. Observation of wildlife is a prime reason people take to the Wilderness. While most animals are fairly elusive, a sharp eye frequently pays off.

I've left bird descriptions to Andy's chapters because he is much more attuned to them. Remember, however, that birds tend not to hang around. Just because Andy spotted one, it doesn't mean you will. The reverse is also true, of course.

Mammals also tend not to hang around. I guarantee that if you drive the road where I saw three cougars last summer, you will not repeat the experience. You will, however, have many amazing experiences of your own.

Here is a brief overview of the more interesting wildlife species you may run across:

Rats and mice are by far the most abundant mammals. They hold the unenviable distinction of occupying the bottom of the food chain. Their populations are so enormous, however, the likelihood of any given mouse getting eaten is not that great.

Despite their numbers, you're unlikely to meet one since they're nocturnal and extremely wary. Don't look for the familiar European house mouse or Norway rat, either. More likely, you'll find an All-American variety with a furry tail, such as a kangaroo rat, harvest mouse or meadow vole.

Since tree squirrels, ground squirrels and chipmunks are day feeders, 90% of observed mammals will fall into one of these nut muncher categories. Tree squirrels are the guys with big bushy tails (except for flying squirrels), who climb trees. Ground squirrels can have small bushy tails or no bushy tails and come in either plain or striped wrappers. Some also climb trees. All chipmunks are striped. Unlike striped ground squirrels, the stripe extends to their head.

As for beavers, you're more likely to see their works than the animal itself. Beaver dams, impoundments and lodges are a unique treat even if their creators never poke their noses out of the water.

Large mammals offer a special thrill, especially deer and elk. Deer are a naturalist's dream and America has long been mesmerized by the "Bambi" consciousness. Although fire is not as threatening to deer as that film depicts, and in fact stimulates growth of browse vegetation, the movie offers a great lesson in compassion.

In the ecological scheme of things, deer have an easy niche to occupy. They prefer mid-successional habitats, with both open browsing areas and forest cover. They abound because forest management practices create ideal habitat. Elk occupy a similar niche but are much larger and less abundant than deer.

As noted, I saw three cougars in researching this book, all from the car. The chances of one of these elusive and intelligent carnivores menacing you on the trail approaches zero.

D. Many wilderness visitors worry about bears, rattlesnakes, yellowjackets and poison oak. The Pacific Northwest trails are amazingly safe, however, and your chances of being carried off or eaten are nil. While it's good to know about things which may accost you, I wouldn't lose sleep over them.

Bear. I've seen only two bears in all my years of wilderness hiking. Bear sign turns up often, however, usually in the form of seed laden droppings.

Black bear, our local species, tends to hightail it if they see a human. While I've never had a black bear enter my camp, or heard of anybody being injured by one in Oregon, they are not to be trifled with. They love to rummage in quest of food and have been known to damage parked cars if they see something edible through the window. The Forest Service recommends you hang all food at night, well out of reach. Bears are intelligent enough to avoid the more heavily trodden paths.

Rattlesnakes. Trust me on this, there's little to worry about when it comes to rattlesnakes. In my half-dozen or so rattler encounters, they've been more anxious than I to avoid confrontation. Keep an eye out for them in grass, brush or when stepping over logs or rocks. Should you spot or hear one, walk a wide berth around it. They're pretty slow and have a striking range of only a couple feet.

Should you get chomped, the recommended treatment is to apply ice and get to a doctor within two hours. Keep in mind that (a), they don't always get the venom out and (b), a healthy adult can usually shake off a snake bite. Victims should avoid walking and either be carried out and/or have help summoned. If a small child or someone with asthsma or a heart condition gets bitten, it should be taken extremely seriously.

The practice of killing rattlesnakes for no reason is, to me, unconscionable. Remember that you're the intruder, not the snake.

Yellowjackets. Unlike rattlers and honey bees, these carnivorous insects can be aggressive. Nevertheless, your chances of being stung are remote, although it's happened to me on a half-dozen occasions. In 1970, I stepped on a below ground nest and got stung six times. Bell bottoms were popular then and the yellowjackets became trapped in my pant leg.

Usually, the result is akin to a mosquito bite. If a large yellowjacket gets a good shot, however, it can be painful and swell badly. If you're allergic to bee stings, carry some anti-histamine or prescribed medication. If you see a swarm of jellowjackets, walk a wide berth around it.

Poison oak. While poison oak is uncommon in the Portland region's moist climate, it does turn up. Look for three irregularly toothed or lobed leaflets radiating from a central stem. The side leaflets are toothed only on their outside edge.

While many people are immune to poison oak, it can cause a nasty rash. If you think you've been exposed, avoid touching or scratching the area and wash it thoroughly in strong soap as soon as possible. Wash your clothes, also.

VIII. Fishing.

Since I couldn't catch a fish to save my life, any assessment I might make on fishing the lakes and rivers around Portland would be useless. To most outdoors types, the streams and high lakes of northwest Oregon and southwest Washington offer some of the world's premiere angling.

The vast majority of the region's alpine lakes contain Eastern brook and/or rainbow trout. In the major streams and rivers, look for brook and rainbow trout higher up; with steelhead trout and chinook, coho and sockeye salmon lower down. Bass and sunfish sometimes turn up in low elevation, warm waters. Lucky anglers may land a green sturgeon in the main coastal rivers.

Most mountain lakes are stocked regularly since few such lakes boast honest to gosh native fish populations. Furthermore, there is little natural reproduction in most lakes, either by planted or native stock.

The best fishing lakes have greenish water and much shoreline and aquatic vegetation, but not so much that the lake is unfishable or inaccessible. Ideally, they will contain shallow areas along the edge, a few logs, a fair amount of cover and a deep spot. In streams, look for ledges and still collecting pools at the base of fast moving areas.

IX. Acknowledgments.

This book would not be nearly as thorough or interesting without the considerable assistance of a number of individuals and resources. Above all, Andy and I must again acknowledge the patience and helpfulness of the staff of the USDA Forest Service. Among their many employees I've pestered, a few stand out: Venita Mills at the Detroit Ranger District, Bruce Haines at the Zig-Zag Ranger District, Mark Shepard at the Estacada Ranger District, Stan Hinatsu at the Hood River Ranger District, Bob Radcliffe at the Salem BLM office and Peter Frenzen at Mount Saint Helens. Those are people whose names we remembered to write down. There were many others.

I (Art) should also acknowledge the assistance and encouragement of Gary Newbold, Amy Norton, my wife Patricia, my daughter Anna and especially my daughter Sara, who accompanied me on a couple hikes and wrote Chapter 8.

This book might never have come to pass were it not for Sara. There are precious few things in life which I find preferable to hiking. Spending time with my children happens to be one of them. Since I live in southern Oregon, visiting Sara in Portland after completing my various excursions profoundly increased my motivation to pursue the project.

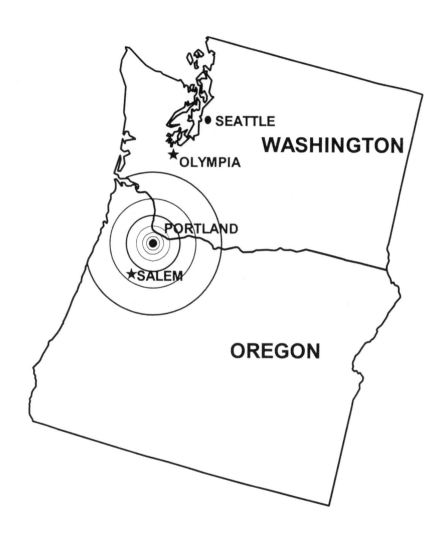

Saddle Mountain, Saddle Mountain State Park, Oregon.

Introduction

Coastal Hikes

Trail to Saddle Mountain.

Another view of Saddle Mountain.

1.

Saddle Mountain

(Saddle Mountain State Park)

Lenght:	21/2 miles
Difficulty:	Difficult
Elevation:	1650 to 3283 feet
Season:	All seasons
Water:	One creek
USGS 7.5" Topo:	Saddle Mountain
Location:	T6N-R8W-Sec. 33
Ownership:	Saddle Mount State Park
Phone:	(503) 861-1671
Camping:	At trailhead
Use intensity:	Heavy

Directions: *Take US-26 west from Portland to the Saddle Mountain State Park turnoff, nine miles east of Highway-101. Follow the park signs seven miles to the campground, picnic area and trailhead.*

鉄鉄鉄

An easy hour from Portland and ten miles from the ocean, Saddle Mountain is the one peak every Portlander should climb. Between vistas of sea and mountains, spectacular rock formations and botanical rarities, the rewards are unsurpassed. While it is a challenge, it is only two or three hours out of your life.

Let's be honest; at 3283 feet, Saddle Mountain is puny compared to the Oregon Cascades, which top out at more than 11,000 feet. However, Saddle Mountain's bald, twin summits comprise the major landmark on Oregon's northwest peninsula, between the Columbia River and the coast. Jutting above the surrounding peaks, it can be seen for miles. Of all the trails in this book, this one is my favorite.

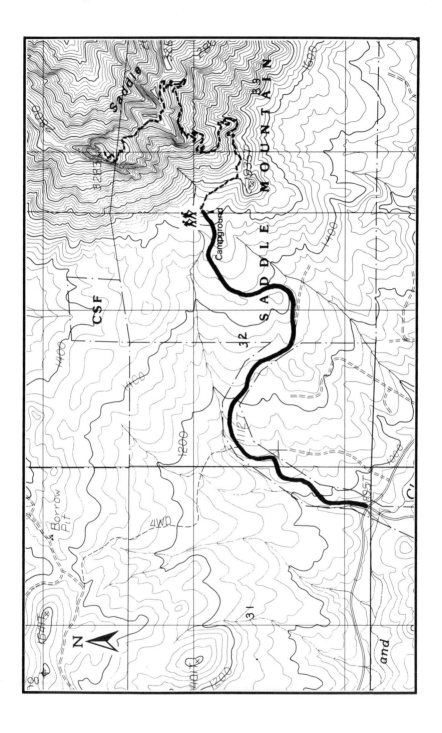

Saddle Mountain

The basalt outcropping forming Saddle Mountain is actually a tiny volcano, one of several in the vicinity. A geologist would identify its rounded billowing rock as "pillow lava," indicative of underwater eruptions. Humbug Mountain, immediately south, has an identical history, as do several north coast capes.

With so much to be seen from the summit, in an area receiving 100 inches of rain annually, check the weather for visibility before heading out.

At the trailhead, a sign warns that only "experienced" hikers should tackle the path's upper end. Presuming normal common sense, I encountered nothing requiring "experience." Anyone in reasonable health, who doesn't have a problem with heights, should do fine. If you're out of shape, go slowly. And be aware that the upper climb can be frightening in high winds.

From the parking lot, the mountain's rounded, black to red, moss highlighted facets soar upward in a nearly vertical, stepped wall. The highest point visible from the parking lot is an exposed basalt dike, passed halfway up the trail.

The initial mile winds in long switchbacks, at gentle to moderate grades, through a typical coastal forest of Douglas-fir, Western hemlock, Western redcedar and red alder. Look for hemlock, an exceedingly shade tolerant species, growing from "nurse" stumps in this second growth stand.

Mile one's gloomy understory is crammed with vegetation; including fern, Queen Anne's lace, vine maple, ceanothus, sorrel, dwarf Oregongrape, thimbleberry, devil's club, *ad infinitum*. And you haven't even gotten to the rare stuff yet.

Towards the end of the first mile, the grade steepens and the switchbacks shorten. At mile 11/4, the route breaks out of the woods, near the volcanic dike mentioned earlier, next to a large rock spire. This is the halfway mark only in distance. Time-wise, it is only one third of the way. But the scenic quality jumps up several notches here and improves with every step.

During mile two, the path winds around rock faces, past floral meadows and in and out of the woods. The steep meadows, in spring through mid-summer, are emblazoned with wildflowers; notably Indian paintbrush, iris, monkeyflower, delphinium, and (on the rocks), sedum and saxifrage. Forested areas have evolved since mile one, with Douglas-fir, Sitka spruce and noble fir dominating.

Botanically, Saddle Mountain is a glacial island. During the last Ice Age, advancing glaciers pushed the range of many species far to the south. When the glaciers retreated, the species moved back northward, lingering in a few isolated, high elevation locations. Some remnant populations evolved into new species. Glacial relics and unique species on this trail include Saddle Mountain bittercress, Saddle Mountain saxifrage, alpine lily and others.

Eventually, mile two makes its way to the head of a steep canyon, where it crosses the trail's only water (unless you go in winter). While mile two offers spectacular vistas of the surrounding peaks and the emerging ocean, they hardly compare with the view from the top.

When I visited, during a wet June, I found the path badly eroded in a couple spots. Only one posed a problem, however, where the trail disappeared over a cliff, leaving a four to five foot gap. An obvious way trail led downhill about eight feet, then across the gap and back up. While it made for a little extra work, it wasn't as dangerous as it looked.

Near the end of mile two, the trail hits the ridgetop at a wooded saddle which, while impressive, is not "the" saddle after which the peak is named. Soon after, the route breaks into the open for good. Both the main summit and South Saddle Mountain come into view for the first time here. The latter is 16 feet lower than the former and even more precipitous, if possible.

The last half-mile is marked by long vistas and some extremely steep ups and downs as two large gaps are spanned. The second and deepest is the main saddle. The most difficult areas in this section are fortified with wooden walkways, railings, stairsteps, hand-hold cables, etc.

Rounding a point, the trail drops several hundred feet in a series of stairways to a footbridge at the main saddle. Immediately beyond, the steepest and most difficult pitch ascends a gravelly rock face to a cluster of trees. Beyond that, the remaining zig-zag pitches to the summit have been stair-stepped with railroad ties. It looks imposing from the saddle but goes by quickly.

The summit consists of a flat the size of an infield, surrounded by a railing. To the west lie the Pacific Ocean, Nehalem Bay, Seaside and Tillamook Head. To the south, a sea of trees spreads to the horizon, welling up at Humbug Mountain, Onion Peak and the backbone of the Coast Range. To the north, Astoria is easily seen, with its tower and its bridge over the Columbia. Across the Columbia rise the mountains of Washington. And on a clear day, the high Cascades can be seen to the east, including Mount Hood, Mount Adams, Mount Saint Helens and, with luck, Mount Rainier.

The real challenge, of course, would be to climb Mount Hood, Adams, Saint Helens and Rainier and see if you can pick out Saddle Mountain.

2.

South Jetty/Columbia Mouth

(Ft. Stevens State Park)

Difficulty Easy
Length: 2 miles
Elevation: Sea level
Season: All seasons
Water: None potable
USGS 7.5' Topo: Warrenton, Clatsop Spit
Location T9N-R11W-Sec. 23
Ownership: Fort Stevens State Park
Phone: (503) 861-1671
Camping: Fort Stevens Campground

Directions: *Leave Highway 101 west of Astoria, at signs to Fort Stevens State Park. Follow signs into park, then to the South Jetty day use and parking area.*

🚶🚶 🚶🚶

Having hiked in Oregon since 1966 and written nine books on hiking trails, it is a rare event to discover a magnificent place I'd never heard of. Clatsop Spit, at the mouth of the Columbia River, is such a place.

With its dunes and stunted shore pines, the two mile sand bar forming Oregon's northern tip evoked visions of Cape Cod, where I once spent a summer. The Oregon State Parks has built a viewing platform at the parking area near the tip, offering one of the state's more stunning panoramas. The ocean crashes against the dunes on one side while the immense Columbia River estuary laps against the opposite shore, 1/8 mile away. The City of Astoria can be seen in the distance, as can Saddle Mountain and the peaks of the Washington Coast Range.

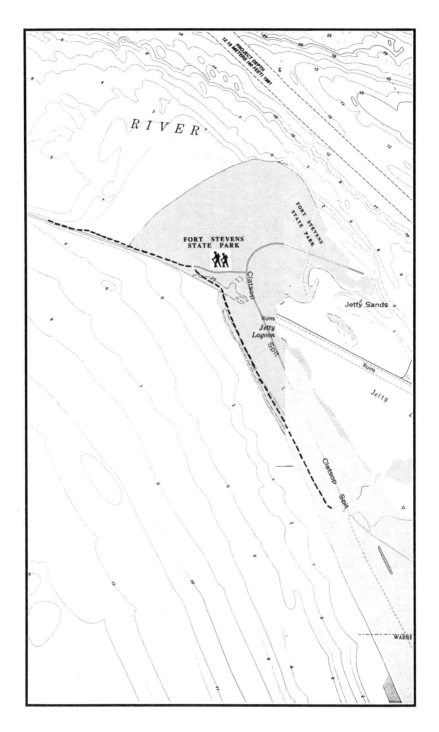

South Jetty/Columbia Mouth   33

South Jetty is an outstanding winter destination. Storms can be spectacular, although I'd avoid the beach and breakwater when they're putting on a show. Tundra swans frequent the area in November and December.

Geographically, the name "Clatsop Spit" is confined to the sandbar poking into the Columbia Mouth. Geologically, it includes the entire chain of beach dunes extending 20 miles to the Necanicum River, just south of Seaside.

The South Jetty, a breakwater beginning at the parking area near the tip of Clatsop Spit, extends into the river mouth for two miles. A quarter-mile trail leads from the parking lot, along the base of the breakwater, to land's end. To continue, one must walk out the jetty, which is difficult because of its large boulders. Scattered planks along the top make the going a little easier.

The South Jetty viewing platform marks "Mile Zero" of the Oregon Coast Trail. While nearly every inch of this 300 mile path offers first class scenery and adventure, this book has whittled it down to the four best northern chunks. However, the Coast Trail can be picked up just about anywhere on the north coast, for hikes ranging from 1/4 to sixteen miles.

The State Parks has published an indispensable brochure called the *"Oregon Coast Trail Guide."* Here are some tips on using it: First, its instructions assume you're hiking through, not trying to locate intermediate trailheads from your car. Second, the map is very sketchy. I suggest augmenting it with brochures and hikers maps for the individual state parks, showing much more detail. Write or call the State Parks headquarters in Salem.

This chapter constitutes the book's only Coast Trail segment that runs along a beach. While I love walking along beaches, I find myself without incentive to go very far or expend much energy when confronted with a beach trail. Frankly, I'm perfectly happy to remain at the trailhead.

If you wish to make a hike of your South Jetty visit, either walk out the two-mile breakwater or start at the Mile Zero post near the viewing platform and head south, through dunes and dune grass, and along the beach. It's 11/2 miles from Mile Zero to the south parking area on Clatsop Spit.

At the south parking area, a bike trail system takes off which further explores the dunes and beach and visits a number of park landmarks; including the wreck of the Peter Iredale (stuck on the beach since running aground in 1906), Coffenbury Lake, Battery Russell and old Fort Stevens. All of the latter can be driven to.

For you trivia buffs, the campground between Battery Russell and Coffenbury Lake is the nation's largest State Park campground.— I believe it!

South Jetty. Ocean on the left. The Columbia to the right.

3.

Tillamook Head

(Ecola State Park)

Length:	2 to 6 miles
Difficulty:	Moderate
Elevation:	10 to 1100 feet
Season:	All Seasons (avoid stormy weather)
Water:	2 or 3 creeks
USGS 7.5' Topo:	Tillamook Head
Location:	T3N-R10W-Sec. 7
Ownership:	Ecola State Park
Phone:	(503) 436-2844
Use intensity:	Heavy
Camping:	Cannon Beach (private), hikers camp at mile 2.

Directions: Take US-101 to the north Cannon Beach exit. Follow signs to Ecola State Park. Inside the park (day use fee), follow signs to Indian Beach, the suggested trailhead. For the north trailhead, take "U" Street in Seaside to the beach. Make your way south until you come to Sunset Road. The trailhead is located at a paved, ten car parking area where the road ends.

🚶🚶🚶

The six-mile hike over Tillamook Head is heralded as one of the premiere segments of the Oregon Coast Trail. I concur, but only if you limit your trek to the initial 2 1/2 miles from the south trailhead. The northern two miles, in my experience, underscore the fact that "Ecola," the park where this path is located, sounds ominously like "E coli," a bacteria which can cause violent stomach problems.

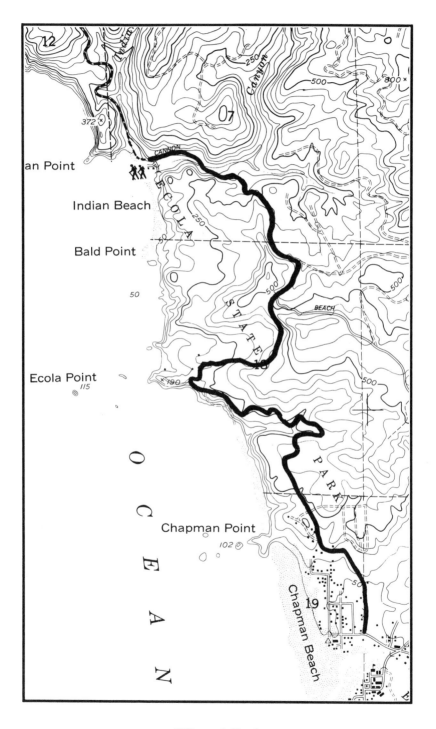

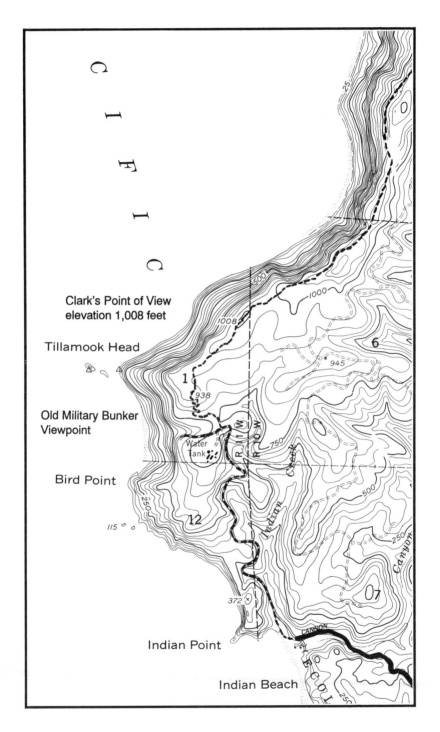

Clark's Point of View
elevation 1,008 feet

Tillamook Head

Old Military Bunker
Viewpoint

Bird Point

Indian Point

Indian Beach

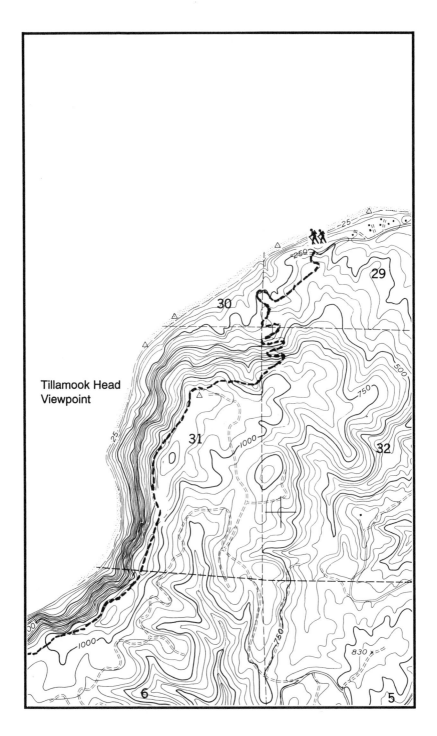

Tillamook Head
Viewpoint

Before getting to the trail's good part, let me fill you in on its infamous northern two miles. According to the *Oregon Coast Guide*, a brochure put out by the State Parks, there are two steep miles separating the north trailhead from a place called the "Tillamook Head Viewpoint." I found the trail not only steep and muddy (in mid-June), but boring, with vistas of nothing but forest understory.

What really soured my grapes was the brochure's failure to mention that the Tillamook Head Viewpoint, the trail's highest point at 1100 feet, looks inland. It's another mile before you come to any ocean views.

For day-hikers, I suggest beginning at the Indian Beach trailhead and hiking north about 21/2 miles to an overlook called Clark's Point of View. The mile beyond Clark's POV also contains superb vistas. Use the north trailhead only if hiking through, you have a ride waiting at the other end, or to avoid the day-use fee at Indian Beach. While the trail from Indian Beach begins at a much lower elevation, the grade is gentler and the route much more interesting.

The six mile path across Tillamook head was pioneered in 1806 by Lewis and Clark (Clark actually, not Lewis), who was searching for an Indian village which supposedly had whale blubber to sell. It marked the southernmost extent of their exploration.

Indian Beach is a gorgeous little cove backed by sea cliffs and enclosed by Indian Point and Bald Point. The trail takes off from the parking area just above the beach. It follows Indian Creek a few hundred feet, then climbs up Indian Point, skirting the edge briefly before cutting inland.

The first mile ascends moderately through a coastal forest of Douglas-fir, Western hemlock, Sitka spruce and red alder. Indian Point remains hidden until you come to a viewpoint, one mile up, where the path finally breaks out of the woods. This is the best southward panorama. South of Indian Point lie Bald Point, Ecola Point and the town of Cannon Beach.

After that, it is back into the woods for a mile. The trail becomes quite steep towards the end of this second mile, scribing a series of short switchbacks. A small hiker's camp sits just beyond mile two. Nearby, a side trail leads uphill to the remnants of some old military bunkers. Since the bunkers were placed for their strategic vantage point, the view of the ocean, coast and headlands is awesome. This is the closest you'll come to Tillamook Head, immediately north. Tillamook Lighthouse sits just off Tillamook Head, on a quarter-acre rock.

From the hiker's camp, it is a half-mile through the woods to an overlook, 1000 feet above the water, called Clark's Point of View. Had it been named today, it would have been called Clark's Viewpoint since "point of view" is now a literary term having nothing to do with vistas. The site was named by William Clark who, on reaching the spot, described it as the most spectacular ocean view he'd ever seen. I'll buy that.

Clark's POV, just past the main head, offers the first vista northward, of Seaside and the Columbia mouth. I nominate it as the ideal turnaround spot for day-hikers, although the path hits the rim and openings of salal brush several more times in the mile beyond Clark's POV.

After that, of course, the woods close in for good. You already know how I feel about the grossly mis-named Tillamook Head Viewpoint, and my point of view regarding the trail's last two miles.

Elmer Felderheim Area entry sign.

4.

Falcon Cape

Length:	2 1/2 miles
Difficulty:	Moderate
Elevation:	50 to 250 feet
Season:	Any (avoid storms)
Water:	3 creeks, probably potable
USGS 7.5' Topo:	Arch Cape
Location:	T3N-R10W-Sec. 7
Ownership:	Oswald West State Park
Phone:	(503) 368-5153
Use intensity:	Medium
Camping:	Walk-in campground at park.

__Directions__: Take US-101 to Oswald West State Park, 15 miles south of Cannon Beach. The trailhead is located at the northernmost of the park's three paved parking areas, immediately north of Short Sand Creek. The other two parking lots access a picnic area and walk-in campground.

𝅘𝅥 𝅘𝅥 𝅘𝅥 𝅘𝅥

Of the three hikes in this book which access headlands jutting into the Pacific, all of about equal length, this is the easiest. While the Tillamook Head (Chapter 3) and Cape Lookout (Chapter 6) trails are a tad more scenic, this is no slouch by any stretch of the imagination.

Trails in the vicinity of Falcon Cape also lead to a gorgeous beach cove. And if cape and beach don't offer a sufficient workout, the trail up Neahkahnie Mountain (Chapter 5), second highest spot on the Oregon coast (after Curry County's Humbug Mountain), lies within the same park and connects with the Falcon Cape trail.

Oswald West State Park was named for a Governor of Oregon

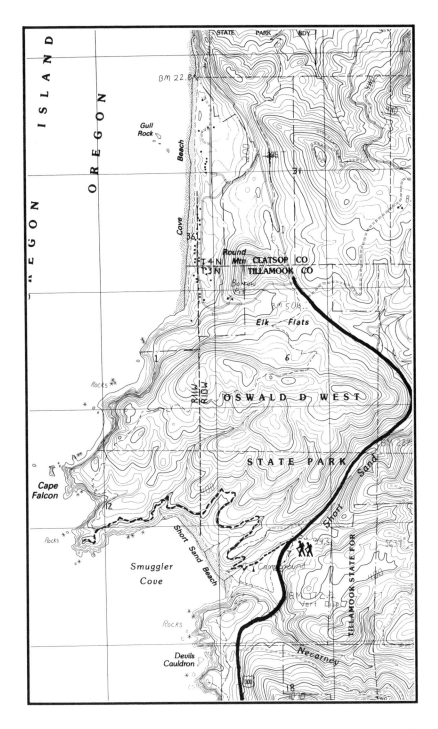

Falcon Cape 43

who served from 1910 to 1915. The State Park people would like you to call him "Os West" but I personally don't feel I know him well enough.

From the parking lot on Highway-101, the trail's initial segment is level at first, then descends gradually as the ocean is approached. It traverses a dense, old growth rainforest, several hundred feet uphill from Short Sand Creek. The usual species are present with Sitka spruce, Western hemlock and red alder predominating, along with Douglas-fir, Western redcedar, evergreen huckleberry, salal, sorrel, etc. While many of the trees are huge, none are as immense as the numerous decaying stumps.

After a half-mile, the path from the parking lot meets the Oregon Coast Trail. Head right (north) for Falcon Cape. For the beach, walk-in campground and the 1 mile connecting link to the Neahkahnie Mountain trail, head left (south). Neahkahnie Mountain is reached much more easily from a trailhead on Highway 101, a mile south of the Short Sand Creek parking area.

Before ascending the cape, the trail spends a mile dropping and rising three times as it spans three creeks, each at a slightly higher elevation than the last. It crosses the first creek, near sea level, in a muddy skunk cabbage bog. In fact, the entire path contained numerous muddy patches during my June visit.

Soon after the third creek, the trail hits its first vista point, looking southward to the secluded cove of Short Sand Beach. The beach is hemmed in by the towering cliffs of Falcon Cape, dropping off 200 feet just below your feet, and the cape formed by Neahkahnie Mountain, with its arched rock just offshore. The zig-zag trail up Neahkahnie Mountain is easily discerned from here.

For its final mile, the trail climbs gently in and out of woods and though openings of dense salal brush. Look for ever widening vistas to the south, with Nehalem Bay eventually coming into view. Near the end, the path jumps over the top of the cape and continues north. A short side path leads to the point. If you continue north on the Coast Trail, you'll cross Highway-101 in 31/2 miles, just south of the town of Arch Cape.

The narrow path to the point pushes its way through salal brush, trees clumps and grass, branching several times. Eventually, it hits the tip at a grassy overlook offering the first real view northward. With binoculars, you can pick out Cannon Beach,

Tillamook Head and Tillamook Lighthouse, to the north, with Neahkahnie Mountain and Nehalem Bay to the south.

I was impressed!

Rock at Falcon Cape. Oswald Wilderness Area.

5.

Neahkahnie Mountain

(Oswald West State Park)

Length:	11/2 miles to summit
Difficulty:	Difficult
Elevation:	300 to 1600 feet
Season:	All seasons
Water:	None
USGS 7.5' Topo:	Arch Cape, Nehalem
Location:	T3N-R10W-Sec. 17, 18
Ownership:	Oswald West State Park
Phone:	(503) 368-5153
Use intensity:	Medium
Camping:	Walk-in camp 1 mile north

Directions*: The two trailheads to Neahkahnie Mountain are a mile apart on US-101, between Nehalem and Arch Cape. From the Oswald West camping and day-use area, proceed south one mile on highway 101 to an overlook/turnout. A trail comes up from the beach and, across the highway, the Neahkahnie Mountain trail's north end takes off. The latter is marked by a post denoting the Oregon Coast Trail. A mile farther south on highway 101, at Neahkahnie Meadows, there's a similar post, near a dirt road heading inland. The trail's south end is found a half-mile up the dirt road.*

🚶🚶🚶

For a really mind boggling view of the Oregon Coast, forget about climbing out capes or parking at overlooks. This is a good as it gets. At 1632 feet, Neahkahnie Mountain is the second highest point on the Oregon Coast rising directly from the ocean. It is surpassed only by Humbug Mountain (1756 feet), near Port Orford,

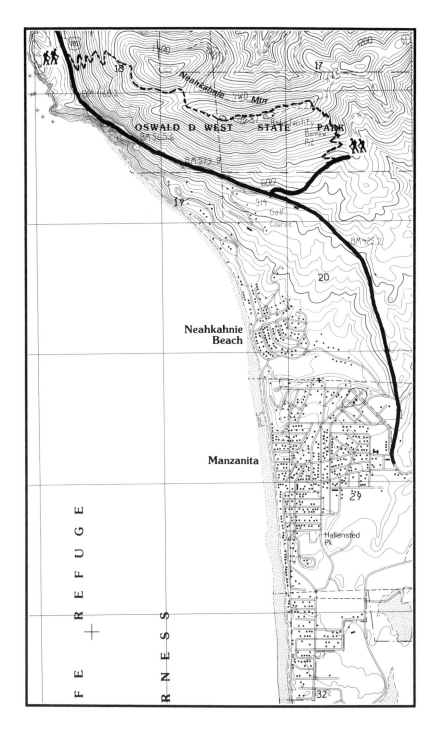

a couple hundred miles south.

Neither summits compare to the Pacific Coast's highest point, Kings Peak, on Cape Mendocino south of Eureka, California. It rises 4087 feet from sea level in a horizontal distance of three miles.

A three mile chunk of the Oregon Coast Trail climbs Neahkahnie Mountain from US-101, then returns to the highway. If not hiking through, take your pick as to which trailhead to use since both reach the top in 11/2 miles. Elevationally, the north trailhead begins 300 feet lower. The south trail is a little drier and brushier and thus has slightly better vistas. Obviously, the path up the north side offers views to the north while that on the south...

A third option is to walk up the gated park road just north of the north trailhead. It reaches the top in the same distance as the trail but swings way inland and has only a couple of switchbacks. It is much more open than the trails.

The north trailhead parking area on 101 ranks among the better grey whale viewing sites, in season. If you follow the trail in the opposite direction from the north trailhead, you'll find yourself on a beautiful one-mile connecting link which climbs down the rocky headland forming the base of Neahkahnie Mountain, to the Oswald West beach and campground.

Whichever trailhead you use, expect dense forest most of the way, with a frustrating dearth of vista points. While the local native tribes used to burn in this area to enhance deer and elk habitat, the forest has rebounded in most places. The mountain's name, which mean's "place of fire," refers to this practice.

The paths on both sides of the peak climb 1200 feet in about 11/2 miles in an endless series of short switchbacks. That's a rise of 800 feet per mile, which is getting up there on the difficulty scale. Carry water. Fortunately, the route isn't very long and does offer a few vistas. Most occur at openings where the forest yields to salal brush.

The trail does not quite reach the summit. Where it crests, scramble uphill to a cleared flat containing a microwave repeater and other electronic equipment. With a good map and binoculars on a clear day, you should be able to pick out Tillamook Head, Tillamook Bay, Tillamook, etc. With a little effort and imagination, you will also see Seattle, San Francisco, Fairbanks, Bogota, the Eiffel Tower, and the North Pole.

6.

Cape Lookout

(Cape Lookout State Park)

Length:	2 1/2 miles
Difficulty:	Moderate
Elevation:	900 to 400 feet
Season:	All seasons
Water:	None available
USGS 7.5' Topo:	Sand Lake
Location:	T3S-R11W-Sec. 1
Ownership:	Cape Lookout State Park
Phone:	(503) 842-4981
Camping:	Cape Lookout State Park
Use Intensity:	Heavy

<u>Directions</u>: From Tillamook, on US-101, follow signs for the Three Capes Scenic Drive (Capes Meares, Lookout and Kiwanda). Proceed west, around Tillamook Bay and past Cape Meares, to Cape Lookout State Park. Continue past the Cape Lookout campground and beach to the paved trailhead parking area at the hilltop, which holds 50 cars.

South of Tillamook on US-101, roads at Hemlock and Cloverdale also lead to Cape Lookout and the Three Capes Scenic Drive.

🚶🚶 🚶🚶 🚶🚶

First, let me list the many compelling reasons why one might hike this trail. After that, I'll share the difficulty encountered in my 1993 visit.

While Cape Lookout may not be quite as dramatic as the Tillamook Head and Falcon Cape Trails (Chapters 3 and 4), the narrow rock finger offers a tremendous panorama of the Oregon

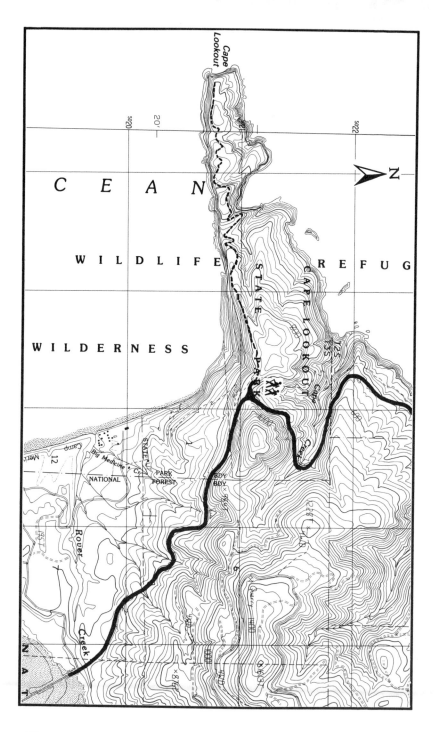

Cape Lookout

Coast. When you combine the Cape Lookout Trail with car visits to Cape Meares and Cape Kiwanda, the other state parks of the Three Cape Scenic Drive, the results are memorable.

Three pathways converge at Falcon Cape's hilltop trailhead. A two mile section of the Oregon Coast Trail leads south from the parking area, down a nightmarish grade, to secluded Sand Lake Beach. The Coast Trail also heads north, much more gently, arriving at the park campground and Netarts Beach after 21/2 miles. The Cape Trail lies between the two and is not part of the Coast Trail.

For its first mile, the Cape Trail is lovely, nearly level and deceptively innocent. It traverses high above Sand Lake Beach, offering spectacular views from atop a nearly vertical bluff. After a half-mile, it passes a plaque commemorating the 1943 crash of a military B-17 airplane into the cape.

The forest throughout is dense and coastal. It consists, not surprisingly, of Sitka spruce, Western hemlock and red alder, with a few Douglas-firs and Western redcedars thrown in.

Somewhere near the plaque, the path begins to descend, gradually at first, then somewhat more obviously. Near the start of mile two, it inscribes a series of steep switchbacks to the bottom of a little dale, then climbs out the other side and continues uphill for nearly a mile. Shortly beyond the dale, crossing to the cape's north side, an excellent vista to the north emerges as the trail makes its way around a deep inlet of perpendicular cliffs hundreds of feet high.

It is important to know, in light of the miserable trail conditions shortly beyond this spot, that in December, 1992, during a tremendous storm, 300 feet of the Cape Lookout Trail slid over these cliffs and crashed into the ocean. Had anyone been there, it would have been tragic.

In February, 1993, the trail was rerouted around the inlet, over a hill farther inland. In my mid-June visit, this segment had deteriorated to a steep, a half-mile long trough of foot deep mud. One would be hard pressed to even call it a trail. In the hundreds of trails I've been on, throughout the West, I've never seen anything quite like it.

The Cape Lookout management hopes that with drier weather and heavy summer use, things will settle down and get packed in. If not, they will take measures to help it along. Meanwhile,

I suggest: (1) Wear hiking boots, not sneakers. (2) Inquire into trail conditions at the campground.

As noted, climbing up and away from the inlet, the trail steepens. Soon after, the spectacular mud begins. The path crests a half-mile from the trail end. The mud bath continues a short (but steep) ways down the other side, levelling off when the old trail is rejoined.

From there on, it is smooth, gorgeous hiking. For its last 60 feet, the trail heads out over bare rock to the point, where there is a bench and a cable railing. While salal brush blocks the view north, the rocks and cliffs are inspiring and the vista west and south is unimpeded to the horizon. Maybe...just maybe...it was worth the trouble.

The Columbia River

7.

Wildwood/Macleay Trail

(Portland Forest Park)

Length: 11/2 to 28 miles
Difficulty: Easy
Elevation: 400 to 1000 feet
Season: All seasons
Water: Some
USGS 7.5" Topo: Portland, Linnton
Ownership: Portland Parks and Recreation
Phone: (503) 832-5123
Camping: No designated areas
Use intensity: Heavy

Directions: For the Wildwood/Lower Macleay trailhead, in Portland's Forest Park, take NW Burnside west to 23rd. Go north on 23rd to Lovejoy Road and proceed west to Cornell Road. Turn right on Cornell and continue to the Macleay Park parking area. Or follow NW Burnside west to Skyline, Skyline to Greenleaf and Greenleaf to Cornell Road. Turn right on Cornell and continue to the Macleay parking area. A large sign indicates trails in the vicinity. There's parking for 50 cars.

The Wildwood Trail passes numerous developed trailheads in addition to Macleay Park. These include Hoyt Arboretum, Pittock Mansion, 53rd Drive, Springville Road, Germantown Road and many other access points. For a map of the Wildwood and Macleay Trails, write the Portland Parks and Recreation Department.

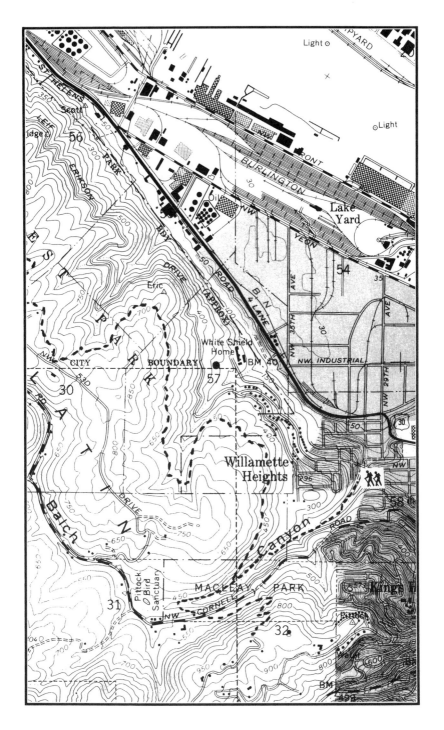

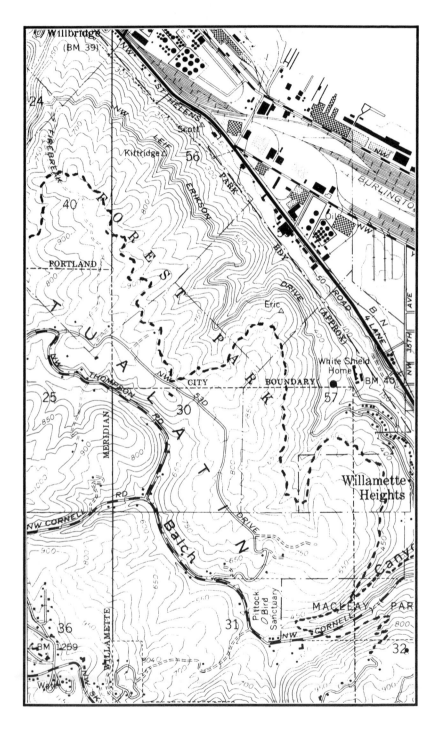

𝓍𝓍 𝓍𝓍 𝓍𝓍

As most Portlanders are aware, the Rose City is crammed with parks, boasting hills, forests and miles of outstanding trails. The paths decorating Portland's city green enclaves would make a worthy book in their own right.

In terms of mind boggling scenery and a sense of wilderness, however, it would be misleading to compare these parkland walks to trails, for example, on Mount Hood or Mount Jefferson. City parks fall into an totally separate category with, by and large, a range of experiences outside the scope of this book.

There are some notable exceptions. Two Portland park pathways are outstanding enough, with enough of a non-urban feel, to merit inclusion among the region's very best day-hikes. These are (1) the loop trail at Tryon Creek State Park (Chapter 8), and (2) Forest Park's Lower Macleay Trail.

Forest Park is the largest city park in the United States, covering nearly 5000 acres in the city's northwest corner. Its densely wooded, northeast facing hillside extends for eight miles and is cut by many narrow ravines and small creeks. Occasional grassy openings offer panoramic cityscapes, with Mount Hood nearly always rising in the background.

Forest Park's main hiking route is the Woodland Trail, which begins at Hoyt Arboretum and winds for twenty eight miles across the length of the park, to Germantown Road and beyond. Beautiful Skyline Drive parallels the a half-mile up the hill and hits the ridgetop several times, which the drive does not. Skyline Drive constitutes one of Portland's major scenic thoroughfares.

The Wildwood Trail, along with peripheral trails and fire roads, contains many segments in excess of three or four miles without a road crossing. A typical segment winds through a Douglas-fir, Western hemlock, Western redcedar, bigleaf maple and red alder forest, hitting vista openings from time to time and crossing shaded, cedar lined creeks every now and then.

The only Wildwood Trail portion to vary significantly from this is its spectacular but urban influenced initial segment. Running from Pittock Mansion to the Macleay Park trailhead, it drops 900 feet in 11/2 miles.

Forest Park's prettiest and most "wilderness" path, following the Wildwood and Lower Macleay Trails, begins at a busy, manicured trailhead. From there, the Wildwood Trail inscribes a series of switchbacks to the bottom of a steep, narrow, rock lined ravine.

At the bottom, all reminders of the city vanish. The trail crosses a rustic footbridge, then takes up a course along an ample, fast moving creek, shaded by large Douglas-firs, alders and maples.

The route follows the creek for a half-mile to Stone House, which is the shell of an old...stone house. Stone House marks the lowest elevation on the Wildwood Trail's twenty eight mile route. From there, the pathway peels off left and uphill, on its way to the rest of the park.

Beyond Stone House, the Lower Macleay Trail continues along the creek for another mile, crossing it twice. This serene and beautiful route, the park's highlight in my opinion, could just as easily be Trapper Creek (Chapter 55) or the Salmon River Trail (Chapter 30), as the middle of Portland.

Then, all of a sudden, you find yourself not in a wilderness canyon but on Portland's Thurman Street. While it is a fairly jarring experience, I enjoyed the contrast. There are, after all, worse places to be than the middle of Portland.

8.

Tryon Creek

(Tryon Creek State Park)

Length:	Up to 2 miles
Difficulty:	Easy
Elevation:	75 feet
Season:	Any
Water:	Yes
USGS 7.5" Topo:	Lake Oswego
Ownership:	Tryon Creek State Park
Phone:	(503) 653-3166
Camping:	None
Use intensity:	Heavy

__Directions__: In Portland, follow SW Terwilliger to the park entrance and main parking area (11321 Terwilliger Blvd.). The route and entrance are well signed. Several other trailheads provide access from road-ends along the park periphery. There are two other trailheads on Terwilliger, two on Boones Ferry Road, one on State Street, one on 4th Avenue, one on Englewood Drive and one on Iron Mountain Road.

ﾀﾀ ﾀﾀ ﾀﾀ

For my first twenty years in Oregon, I called Tryon Creek Park "Fort Tryon Park" and found it remarkable that a park in Portland had the same name as one in New York City. It wasn't until my daughter, Sara, enrolled at Lewis and Clark College, adjacent to Tryon Creek Park, that I noticed the difference in the names.

On discovering that Sara was spending much time tromping around this pastoral paradise (when not studying, of course), I asked her to write it up for me. The result reaffirmed my belief

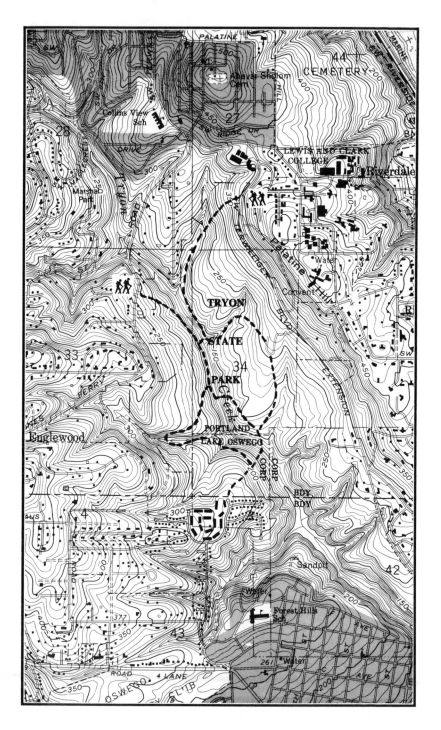

Tryon Creek

that people take to the trails for many reasons. Who is to say whether one person's motive is more valid than another?

Sara couldn't care less about things like identifying trees or which trail leads where. Her joyful description of Tryon Creek forced me to ponder whether I am overly hung up on such things. With hardly a mention of natural history, she captured the essence of a Sunday afternoon at Fort Tryon Park from the prespective of a teenager and college student. I must admit, I am envious.

It would be interesting to have her rewrite the chapter in twenty years and see if her enthusiasm and sense of adventure has bogged down in the trivial details of life. For now, however, if you have an overwhelming need to know which trail leads where, check the accompanying map.

𝍐 𝍐 𝍐

Once my father saddled me with the task of formally investigating Tryon Creek, all available time suddenly vanished like moondogs in a monsoon. I meant to go there all summer but something always came up. I'd have to study, or it would rain, or there'd be no transportation, or the preliminary ten block hike to my friend Todd's apartment would wear me out.

It wasn't exactly procrastination. I was just waiting for the elements to "fall into harmony." I'd never forgive myself if the day was lost because I chose to get the thing over rather than bask in the experience.

On a sunny, late September day, I finally managed to fall off my futon, turn off Oprah and bribe Todd, along with my roommate Brenda, into doing the same. We left early, at 2:30 PM, and soon found ourselves speeding along Barbur Boulevard, listening to the Cajun hoedown of Buckwheat Zydeco at full volume.

You need to know that while Todd is a splendid fellow, he has ideas others on the planet can't quite grasp. One is that everyone around him is as interested in what he is saying, doing and listening to as he is.

As Todd pulled into the Tryon Creek State Park parking lot, Brenda and I had slid as far down in our seats as we could without landing on the floor. Rather than turn down his music, he decided that all the assembled retired couples and college

Tryon Creek 61

kids must know Zydeco.

I forgot to mention that Todd was driving his brother's car. The main feature of this automobile is what is known in these parts as "kickass stereo."

I got the courage to lift my head to window level just in time to see a Saab full of Lewis and Clark students pull up. It's a small school and luckily, they happened to be friends of mine. That's the only thing which prevented a confrontation.

Tryon Creek State Park is made up of dozens of short trails, most between a quarter-mile and a mile. They form a network of loops, connecting with other loops every few hundred yards or so. While it may not be entirely honest to call any of them "hikes," they were interesting, easy and mellow enough to keep even Todd from complaining very much. If you play your cards right, you can walk two or three miles without hitting a road.

Describing nature isn't really my forte but the place is certainly beautiful; very green with lots of plants and stuff. Of course this isn't exactly the High Sierra as far as "take your breath away" scenery. But it is nice. Very nice, in fact.

There are some rare flowers scattered around which you can read about in the gift shop (I forgot to mention, the park has a gift shop). There are also lots of really cool, super huge spider webs, several thousand trees and a creek. My dad says the trees are mostly Douglas-fir and hardwoods.

The attraction of this uniquely located state park is more where it is than what it is. Where it is is the middle of Portland. What a great idea for a Sunday afternoon with the kids. And that's exactly what you'll find swarming in anxious anticipation of their first glimpse of the much advertised Beaver Bridge. It's a perfect destination to introduce the kids to the wonders of nature...even if they do spend the entire trip whining like stuck police sirens.

Trails, and signs along the trails, are short and abundant. If you listen carefully, you can hear the magical sounds of...was it a dancing stream? A scurrying bunny? A new Isuzu Trooper speeding along Terwilliger, bound for Lewis and Clark?

Which brings me to the only wildlife you are likely see. They come from prep schools in Massachusetts and Vermont. Like army worms, they descend on the area. You can spot them by their carefully ungroomed hair, their soiled *REI* and *Patagonia* wardrobe and the Lewis and Clark stickers on their Land Cruisers, Troopers and Cherokees.

Most of the time, these classmates of mine are solid, relatively normal people. But something in the air or water at Tryon Creek seems to skew their sense of reality. They love to wander aimlessly on and off the path, becoming "one with Oregon."

The best way to get rid of them is to casually say something like, "Honey, what do you suppose was in that plastic bag on the trail back there?" Should that fail, do what we did. Smile and say, "Hey man. Nature. Dig it."

They'll smile back, then amble off muttering things like, "Yeah man. Wow."

Our Sunday sojourn proved frighteningly domestic. I had to remind Todd repeatedly that the trail is not an ashtray. And once or twice, we were forced to physically restrain Brenda, who has a passion for stealing flowers, from messing with the endangered, protected-by-heavy-fines flora.

We left feeling good, glad we'd gotten away from the pavement, if only for a short time. And glad also that the same pavement was waiting for us at the end of the trail and that we could be at the Dairy Queen, for a post-hike Mr. Misty, in less than ten minutes.

9.

South Falls

(Silver Falls State Park)

Length:	1 1/4 miles
Difficulty:	Moderate
Elevation:	1500 to 1200 feet
Season:	All seasons
Water:	Plentiful
USGS 7.5" Topo:	Drakes Prairie, Stout Mountain
Ownership:	Silver Falls State Park
Phone:	(503) 873-8681
Camping:	Silver Falls State Park
Use intensity:	Very popular place

Directions: *Take Highway-22 east from Salem, towards Detroit Lake. Turn onto Highway-214, following signs to Silver Falls State Park. Continue to the South Falls day use area. Park in the lot on the left, which has room for a million cars (100 anyway). The trailhead is at the lot's west end. A well marked, asphalt walkway leads past the restrooms and lodge to the falls overlook and trail.*

𝀥𝀥 𝀥𝀥 𝀥𝀥

Although the South Falls Trail's initial quarter-mile may be the most hiked in Oregon, and the next mile isn't much better, there's a good reason for this. Silver Falls State Park ranks among Oregon's premier scenic wonders. And the principle attraction is South Falls. Even the drive to Silver Falls State Park is gorgeous as Highway-214 winds through rolling farmland with long vistas of the Willamette Valley and the Cascades.

On peak weekends, use intensity at South Falls is beyond heavy. The non-stop stream of hikers brings to mind theater

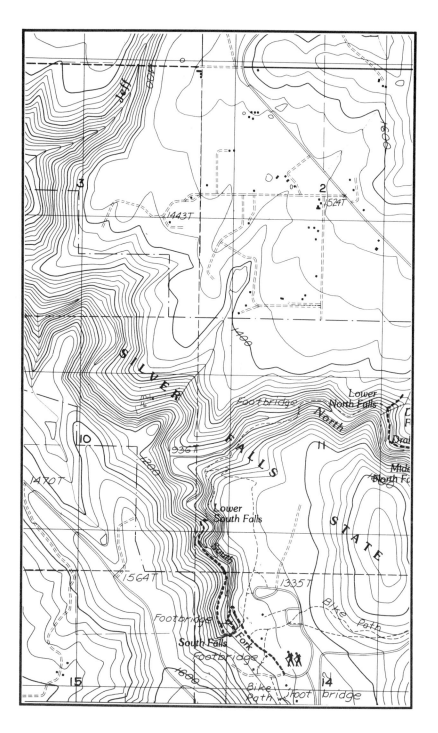

South Falls   65

lines in New York City. To buck the crowds, go midweek or in the off-season. To avoid day-use fees, go between October and April. Or begin your hike at the North Falls area (Chapter 10).

Actually, the crowds didn't bother me. What did bother me was the fact that despite posted signs that dogs are not allowed on the South Falls Trail, one party in ten packed a pooch. Enforcement would appear in order.

My other complaint is that not one of the park's ten waterfalls contains the word "silver" in its name. In fact, most Silver Falls waterfalls have unbelievably pedestrian names. They surely could have done better than "North" and "South." Where are the Wahkeenas and Oneontas of Silver Falls State Park?

Even the name "Silver Falls" isn't that original. Coos County boasts a Golden and Silver Falls while one of the scenic wonders of Josephine County is Silver Creek Falls.

From the extremely well marked trailhead, the asphalt path passes trimmed lawns, restrooms, a historic lodge and side paths to the upper South Fork of Silver Creek, all in the first 1/10th mile. Just beyond the lodge, you arrive at the South Falls overlook, revealing a sheer, 177-foot plunge, over an overhanging cliff of basalt lava, into an emerald grotto. The trail can be seen, halfway down the cliff, following an eroded seam between two lava layers.

From the overlook, the path cuts a long switchback down the cliff, at a somewhat less vertical spot, quickly making its way onto the narrow ledge which takes you behind the falls and one of the greatest scenic "rushes" you're likely to experience.

Emerging on the other side, the path shoots sharply downward to the creek. The combination of asphalt, steepness, accumulated mud and constant mist makes this segment slippery. The pavement ends at the bottom of the descent, where the path levels off at the creek. A nearby footbridge offers an excellent view of South Falls. It connects to a short, steep trail back up to the overlook.

For the next half-mile, the path follows a level route along the South Fork of Silver Creek, through a forest of Douglas-fir, Western Hemlock and Western redcedar. The water looks amazingly placid, considering the trauma it just experienced. And the trauma it is about to experience.

Soon, the trail crests a small rise, turns away from the creek and begins a dizzying descent. The top of Lower South Falls comes into view just beyond the crest. To fully appreciate it, follow the path to the bottom. Since the falls are nearly 100 feet high, and the path crests 50 feet above their top, the trail drops 150 feet in a quarter-mile. It seems much steeper as it makes its way down a series of stairways.

Although only a little more than half as high as South Falls, at 93 feet, Lower South Falls more than holds its own against its heralded upstream neighbor. For one thing, the creek immediately above Lower South Falls occupies a rather odd canyon. Despite its nearly vertical walls, the creek bed is extremely wide and table-like as it approaches the falls' rim. Lower South Falls is thus much wider than South Falls.

After a tremendous drop over yet another overhanging basalt cliff, the water hits a rounded rock bulge, over which it fans for its last 40 feet. The trail runs behind the falls, on the seam between the overhang and the bulge.

The Ridge Trail breaks away to the right, 1/4 mile beyond Lower South Falls. It follows an extremely steep, one mile route out of the canyon and through the woods, back to the starting point. To visit the park's other eight waterfalls, continue ahead instead of turning onto the Ridge Trail. You will end up at Lower North Falls in a mile, via a route away from the creek.

10.

Middle North Falls

(Silver Falls State Park)

Length:	11/2 miles
Difficulty:	Easy
Elevation:	1500 to 1300 feet
Season:	All seasons
Water:	Certain, always available
USGS 7.5" Topo:	Elk Prairie, Drakes Crossing
Ownership:	Silver Falls State park
Phone:	(503) 873-8681
Camping:	Silver Falls State Park
Use intensity:	Heavy

Directions*: Take Highway-22 east from Salem. At the junction with Highway-214, follow the signs to Silver Falls State Park. Continue past the South Falls day use area to the Winter Falls parking lot, which holds 20 cars. The Winter Falls trailhead is well marked.*

𝆕𝆕 𝆕𝆕 𝆕𝆕

At least five waterfalls, ranging from the really, really pretty to the downright mind boggling, adorn this marvelous trail through Oregon's most popular state park. An energetic hiker could throw in up to five additional falls, the park's entire complement, without exceeding the definition of a reasonable day-hike.

Both the Winter Falls trailhead, and the nearby North Falls trailhead, boast far fewer visitors than those thronging the South Falls area (Chapter 9), although use remains heavy. One can avoid the summer day-use fees imposed at the South Falls day-use area by beginning at the Winter Falls (or North Falls) trailhead and hiking three miles (or 41/2 miles), to South Falls.

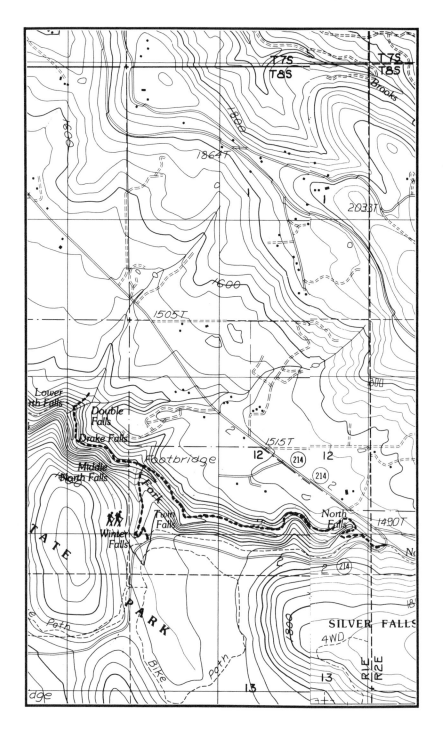

Middle North Falls 69

From the Winter Falls Trailhead, the path cuts a long switchback down to aptly named Winter Falls (which tends to dry up in late summer). It's only a five minute walk to Winter Falls, on a side creek immediately below the trailhead parking lot. At 134 feet, the tumble is impressive when there's water present.

Below Winter Falls, the trail levels off and follows the side creek a half-mile, to a foot bridge over the North Fork of Silver Creek. Across the bridge, turn left for Middle North Falls, Double Falls and South Falls. Hang a right for Twin Falls, 1/4 mile away, and North Falls, 11/4 miles away. Twin Falls is a 31 foot drop whose flow is split in two by a jutting rock. More on North Falls shortly.

Taking a left at the bridge, it is 1/4 mile to Middle North Falls, the highlight of this chapter. The 106 foot plunge crashes into a huge and lovely grotto, accessed by a short side trail. The segment between the bridge and Middle North Falls gets a little muddy in winter.

Drake Falls makes an appearance 1/4 mile beyond Middle North Falls. Drake is the lowest of the park's ten waterfalls at twenty-seven feet. Its water cascades over a rounded rock surface.

From Drake Falls, it is another 1/4 mile to the short turnoff to Double Falls, the park's highest at 178 feet. While South Falls is the more popular and spectacular, Double Falls exceeds it in height by a foot. Double Falls' sheer cliff basin is well worth visiting, although it is far more confining than the basin surrounding South Falls.

The main difference between Double and South Falls is that since Double Falls is located on a side creek, the water volume is much less. Double Falls has an upper drop of 50 feet. A short cascade then leads to the lacy lower drop, where the water hugs the rock surface rather than falling freely.

Lower North Falls lies immediately beyond the Double Falls turnoff. While Lower North's vertical plunge is considerably more voluminous than that of Double Falls, it is only 30 feet high. Should you continue beyond Double Falls, you'd be marching smack into Chapter 9.

Most visitors consider North Falls the park's second most beautiful after South Falls. While North Falls is easily visited via the Winter Falls trailhead, it is best approached from the North Falls trailhead. It is also visible by car. From the Winter Falls trailhead, a 3/4 mile drive on Highway-214 leads to the North Falls overlook. Another 1/4 mile lands you at the North Falls trailhead, where Highway-214 crosses the North Fork of Silver Creek before continuing on to Silverton.

A steep, quarter-mile path leads from the North Falls trailhead to the base of thundering, 136 foot North Falls, with its undercut cliff of basalt lava. As at South and Lower South Falls, the trail cuts behind the water, except in this case, it does so at ground level. The North Falls Trail connects to the Winter Falls Trail after 11/2 miles.

Also from the North Falls trailhead, an easy, quarter-mile hike upstream, along the North Fork of Silver Creek, takes you to 65 foot Upper North Falls, the park's least visited.

11.

Angels Rest/Bridal Veil/Latourel

(Columbia Gorge Scenic Area)

Length:	21/4 miles (to Angel's Rest)
Difficulty:	Moderate to difficult
Elevation:	100 to 1600 feet
Season:	Any
Location:	T1N-R5E-Sec. 22
Water:	A little
USGS 7.5" Topo:	Bridal Veil
Ownership:	Hood River NF and Oregon St. Parks
Phone:	(503) 695-2276 or 386-2333
Camping:	Talbot State Park
Use intensity:	Moderate

Directions: *For Angel's Rest, leave I-84 at the Bridal Veil Exit (#28). There's a large gravel parking area, with room for 15 cars, where the freeway exit ramp meets the Scenic Highway. The trailhead is across the road, marked by a wooden sign on a tree. For Bridal Veil Falls, Shepperds Dell, Latourel Falls and Talbot State Park, follow the Scenic Highway west from Bridal Veil.*

🚶🚶🚶🚶🚶

For real exercise, and a view of the Columbia River Gorge that makes popular Crown Point look like Chicago back alley, try hiking to Angel's Rest from the trailhead near Bridal Veil Falls. While the path climbs to 1500 feet above the river in 21/4 miles, at a gradient of 667 feet per mile, its beauty and variety more than compensates for the unrelenting upgrade.

Angel's Rest can be seen towering above I-84 beginning at

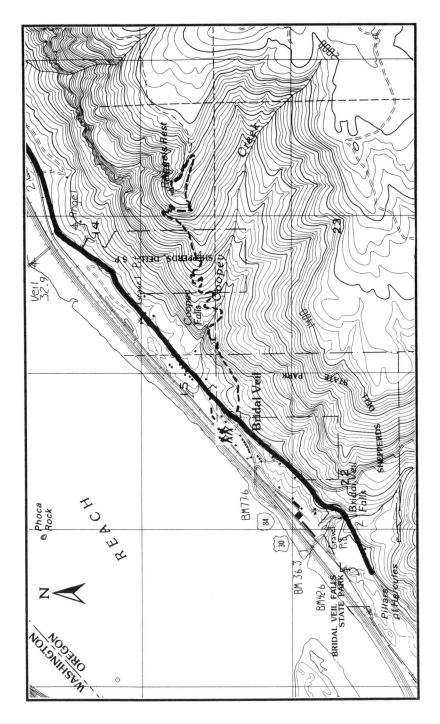

Rooster Rock. It looks discouragingly high and far away from there. Once on the trail, however, things progress quickly.

From the trailhead, the route climbs a half-mile, through old growth woods and across a couple boulder slopes, to a little bridge across Coopey Creek, just above Coopey Falls. Despite its 100 foot height, Coopey Falls is easily missed since the trail doesn't get very close and the best view is obscured by trees.

Beyond Coopey Falls, the path inscribes a series of long switchbacks up the side of Coopey Creek's wide canyon. According to the "Trails of the Columbia Gorge" contour map, the path remains entirely within the canyon until reaching the top. Actually, it swings around several times to the slopes above the Columbia, offering ever improving panoramas.

Halfway up, the route breaks out of the dense forest of Douglas-fir, Western Hemlock, Western redcedar and bigleaf maple, entering a huge burn area. In between the dead and blackened trees, a wonderland of wildflowers has taken hold, the most prominent of which are columbine and tiger lily. The rockier areas take on the look of a Japanese garden.

The precipice which is your objective comes into view a mile up from the trailhead, still looking far off and high up.

When the path curves into the canyon, then breaks out onto some shale rock high above the Columbia Gorge, you know you're approaching the last switchback. Look for an occasional quaking aspen here, clinging to the most exposed outcroppings. Aspen generally isn't found in western Oregon, preferring the bitter cold of the High Cascades and eastern Oregon. It's presence atttests to extremely harsh winter conditions.

Angel's Rest itself is an oblong tower connected to the Gorge's main wall by a narrow, rocky ledge. It's flat summit covers about an acre and is vegetated with scrub white oak. Vistas, needless to say, abound. Were I an Angel, I could think of no better place to take a load off.

Just before crossing the narrow ledge, which requires a little scrambling; the trail to Devil's Rest, Wahkeena Falls and Multnomah Falls (Chapter 12), peels off to the right (I didn't see a sign). It's five miles to the Wahkeena Falls trailhead from the Angel's Rest trailhead.

The west end of the Columbia Gorge Scenic Highway boasts several short, exquisite hikes in addition to Angel's Rest. In fact, you could fill a satisfying day with short trails to waterfalls in the Columbia Gorge. Paths to Latourel Falls, Bridal Veil Falls, Wahkeena Falls, Multnomah Fall (Chapter 12), Oneonata Gorge (Chapter 13), Horestail Falls, Elowah Falls (Chapter 14) and Wahclella Falls (Chapter 15), are all less than a mile.

Of the 70 or so Gorge waterfalls, my favorite is the very first one encountered coming east from Portland. While Latourel's 249 foot plunge ranks second to Multnomah, nothing in the Gorge quite equals the exquisite basin of undercut rock into which Latourel Falls...er, ah...falls.

From the Latourel Falls parking area in Talbot State Park, two miles east of Vista House, a quarter-mile trail visits the falls' splash pool. If you follow the uphill path from the parking area, you'll hit the top of the falls in a mile, only to discover an upper falls just above. By the Bernstein rating system, a rise of 300 feet in a mile isn't that bad.

A mile east of Latourel Falls on the Scenic Highway, you'll find Shepperd's Dell State Park, where a short trail into a little alcove reveals a couple more waterfalls.

Two miles east of Shepperd's Dell, Bridal Veil Falls turns up. Bridal Veil is popular for its short access trail and for having its own freeway exit. It is the only major Gorge waterfall below the Scenic Highway.

Bridal Veil Falls annoyed me. It might have had something to do with the fact that I hiked 41/2 miles up Eagle Creek and climbed to Upper Multnomah Falls the same day. To illustrate how tired I was, the trailhead sign said it was 2/3 of a mile round trip to Bridal Veil Falls. It took me most of the hike to calculate how far that is one way.

And yes, Bridal Veil cuts a fine figure of a fall; a towering double horsetail careening down a moss covered cliff.

12.

Multnomah & Wahkeena Falls

(Columbia Gorge Scenic Area)

Length: 13/4 miles
Difficulty: Moderate to difficult
Elevation: 100 to 1200 feet
Season: All seasons
Location: T2N-R6E-Sec. 7
Water: Plentiful
USGS 7.5" Topo: Bridal Veil, Multnomah Falls
Ownership: Hood River NF
Phone: (503) 695-2276
Camping: At Wahkeena Falls
Use intensity: Heavy to moderate

Directions: For Multnomah Falls, take I-84 east from Portland to the Multnomah Falls exit and viewing area. For Wahkeena Falls, drive west a half-mile from Multnomah Falls, on the Columbia Gorge Scenic Highway.

****

At 620 feet, Multnomah Falls is America's highest waterfall outside Yosemite National Park. As such, it ranks among Oregon's premiere scenic attractions. Visitors find not only an awesome display of nature, but vast parking lots, teeming masses of humanity, restaurants, etc.

A fine pathway, called the Larch Mountain Trail, leaves the Multnomah Falls viewing and parking area and ascends the falls in 11/4 miles. On my June, 1993 visit, I found this path closed for repairs. It turned out to be a stroke of luck because otherwise, I'd never have discovered the Wahkeena Falls/Perdition Trail, that climbs Multnomah Falls in an identical distance,

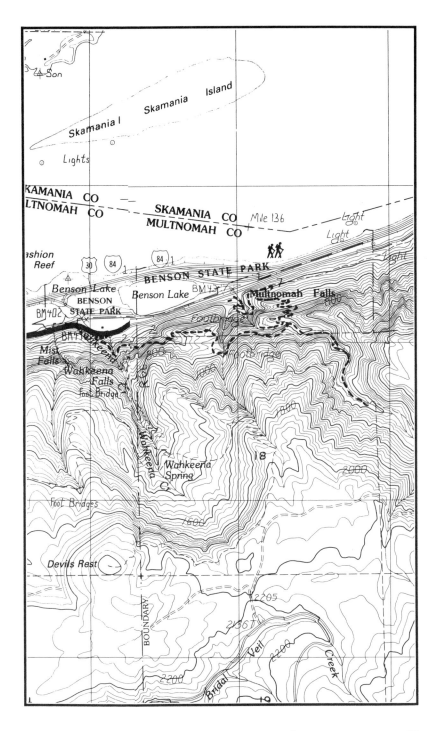

over a much less traveled and more varied route.

Be aware that the plethora of books and maps on the Columbia Gorge contain numerous inconsistencies. Multnomah Creek is a particular hotbed of misinformation. For example, one book rates both the Multnomah and Wahkeena Falls hikes as "easy." In my rating system, which disregards differences in individual ability, they are considered "difficult" because the gradient exceeds 500 feet per mile.

Another book lists the falls on Multnomah Creek as follows: Multnomah Falls (lower and upper tier), Dutchman Falls, Double Falls (lower and upper tier), and Upper Multnomah Falls. It claims that Double Falls's lower tier is 75 feet high, its upper tier tops 100 feet and that Upper Multnomah Falls is a 15 foot dribble above Double Falls. Most references, however, make no mention of a "Double Falls" and identify the 75 foot drop as Upper Multnomah Falls.

While I observed only two falls in the canyon above Multnomah Falls, neither I nor the Forest Service categorically rule out the existence of a 100 foot waterfall immediately above the 75 foot drop. It's not visible from the trail. One widely distributed map shows Triple Falls immediately above Upper Multnomah Falls, omitting the real Triple Falls on Oneonta Creek (Chapter 13).

Let's begin hiking at the Multnomah Falls viewing area, location of the Multnomah Falls/Larch Mountain trailhead. This elaborate path, with its fancy stonework and bridges, winds dizzyingly to the bridge between Multnomah Falls' lower and upper tiers. After crossing to the creek's east bank, it inscribes a series of switchbacks up a mostly forested talus slope to a ridgetop 100 feet above the top of the falls.

Several more switchbacks drop the path down to the upper creek. It then follows the creek a quarter-mile north to a railed platform at the lip of Multnomah Falls' 620 foot upper tier. All in all, it is a marvelous outing. Unless the trail is closed for repairs or you seek a slightly different perspective.

🚶🚶 🚶🚶

The Wahkeena Falls Trail begins at the Wahkeena Falls parking and viewing area, a half-mile west of Multnomah Falls. At 242 feet, Wahkeena's upper tier ranks third in the Columbia Gorge after Multnomah and Latourel Falls. Like Multnomah, a concrete bridge spans the creek between the upper and lower tiers.

Shortly beyond the bridge and around a point, the Wahkeena Trail bends uphill to the right while the Perdition Trail continues ahead. I don't care what any guidebook says, there's no way something called the "Perdition Trail" could be easy. Follow the Perdition Trail for Multnomah Falls. I'll get back to the Wahkeena Trail shortly.

The "perdition" part of the Perdition Trail begins a quarter-mile past the Perdition/Wahkeena junction, when the path shoots straight up a rockfall and cliff at a 100% gradient. A steep fan of loose boulders leads to a concrete staircase which is undercut and eroded at the bottom. Another concrete staircase, immediately above, is nearly buried in debris. Fortunately, this segment is only a couple hundred feet long. It was scheduled for badly needed maintenance in 1993.

Past the rockfall, the trail enters a dry, hanging canyon forested with Douglas-fir and flowered with purple pentstemon. Soon after, it hits a narrow ridge, which it surmounts in a steep, interminable series of railroad tie stairs. The view is terrific, with the ridge dropping straight into the Multnomah Falls parking lot.

After all that huffing and puffing, the path loses a couple hundred feet, which it must then regain. Halfway along this downhill pitch, a short spur leads to a rock outcropping with Multnomah Falls just coming into view and a sweeping panorama of the Columbia. You're now eye level with the top of Multnomah Falls.

After bottoming out, the trail makes its way through another hanging, wooded basin, climbing moderately and following the base of a columnar basalt cliff. It levels off after rounding a point. Just before the point, another side spur affords a commanding view of Multnomah Falls.

You soon find yourself in the upper canyon of Multnomah Creek. On the opposite bank, the high end of the trail from the Multnomah Falls parking area can be seen, with its endless queue of hikers. It's a quarter-mile up the canyon, and 1 1/4 miles from the Wahkeena trailhead, to the end of the Perdition Trail at the junction with the Larch Mountain Trail. A little bridge crosses the creek at the junction. Go left, over the bridge, for the Multnomah Falls viewing platform. Continue straight for the various upper falls and Larch Mountain.

Dutchman Falls; a wide, fan shaped formation 20 feet high; appears a quarter-mile beyond the Perdition/Larch Mountain junction. After another slightly uptrending quarter-mile, Upper Multnomah Falls (or lower Double Falls), plunges 75 feet in a vertical drop. The area of overhanging rock along the trail, between Dutchman and Upper Multnomah Falls, is called Dutchman's Tunnel.

Beyond Upper Multnomah Falls, it is five miles to the top of Larch Mountain, with a breathtaking gorge overlook from an elevation of 4056 feet. As with Wahtum Lake (Chapter 16), I'm uncomfortable with Larch Mountain as a hiking destination because you can drive there.

𝞨𝞨𝞨𝞨𝞨

If you're feeling energetic on the way back from Multnomah Falls, the upper portion of the Wahkeena Trail, above the junction with the Perdition Trail, offers some interesting highlights. Alternating between steep switchbacks and gentle contours, it rises 1000 feet in the 11/4 miles between the trailhead and Wahkeena Springs (3/4 miles from the Perdition/Wahkeena junction). *En route*, it passes Fairy Falls and a side trail to yet another vista point.

Should you continue on from Wahkeena's gushing springs, you'll emerge onto the Larch Mountain Trail after a mile, a half-mile above Upper Multnomah Falls. Or, you can branch off to the Devil's Rest Trail, a "moderate," (devilishly steep at first, then angelishly gentle), 11/2 mile climb ending at the Devil's Rest overlook. For the record, Devil's Rest, at 2500 feet, is a mile away from and 900 feet above Angel's Rest (Chapter 11).

13.

Oneonta Gorge

(Columbia Gorge Scenic Area)

Length:	1 mile (Oneonta Falls)
Difficulty:	Moderate
Elevation:	100 to 700 feet
Season:	All Seasons
Location:	T1N-R6E-Sec. 9
Water:	OK
USGS 7.5" Topo:	Multnomah Falls
Ownership:	Mount Hood NF
Phone:	(503) 695-2276
Camping:	Ainsworth St. Park
Use intensity:	Moderate

**Directions**: Take I-5 east to the east end of the Columbia Gorge Scenic Drive. Get off at Ainsworth State Park and follow the drive west, past Horsetail Falls, to the Oneonta Gorge parking area. The Oneonta Falls trailhead lies a quarter-mile west of the Oneonta Gorge viewing area, at a well marked parking area, with room for ten cars.

🚶🚶🚶🚶

Of the Columbia Gorge's many mind-boggling landmarks, my personal favorites are Latourel Falls (Chapter 11) and Oneonta Gorge. Oneonta Gorge can be seen from the highway and is explored by a fabulous a quarter-mile path up the creek bed. The entirely separate Oneonta Trail also ranks high in scenic quality.

Oneonta Gorge is a narrow slit in the towering basaltic lava formations comprising the Columbia River Gorge. Its sheer walls converge above the creek, forming a light starved, 150 foot high,

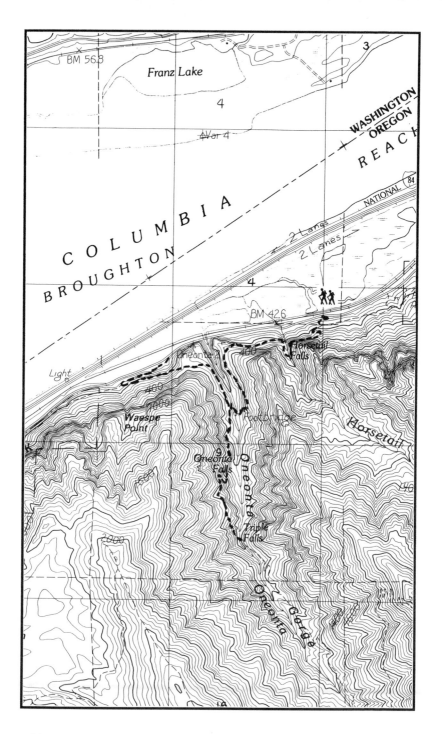

Oneonta Gorge

tunnel-like crevice above the wide, level creek. It's a mysterious and unique environment, enhanced by an array of wildflowers, including several of the 15 species unique to the gorge. The Columbia kittentail falls into the latter category. Flowers are often displayed as hanging gardens clinging to the rock wall.

A quarter-mile trail through the gorge wades the creek to the base of Lower Oneonta Falls. By all means, don't miss this spooky wonderland.

Reaching the thirty foot upper falls, a quarter-mile upstream from the cascading lower falls, requires doubling back to the parking area and following the Oneonta Trail, taking off a quarter-mile west on the Scenic Drive. Don't confuse it with a steep way trail up the rock face, which begins a few hundred feet west of the gorge viewing area and dead ends after a tenth of a mile.

The Oneonta Trail starts as a steep, a quarter-mile spur linking with the Gorge Trail. Turn left where the spur meets the Gorge Trail and continue 3/4 mile into Oneonta Gorge, rising for a ways, then leveling off. All but the last quarter-mile parallels the Scenic Highway and the Columbia River.

Just before entering Oneonta Gorge, the route passes both ends of a side loop offering a fine view of the Columbia Gorge. Soon after, the trail swings into the Oneonta Creek drainage, well above Oneonta Gorge. A mile from the trailhead, you arrive at a junction marked by blue signs. The upper trail leads to Triple Falls (spelled with three P's on the sign), while the lower switches steeply down to the creek, a footbridge and Oneonta Falls.

Oneonta Falls horsetails through a wide rock slit immediately upstream from the footbridge. This is not the region's most impressive falls. To make a real hike of the trip, double back and continue on to Triple Falls, a mile upstream. At Triple Falls, with its three pronged tumble, the path again drops down to and across Oneonta Creek, then climbs the far bank and continues upstream.

Technically, Triple Falls is not a triple fall but a three pronged segmented fall. A triple fall would be three successive waterfalls, not one waterfall divided in three. Taking a cue from Silver Falls State Park's Twin Falls (Chapter 10), Triple Falls would be better called Triplet Falls.

For another variation, continue over the footbridge at Oneonta

Falls to Horsetail Falls. Beyond Oneonta Creek, the path climbs the far bank in a series of switchbacks, emerging at Horsetail Falls. From the bridge, it is a half-mile to Horsetail Creek and a mile to the Horsetail Falls trailhead.

The Horsetail Falls viewing and parking area is a half-mile east of Oneonta Gorge on the Scenic Drive. To start there, look for a trailhead just east of the parking lot for the 175 foot waterfall. The path climbs the falls, then passes behind Ponytail Falls, between water and cliff, immediately upstream from Horsetail Falls, before heading towards Oneonta Creek.

Elowah Falls. Columbia Gorge.

14.

Elowah Falls

Length:	1 mile
Difficulty:	Moderate
Elevation:	250 to 450 feet
Season:	All seasons
Location:	T2N-R7E-Sec. 31
Water:	Plentiful
USGS 7.5" Topo:	Tanner Butte
Ownership:	Mount Hood NF
Phone:	(503) 386-2333
Camping:	Ainsworth State Park
Use intensity:	Moderate

__Directions__: Leave I-84 at the Warrendale exit and proceed east on the frontage road paralleling the freeway's south side, to the well marked trailhead parking area, which holds eight cars.

🚶🚶 🚶🚶 🚶🚶

What Elowah Falls lacks in water volume, it makes up in magical aura. Add to that the fact that it is perhaps the least visited of the major waterfalls off I-84, and you have a truly enticing, if short outing. I must not be the only one who found Elowah Falls special. It is featured on the cover of the photography book "Oregon III," by Ray Atkison.

Bear in mind, of course, that the light use received by the Elowah Falls Trail, by Columbia Gorge standards, translates at least to moderate elsewhere. Possibly heavy.

The path begins at a sign directing hikers to the Columbia Gorge Trail and McCord Creek Trail. For Elowah Falls, head east (left) on the Gorge Trail and/or turn left whenever you come to a junction. Elowah Falls is located on McCord Creek

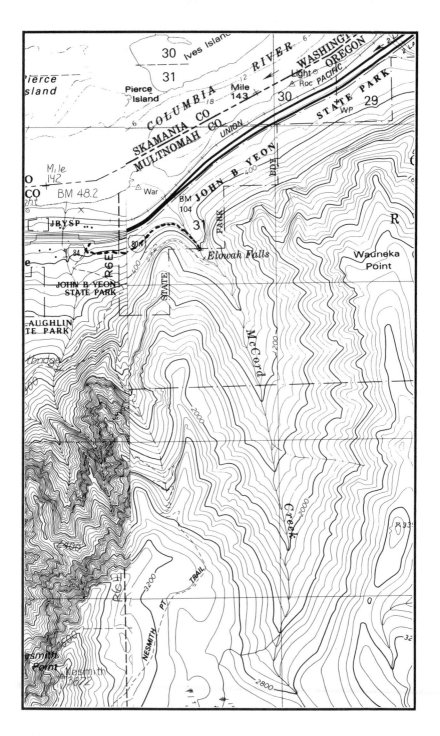

Elowah Falls

but not the McCord Creek Trail.

After climbing steeply past two junctions, the path continues its uphill trek, making its way across the forested bluffs facing the Columbia. After a half-mile, the route crests, then begins a short series of steep switchbacks down to the bowl into which Elowah Falls tumbles.

So I lied. The trail is only 8/10 miles, not one mile. If you're anxious to lengthen your outing, follow the McCord Creek Trail, passed earlier, to the top of Elowah Falls.

With that off my chest, let me describe Elowah Falls, to give you an idea why Mr. Atkison and myself found it so intriguing.

First, it contains less water than other major waterfalls in the region. The water plunges one 150 feet over a table-edge rim, past an undercut wall of basalt, to an emerald collecting pool. Because of the extreme height and low flow, the water dissolves to a lacy mist and ends up more like rain. It also gets to falling extremely fast.

The water doesn't hit the collecting pool but lands on a giant boulder. Also, the flow isn't constant but comes in surges, so the angel hair runoff pattern on the rock changes constantly. Occasionally, wind blows the entire torrent away from the rock.

Unlike the steady crash of Wahclella (Chapter 15) and Multnomah Falls (Chapter 12), Elowah makes a soothing, rain-like sound. It also pushes out a steady breeze, which fills the open, treeless basin.

Many fine sitting rocks line the edge of the collecting pool and a footbridge takes you across the creek. The Gorge Trail beyond the footbridge doesn't really go anywhere. It comes out at the Wahclella Falls Trailhead after three miles.

15.

Wahclella Falls

(Columbia Gorge Scenic Area)

Length:	1 mile
Difficulty:	Easy to moderate
Elevation:	500 to 800 feet
Season:	All seasons
Location:	T2N-R7E-Sec. 28
Water:	Plentiful
USGS 7.5" Topo:	Bonneville Dam, Tanner Butte
Ownership:	Mount Hood NF
Phone:	(503) 386-2333
Camping:	Eagle Creek
Use intensity:	Heavy

Directions: Leave I-84 at Bonneville Dam exit 40. The trail-head is well marked where the off-ramp meets the Scenic Highway, south of the freeway. 20 cars can fit in the well developed parking area.

🚶🚶 🚶🚶

Wahclella Falls lies one canyon west of Eagle Creek (Chapter 16), at the end of a one-mile trail. Actually, the trail is .9 miles, which casts doubt on whether it constitutes a viable day-hike and therefore deserves its own chapter. Especially since the trail dead ends at the falls.

All I can do is forewarn that unless you bring a picnic lunch and walk slowly, Wahclella Falls will take no more than an hour out of your life. But it will be an hour extremely well spent. If you crave more exercise, drive a couple miles down the road and check out the equidistant Elowah Falls Trail (Chapter 14).

The Wahclella Falls Trail begins as an old road. For its

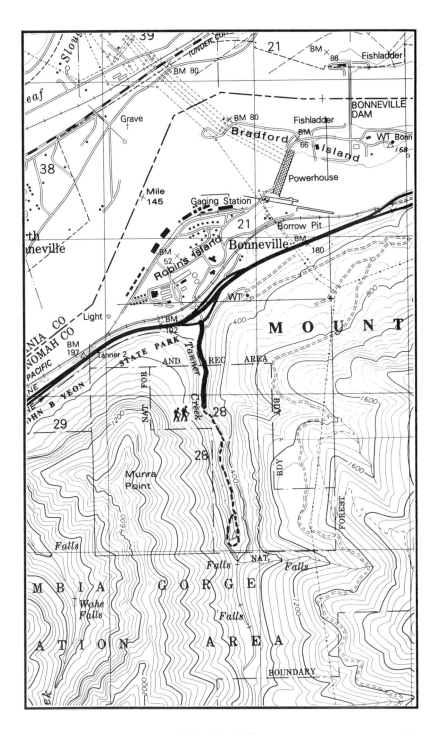

Wahclella Falls   89

first quarter-mile, it follows the wide, level waters of Wahclella Creek upstream along the bottom of a narrow canyon. Look for large Douglas-fir, Western hemlock, Western redcedar and, in October, tons of bigleaf and vine maple resplendent in fall color.

After a quarter-mile, gorge and trail narrow considerably and the path begins a steady uphill climb, which it maintains for the next half-mile. It crests 150 feet above the creek, shortly after passing the far end of the loop trail.

My advice: Stay high (left) at the junction with the loop trail. The approach to the falls from this direction is a little more impressive than via the loop's low side.

Soon after the junction, the trail begins dropping and the falls come into view. The route then takes off downhill much more seriously, through gorgeous old cedars and giant, mossy boulders, snaking its way to a footbridge across the creek.

Wahclella Falls, with its huge water volume, can only be described as "thunderous." At the very top, a short (30 or 40), upper falls crashes through a narrow slit. The lower falls drop 150 feet or so, in a not-quite plunge with water hugging rock all the way down. The play of sunlight in the upper gorge can be spectacular.

As you continue down to the creek, past the collecting pool and over the bridge, a second waterfall comes into view, where a side creek spills into the upper gorge kitty corner to the upper falls.

Beyond the foot bridge, the loop trail continues at creek level, under a lava overhang, before crossing the creek a second time and climbing steeply back to the main trail.

16.

Eagle Creek

(Columbia Wilderness Area)

Length:	31/2 to 6 miles
Difficulty:	Easy
Elevation:	300 to 1200 feet
Season:	All seasons
Location:	R2N-T7E-23
Water:	Plentiful
USGS 7.5" Topo:	Bonneville Dam, Tanner Butte
Ownership:	Mount Hood NF
Phone:	(503) 695-2276
Camping:	Trailhead, Tenas Camp, and others near by...
Use intensity:	Heavy

**Directions**: Take I-84 east from Portland to Exit 41/Eagle Creek. There is no exit westbound. Follow the road south, away from the Columbia, to a parking area at the end. There is a Forest Service campground, a restroom and room for 100 cars.

ᛉᛉ ᛉᛉ ᛉᛉ

This impressive trail, passing numerous major waterfalls in 31/2 to six miles, is the major thoroughfare into the Columbia Wilderness. Not only that, it is one of the region's easier routes. While it penetrates to the heart of the 39,891 acre Wilderness, the area around the lower trail forms a narrow, non-wilderness finger and the Wilderness boundary is not crossed until mile five.

I selected mile 31/2 as the best day-hike turnaround, although one could argue for miles 41/2 and six. The total trail runs 131/4 miles, to Wahtum Lake, a 57 acre pool nestled in a glacial basin at 37 feet elevation. The lake is Mount Hood National Forest's deepest at 175 feet.

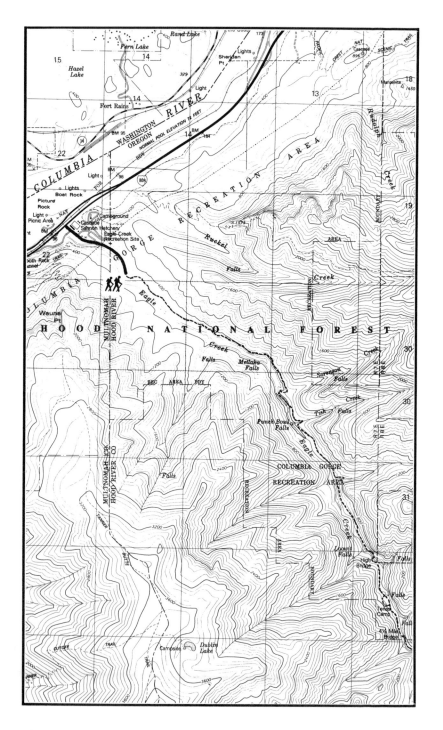

Eagle Creek

Most hikers I encountered on my June visit were headed to Wahtum Lake. As a day-trekker, this jarred my sense of order since one can drive to Wahtum Lake. The lake could make a day-hike destination if you had a ride waiting there. In such a case, it would be easier to start at the lake and hike in the downhill direction toward the gorge trailhead.

The Eagle Creek Trail deserves its status as the Columbia Gorge's most popular pathway, although solitude seekers might do well to avoid it on summer weekends. Also, the route is inscribed into vertical rock faces in many places, especially the first mile, with sheer dropoffs over the trail edge. Although some pitches are augmented with cable hand holds, the path is not for the faint hearted or small children.

Mile one also passes several seep areas where water drips out of the overhanging rock and rains on the trail. Such spots often take the form of enchanted grottoes lined with maidenhair fern.

The first mile from the trailhead rises gradually from creek level to 200 feet above the water. This gentle upgrade is the trail's steepest. From the end of mile one until mile seven, the route follows a nearly level contour.

Vegetation includes lichen draped Douglas-fir, Western Hemlock and Western redcedar, mostly under twenty-four inches in diameter. Look also for bigleaf maple, with Oregon white oak on the drier slopes. Shrubs include scrub alder, vine maple, thimbleberry and Oregongrape. The showiest of the many flowers in the profuse and varied herbaceous understory are tiger lily and columbine.

After a mile, the canyon walls grow somewhat less steep. At mile 11/2, the route passes a short side trail down to the Metlalko Falls overlook. At mile 13/4, a longer side trail leads to Lower Punchbowl Falls.

Punchbowl Falls shows up at mile two, with no side trail. The falls aren't very high but afford a worthy trek as rushing water forces its way down a wavy, moss lined chute into a collecting pool.

Above Punchbowl Falls, the gorge steepens again as the path crosses two side creeks spanned by wooden bridges. The second bridge, at mile 21/2, peers down the narrow, rocky cleft of Fern Creek. Past Fern Creek, the Eagle Creek canyon slopes down to a narrow slit, with perpendicular walls rising fifty feet above the water. The slit is sinuous at first, then becomes an arrow straight crevice culminating at High Bridge. Look for Loowit Falls horsetailing in from a side creek.

High Bridge, at mile 31/2, makes a fine highlight. Spanning 150 feet above the creek, it peers northward into the aforementioned knife slit gorge. To the south, the canyon forms a steep walled grotto.

From High Bridge, it is a short, uphill trek to Tenas Camp and yet another waterfall. A half-mile beyond, the trail re-crosses Eagle Creek, continuing on the east bank past more waterfalls, two more camps and the Wilderness boundary, to Tunnel Falls at mile six. The elevation at Tunnel Falls is only 1200 feet, which calculates to a laughably easy rise of one 150 feet per mile from the trailhead.

Tunnel Falls boasts one of the more unusual examples of trail construction. The 1915 builders of this path actually bored a tunnel into the rock halfway up the falls, passing behind it and out the other side.

At Tunnel Falls, Eagle Creek divides into an East and a West Fork. While Wahtum Lake flows into the East Fork, the trail follows the West Fork for three miles, inscribing a huge switchback (each leg 11/2 miles long), culminating at a marvelous vista at mile nine, called Inspiration Point. The grade steepens markedly at Tunnel Falls and considerably more beyond Inspiration Point.

A true-blue day-hiker, of course, would have turned back long ago and driven to Wahtum Lake.

Oregon Cascades

The Ramona Falls.

17.

Castle Canyon

(Mount Hood Wilderness Area)

Length:	1 mile
Difficulty:	Difficult but very short
Elevation:	1600 to 2300 feet
Season:	All seasons
Location:	T3S-R7E-Sec. 2
Water:	Not reliable
USGS 7.5" Topo:	Rhododendron
Ownership:	Mount Hood NF
Phone:	(503) 622-5741
Camping:	Tollgate Campground
Use intensity:	Light

Directions: Take US-26 east from Portland. At Rhododendron, turn onto East Arlie Mitchell Road (paved) and follow it to East Henry Creek Road #19 (gravel), where you turn left. The trail is well marked, a quarter-mile up road 19, opposite a residential driveway. There's room on the shoulder for one to three cars.

👣👣👣

I nearly didn't include this interesting little path. It's awfully short, for one thing. For another, there's practically no parking at the trailhead, suggesting little use. For another, even though it lies within the Mount Hood Wilderness, it offers none of the spectacular vistas for which the Wilderness is famous.

This is not a path for vistas or even great scenery. What it is, is a hands-on trail, climbing intimately up and around a series of towering rock spires.

It is also a trail for solitary walks in the woods. And quite

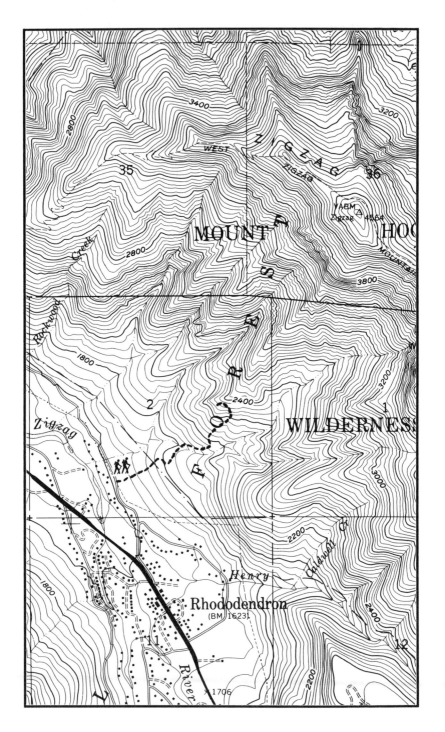

Castle Canyon

a woods they are, consisting of low elevation Douglas-fir and Western hemlock, with an understory indicative of a rainy north slope, including sorrel, salal and fern.

Although the path climbs 700 feet in its brief mile, the first 1/3 is nearly level. The middle 1/3 inscribes a series of short switchbacks up a still densely forested hillside.

Things get interesting in the path's final 1/3, when it crests a knife-edge ridge, then makes its way around the bases of a series of progressively larger rock towers, each with a short side path to the top. There are some extremely steep pitches in this section, none very long. After several false alarms, the three largest spires come into view, each 100 or so feet high and all obscured by the deep woods. The columnar, flat topped outcroppings reminded me of...hmm, let's see...how can I describe them? Well, they sort of looked like the parapets on medieval castles. They must have to at least one other person, as well.

The trail runs along the base of the formation, then around back. It then shoots steeply up the rocks to the top of the highest spire. It isn't a bad view, actually, looking across to the valley area along the Zig-Zag River. But views, obviously, are not why you came.

18.

Burnt Lake

(Mount Hood Wilderness Area)

Length:	31/2 miles
Difficulty:	Moderate
Elevation:	2500 to 4100 feet
Season:	June through November
Location:	T2S-R8E-Sec. 28
Water:	Everywhere you look
USGS 7.5" Topo:	Government Camp
Ownership:	Mount Hood NF
Phone:	(503) 622-3192; (224-5243 f/ Portland)
Camping:	Lost Creek Campground
Use intensity:	Moderate

Directions: Take Highway 26 from Portland. At Zig-Zag, follow the paved E. Lolo Pass Road (# 18). Turn right at road 1825, which is blacktopped to Lost Creek Campground. Continue on the wide gravel past the campground, where the road becomes spur 109. It's a mile to a fork in the road. Take the right hand fork (still good gravel), across Lost Creek and up the hill to the road end. The parking area is a little cramped but accommodates 15 cars.

𝆡𝆡 𝆡𝆡 𝆡𝆡

The Burnt Lake Trail is similar to the Mirror Lake Trail (Chapter 27), in that it offers a lovely lake with close-up views of Mount Hood. As at Mirror Lake, the surrounding lake basin perfectly frames Mount Hood, which is reflected in the lake.

While the Burnt Lake Trail is longer and steeper than the Mirror Lake Trail, it is closer to Mount Hood, less crowded and inside the Mount Hood Wilderness. It follows a beautiful

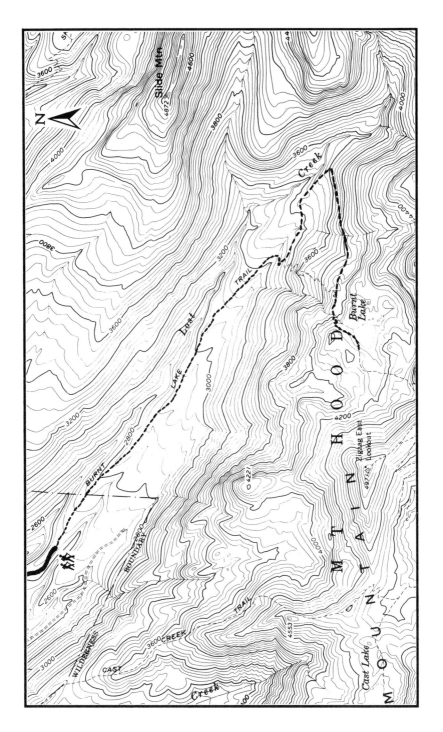

Burnt Lake

creek through a dense forest for two miles, then charges up a hillside for 11/2 miles.

The first two miles seem nearly level, despite a 700 foot elevation gain. The path begins in a young, open stand of Western hemlock, Douglas-fir, Western redcedar, lodgepole pine and red alder. After a half-mile, it enters a much older forest, following a low rise between Lost Creek, just north, and a paralleling tributary to the south. The creek to the south is the more visible.

While the forest has a closed canopy and contains understory species indicative of old growth, such as bunchberry and vanillaleaf, the trees are only middle aged. Remnants of the fire which gave Burnt Lake its name are much in evidence, with huge, burnt out trees lining the route.

After two miles, the path crosses a tributary, inscribes a short switchback, and begins its more serious final leg, rising 900 feet in 11/2 miles. You really get your nickel's worth here, scenerywise, with Mount Hood rising directly across Lost Creek. It's six lineal miles from Burnt Lake to the Mount Hood summit.

On the 1983 Mount Hood Wilderness map, the trail beyond the creek crossing contains at least seven switchbacks. On the actual trail, I counted only one. The path was rerouted in 1992. Instead of zig-zagging straight up the mountain (named, coincidentally, Zig-Zag Mountain), it parallels Lost Creek, itself steeply rising, for another 3/4 mile. It then reverses and contours back towards Burnt Lake.

The old trail was extremely steep and unstable for the use it received. The new one is of much higher quality, a little longer and with a more manageable gradient.

The last mile to the lake contains many open areas with outstanding panoramas. Most occur at brushfields which are unforested due to blowdown on these steep, thin soiled, exposed sites. Areas adjacent to such brushfields are full of downed, jackstrawed trees which tried and failed to gain a foothold.

The trail eventually comes around a point, crosses the lake outlet, and hits the lake. As noted, the outlet of the lake's encircling glacial basin perfectly frames Mount Hood.

Burnt Lake covers eight acres. It's green water reaches a depth of 25 feet and is stocked with brook trout.

Two rocky, treeless summits tower above the lake to the

south. Most impressive is the promontory forming the basin's southeast face, directly above the lake outlet. The other, a little less obvious, is set back from the lake, to the southwest. It constitutes the main bulk of Zig-Zag Mountain, which tops out at 4971 feet.

𖠋 𖠋 𖠋

Above Burnt Lake, the trail passes a marshy meadow, then climbs 500 feet in a half-mile to a forested saddle between the two summits. If you hang a right (east) at the saddle, the path becomes extremely interesting. In short order, it breaks into the open, climbs Zig-Zag Mountain, and drops into the meadowy basin of Cast Lake.

While the Cast Lake basin is prettier than that of Burnt Lake, there is no Mount Hood view. It is six miles from the Burnt Lake trailhead to Cast Lake. Cast Lake covers seven acres at an elevation of 4450 feet. It is seventeen feet deep and stocked with brook trout.

Shortly beyond the saddle above Burnt Lake, you'll pass the upper end of the Devil's Canyon Trail, which begins 900 feet higher than the Burnt Lake Trail and takes 41/2 miles to reach the lake. Views from the Devil's Canyon Trail are mostly south, away from Mount Hood. To reach the Devil's Canyon trailhead by car, continue on Highway 26 past Zig-Zag, to 27 Road. Follow 27's narrow blacktop six miles to the trailhead at the end.

19.

Paradise Park/PCT

(Mount Hood Wilderness)

Length:	51/4 miles
Difficulty:	Moderate
Elevation:	6000 to 4800 to 5800 feet
Season:	July through October
Location:	T3S-R9E-Sec. 6
Water:	Torrents
USGS 7.5"Topo:	Gov't. Camp/Mount Hood So.
Ownership:	Mount Hood NF
Phone:	(503) 622-3191 (224-5243 f/ Portland)
Camping:	Alpine Campground
Use intensity:	Heavy

Directions: Take US-26 from Portland to the Timberline Lodge turnoff just past Government Camp (road 50). The road ends, after six miles, at Timberline Lodge, with parking for hundreds of cars. The trailhead is behind the main lodge.

🚶🚶 🚶🚶

If I had to pick a "most spectacular trail" in this book, the Paradise Park Trail through Mount Hood's treeline region would be a prime candidate. The five mile stretch from Timberline Lodge to Paradise Park offers closeups of Oregon's highest peak; passing mighty canyons, great glaciers, towering waterfalls, vast wildflower meadows and any other superlative adjective you can think of.

On arrival at Timberline Lodge, don't be discouraged to encounter 500 cars in the parking lot. Timberline is a prime tourist destination offering mountaineering, snowboarding, summer skiing, lodging, stores, restaurants, bars, etc. While I classified Pacific Crest Trail use in the vicinity as "heavy," it is minuscule

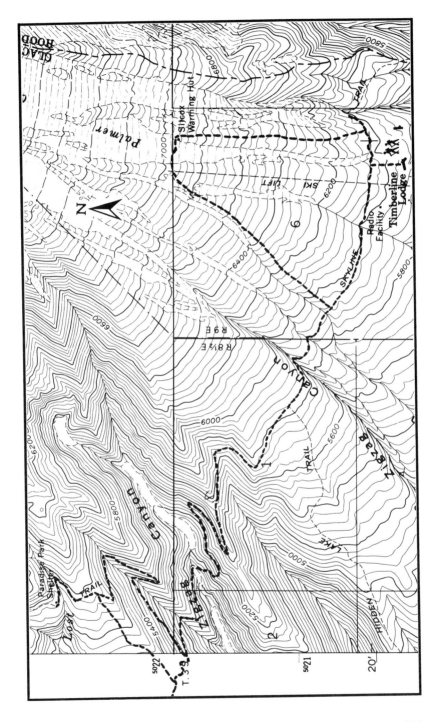

compared to the use received by the rest of the Timberline Lodge complex.

Finding the PCT from Timberline Lodge can be a challenge. For the westbound direction, walk uphill on any of the blacktopped trails behind the lodge. Where they all converge and the blacktop ends, take the trail left. Depending on where you pick it up, you should see a small PCT emblem and/or a stone cairn. It's not well marked.

This trail's "moderate" difficulty rating is a little deceptive. The first 21/4 miles, which seem nearly level, actually drop 400 feet. This may not appear much compared to the subsequent 600 foot drop into Zig-Zag Canyon, or the 1000 foot climb out to Paradise Park. However, on the way back, after having negotiated Zig-Zag Canyon twice, the gentle but persistent rise over the last 21/4 miles can look monstrous.

From the trailhead; on a glacial moraine of loose rock, ash, sand and scattered belly flowers; the path heads into the woods and under two ski lifts. The trees are mountain hemlock and Pacific silver fir; stunted from high elevation, short growing seasons and snow. In non-forested areas, the often sparse vegetation consists mainly of lupine and grass until you reach Paradise Park.

To the north rises the main bulk of Mount Hood, topping out at 11,235 feet. The snowfields above Timberline Lodge are the Palmer Glacier. Those above Zig-Zag Canyon and Paradise Park are the Zig-Zag Glacier.

For its first two miles, the path crosses several draws and canyons, each a little bigger than the last. Sand Canyon and Little Zig-Zag Canyon are the most notable. Despite its bulk, Mount Hood is surprisingly fragile. From the looseness of the sand and gravel, and the lack of vegetation, it is obvious that rapid erosion is occurring. To discover how Mount Hood might look after a couple million more years of erosion, barring further eruptions, take a look at Table Rock (Chapter 46).

Although the smaller canyons were dry when I visited in late August, don't count on this. Water volume fluctuates markedly and is heaviest in the early season and in the afternoon. Flash floods may occur early in the season and in stormy weather. Be aware that the mountain can create its own weather and that an otherwise sunny day can change in a hurry. It is advisable always to carry a jacket.

Early in the season, look for "glacial milk" in the water. The characteristic milky cloudiness is caused by pulverized rock particles.

The first half-mile from the trailhead offers an outstanding view of Trillium Lake. The remainder of the route looks across to Tom Dick and Harry Mountain, with the glaciers of Mount Jefferson, the state's second highest peak, on the horizon. On the east side of Tom Dick and Harry Mountain, the Mount Hood Ski Bowl, with its long, wavy "Alpine Slide," can be seen. West of it lies the basin containing Mirror Lake (Chapter 27), although you'd have to climb a little higher to make out the actual lake.

It is 3/4 mile from the trailhead at Timberline Lodge, to the junction with the Mountaineer Trail (Chapter 20), even though the sign says "1/4 mile." After that, it is another 3/4 mile to the Hidden Lake Trail and yet another 3/4 mile to the Zig-Zag Canyon overlook.

The overlook, 21/4 miles from the trailhead, offers a splendid destination for those not up to following the trail to the canyon bottom or up the other side. The canyon's sheer, barren walls rise 1000 feet or more on three sides, below the Zig-Zag Glacier and the Mount Hood summit.

Beyond the overlook, the path begins a series of long switch-backs as it drops 600 feet in a mile to the Zig-Zag River. Look for a couple of subalpine firs as you approach the crossing, a step-across which can be tricky early in the season. Look also for a roaring waterfall a half-mile upstream from the crossing.

Heretofore, the entire trail has been downhill, dropping 1200 feet in 31/2 miles. For the final 13/4 miles, the honeymoon ends. After trucking up the far side of Zig-Zag Canyon, well downstream from the overlook, the path re-enters the woods and meets the Paradise Loop Trail. Since the PCT misses Paradise Park, you must turn right either onto this side path, or on the next one, a quarter-mile beyond. Go right at the second junction for Paradise Park, left for the Zig-Zag Canyon Trail and straight for the PCT.

The Zig-Zag Canyon Trail is a five mile route, mostly in the woods, following the canyon rim from an access road off Highway 26 (road 2639, marked "Mount Hood, Kiwani's Camp"), to the PCT. It climbs from 2800 feet to 5600 feet.

The twin side trails accessing Paradise Park parallel one another a quarter-mile apart and are of equal length. I made a little loop of them. The first is far more scenic as it winds in and out a deep side canyon. The second charges straight uphill through a series of forest clumps and grassy openings offering a preview of Paradise Park.

Eventually, you'll meet a trail junction in the middle of a vast meadow with, as always, the Mount Hood crest rising immediately above. From the junction, go left (west) for Paradise Park, now only a half-mile away. Were you to follow the meadow uphill, off the trail, you'd end up at 6800 feet at the base of Mississippi Head, a thumblike projection visible from Portland.

The last half-mile to Paradise Park more than justifies the effort. After wandering back into the woods, the path drops into the canyon of Lost Creek, the same creek the Burnt Lake Trail follows for two miles (Chapter 18). While not nearly as deep as Zig-Zag Canyon, Lost Creek Canyon is exquisite and the stream is much prettier. The Zig-Zag River is lined with brush, whereas the banks of Lost Creek are adorned with grass and wildflowers. Expect patches of snow at Lost Creek any time of year since you're now on the mountain's west side rather than its less snowy south side.

Despite the name, Paradise Park is a bit anti-climactic. It boasts a little stone shelter, in a clump of trees surrounded by meadow. Indian paintbrush and corn lily have joined the ever present lupine, along with several other wildflower species. The view of Mount Hood is blocked by an orange outcropping.

Paradise Park actually includes the entire meadow complex, from where the Paradise Loop Trail leaves the PCT to where it rejoins it a mile beyond the shelter. This despite the fact that the map confines it to a spot a half-mile beyond the shelter.

If you thought Zig-Zag Canyon was impressive, continue past the shelter for one mile, to where the Paradise Loop rejoins the PCT at the edge of the Sandy River Canyon, Mount Hood's most extensive erosion. The Sandy Canyon forces the PCT almost completely off the mountain. To visit the spot where it bottoms out, at the 3200 foot mark at the Sandy River, 41/2 miles from the Paradise Park shelter, see Chapter 23.

20.

Mountaineer Trail

Length:	23/4 mile loop
Difficulty:	Difficult but short
Elevation:	6000 to 7000 feet
Season:	July through October
Location:	T3S-R9E-Sec. 6
Water:	At Silcox Hut
USGS 7.5" Topo:	Mount Hood South
Ownership:	Mount Hood NF
Phone:	(503) 622-3191; 224-5243 f/ Portland
Camping:	Alpine Campground
Use intensity:	Heavy

Directions: *Take US-26 from Portland to the Timberline Lodge turnoff just past Government Camp (road 50). The road ends, after six miles, at Timberline Lodge, with parking for hundreds of cars.*

🚶🚶 🚶🚶

For those wishing for a strong dose of the Mount Hood alpine area without the major undertaking involved in trails such as Paradise Park (Chapter 19) or Cooper Spur (Chapter 22), check out the Mountaineer Trail. Although it begins in the Timberline Lodge complex and cuts through heavily used recreation sites, it visits some incredible back country while offering a compact but vigorous workout.

Timberline Lodge is a popular tourist destination offering mountaineering, summer skiing and snowboarding, lodging, stores, restaurants, bars, etc. Most summer snow activities take place on the Palmer Glacier, which comes within a mile of the Lodge's back door.

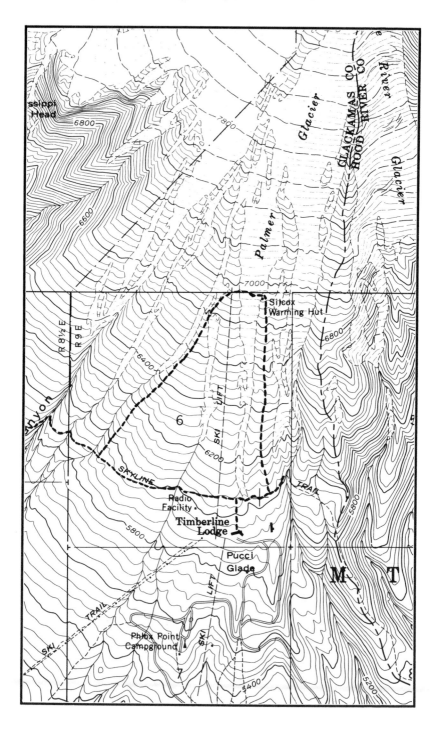

The Palmer Glacier is the most climbed route to the 11,235 foot summit of Oregon's premier peak. It is a grueling, technical ascent outside the realm of this book. The entire Palmer Glacier climbing route can be seen from the Mountaineer Trail, as well as from Timberline Lodge and Highway 26. It follows the glacier along the edge of the Steel Cliffs to a narrow gap, then up a glaciated basin known as the Hogsback to a place called the Chute, a steep snowfield leading to the summit.

The Mountaineer Trail begins 3/4 mile west of Timberline Lodge, as a turnoff from the westbound Pacific Crest Trail. To locate the westbound PCT, walk uphill on any of the blacktopped trails behind the lodge. Where they all converge and the blacktop ends, take the path left. Depending on where you pick it up, you should see a small PCT emblem and/or a stone cairn. It's not well marked.

Fom the PCT trailhead; on a glacial moraine of loose rock and scattered clumps of belly flowers; the path heads into the woods and under two ski lifts. The trees are mountain hemlock and Pacific silver fir. In non-forested areas, the main, often sparse vegetation, consists mainly of lupine.

It's a level 3/4 mile from the trailhead to the Mountaineer Trail junction, even though a sign at the junction claims it is a quarter-mile. From the junction, the path shoots straight uphill for a mile. The 1000 foot elevation gain makes it this book's steepest pitch. It didn't seem that steep to me.

The uphill trek makes its way over loose ash, brecchia (rocky debris) and glacial till. Most of the climb traverses a treeline forest extending like a finger along the lip of a narrow draw. The higher you get, the smaller the trees become, stunted by a short growing season and heavy snows. At the upper end, all that remains are a few windswept hemlocks. Above, scattered whitebark pines grow as a gnarled mat wherever they find sufficient shelter. And above that, the forbidding summit of Mount Hood watches in bemused splendor.

The trail tops out near the upper terminal of the Magic Mile chairlift, which can also be ridden to the same spot. Check at the lift ticket window in the Wy'east Day Lodge, below the main lodge, for summer hours.

The view from the trail's upper end offers a southward panorama of Mount Jefferson, the Three Sisters and Broken Top. Look also for Trillium Lake and Tom Dick and Harry Mountain.

From terminal, make your way across the snowboard and skiing areas at the foot of the Palmer Glacier, to the Silcox Hut, a fascinating structure built in 1939 and restored and reopened in 1993. The hut offers group lodging, with full kitchen and bunkroom. Guests are driven up by snowcat.

From the Silcox Hut, a trail/road shoots straight downhill, back to the lodge, following a ridge just east of a snow filled ravine and emerging at the parking lot.

Newton Creek. Mount Hood Wilderness Area (Chap.21)

21.

Newton Creek Loop

(Mount Hood Wilderness)

Length:	7 mile loop
Difficulty:	Moderate
Elevation:	4600 to 5800 feet
Season:	July through November
Location:	T3S-R9E-Sec. 11
Water:	Plentiful
USGS 7.5" Topo:	Mount Hood South, Badger Lake
Ownership:	Mount Hood NF
Phone:	(503) 352-6002; (666-0701 f/ Portland)
Camping:	Hood R. Meadows, Elk Meadows, upper Newton Creek
Use intensity:	Moderate

Directions*: From Highway 26, turn onto Highway 35, just past Government Camp, towards Hood River. A mile past Bennett Pass, turn left, onto road 3545, marked "Hood River Meadows," (not "Mount Hood Meadows"). The three trailheads will be described in the text. There is room for 30 cars among them.*

𝄃𝄃𝄃𝄃

This seven mile loop culminates, halfway along, with one of the more breathtaking closeup views of Mount Hood, far up Newton Creek at the base of the Newton Clark Glacier.

The path's difficulty is hard to rate because it bobs up and down like jackrabbit on a roller coaster. The first miles is level, the second rises 700 feet, the third rises 500 feet, the fourth drops 400 feet, the fifth rises 200 feet then drops 400 feet and the sixth drops 600 feet. The final mile, retracing the initial

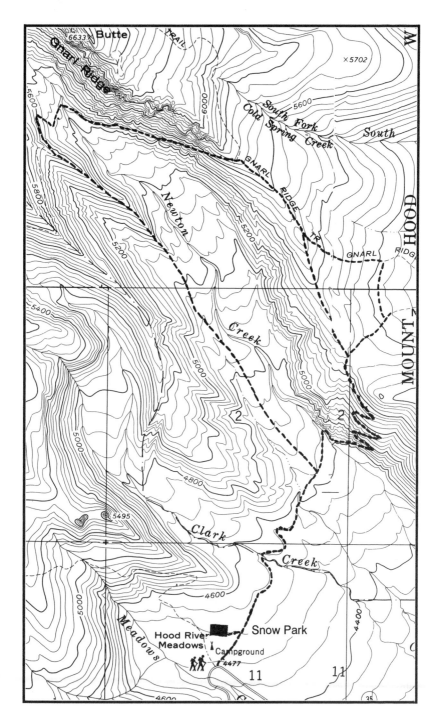

Newton Creek Loop

mile, is level. To me, that all translates to "moderate."

This trail's biggest problem is choosing among its three trail-heads. The main one lies just up road 3545, off Highway 35, at the parking area for the Sahalie Falls Trail. Hike north, towards Elk Meadows, in the opposite direction from Sahalie Falls. Of course, if you're dying to see Sahalie Falls, I won't stop you. It lies across the road, an easy mile from the trailhead.

The shortest route to Newton Creek and Elk Meadows begins at the sno-park just up road 3545 from the Sahalie Falls trailhead. In summer, you may have to park at a locked gate and walk in. Look for an unmarked spur trail at the parking lot's east end (on the right). The spur ends after 1/8 mile, where it joins the Elk Meadows Trail. Turn left for Newton Creek and Elk Meadows.

The third trailhead is along Highway 35, just past the Hood River Meadows turnoff. It is marked "Clark Creek, Elk Meadows Sno-Park," and has by far the most parking spaces, at least 20. It is a quarter-mile longer than the route from Sahalie Falls. It is also a little more scenic because it follows Clark Creek. It is also a little steeper. It is not, however, shown on any maps I know of. It joins the Elk Meadows Trail a mile from the Sahalie Falls trailhead, at the Clark Creek foot bridge.

However you go, the first half-mile traverses a level plateau through a forest of Pacific silver fir, Douglas-fir, Western hemlock and lodgepole pine. The three trailhead routes converge at Clark Creek, which is also the Wilderness boundary. The flood reamed creek channel is spanned by a railed footbridge. As always, look for glacial milk in the water.

Beyond Clark Creek, the path continues its level course for another half-mile, emerging at the much wider, rockier and more desolate channel of Newton Creek. There is no bridge at Newton Creek, a volatile stream subject to great fluctuation and flash floods early in the season.

When I visited, somebody had laid some small logs across the main channel, several hundred feet upstream. It kept my shoes dry.

Just across Newton Creek, the trail begins a series of grunting switchbacks up the wooded flank of Gnarl Ridge. At the top, you come to a four-way intersection. The trail right (east), leads to the top of Elk Mountain after a mile. Go straight for Elk Meadows, a quarter-mile away and 300 feet down.

Elk Meadows, Mount Hood's largest natural meadow, is ringed in trails. At the far end, a four mile continuation of the Elk Meadows Trail runs into the Tamanawas Falls Trail (Chapter 26). To visit Elk Meadows, drop down to the circle trail by going straight at the junction atop Gnarl Ridge. At the meadows, turn left and follow the meadow edge to Trail 652A, which leads (steeply) back up Gnarl Ridge. This Elk Meadows side loop adds a quarter-mile to the route, plus some downs and ups.

Should you omit Elk Meadows, hang a left at the junction back up on Gnarl Ridge, following the Gnarl Ridge Trail. This segment remains in the woods as it winds along the ridgetop, rising gently for a mile.

The Gnarl Ridge Trail ends at the Timberline Trail, coming in from Cooper Spur (Chapter 22) and Lambertson Butte. Head south (left), for the remainder of the Newton Creek loop.

The next mile crosses woods, rock outcroppings, meadows and brush as it descends sharply to Newton Creek. En route, note the huge slide scar soaring up from the creek's opposite bank. Comfort yourself with the knowledge that you'll eventually have to climb to its top. While the slide rises 300 feet above the river, the trail bottoms out upstream from it and only climbs 200 feet.

When the Timberline Trail hits Newton Creek, you've come to the journey's climax. It is obvious that the Newton Clark Glacier occupied the valley fairly recently and has shaped the treeless, forbidding, boulder strewn basin. The valley cuts a wide swath to the top of Mount Hood, with the present Newton Clark Glacier hanging below the summit. Immediately below the glacier, two miles upstream, the creek spills over two immense, barren rock faces. The twin falls can be seen for miles.

Several spectacular campsites adorn this upper crossing of Newton Creek. All lie within view of Mount Hood, the Newton Clark Glacier and the falls.

The creek is wide, fast and a little dangerous. As at the lower crossing, the best ford occurs upstream a short distance, where somebody laid some small logs across when I visited. On the far bank, the trail continues directly opposite from where it first hit the creek, at large boulder pile.

Rising from the creek, the trail inscribes a series of steep switchbacks, through some wooded patches and across a couple small meadows. Soon after, it levels off at the top of the slide scar. This presents an outstanding vista of the rushing creek and the glacier and flood scoured creek bed.

Manzanita and whitebark pine cover the hilltop area above the slide. The elevation is extremely low for whitebark pine, which grows taller and straighter here than its cousins on the high treeline ridges. They're lovely trees; wide apart, stubby and thick trunked. They're also quite short lived, as the many sun bleached snags attest.

Beyond the ridgetop a straight, 1 1/2 mile shot, downhill through the woods, returns you to the Elk Meadows Trail, where the loop comes full circle. This longest and most boring segment follows Newton Creek but offers few views of it. Mostly, it runs along a much smaller, paralleling side creek. Turn right on the Elk Meadows Trail for the trailhead.

The only possible problem in the final leg to the trailhead, comes just across Clark Creek. To return to the Sahalie Falls trailhead, take the path marked, "Umbrella Falls." The trail marked "parking lot," leads to the Clark Creek sno-park on Highway 35. A side trail to Umbrella Falls leaves the Elk Meadows/Sahalie Falls Trail a quarter-of-a-mile down from Clark Creek.

22.

Cooper Spur

(Mount Hood Wilderness Area)

Length:	3 miles
Difficulty:	Difficult
Elevation:	5700 to 8500 feet
Season:	July through October
Location:	R9E-T2S-Sec. 15
Water:	Not a drop
USGS 7.5" Topo:	Mount Hood No.
Ownership:	Mount Hood NF
Phone:	(503) 352-6002 (666-0701 f/ Portland)
Camping:	Cloud Cap, Tilly Jane
Use intensity:	Moderate/heavy

Directions: Take US-26 from Portland, past Government Camp, to Highway 35, the road to Hood River. Turn left at the junction with the Cooper Spur Road 3510 (paved). Proceed to the Cooper Spur turnoff (3512) and follow signs past the Cooper Spur ski area to Tilly Jane Campground. The ten-mile gravel road, with its eleven switchbacks, is wide but gets badly washboarded. A couple dozen cars can park at the campground, where the trail begins.

🚶🚶 🚶🚶 🚶🚶

Of all the paths in this book, the trek to the summit of Cooper Spur is by far the highest, topping out at 8500 feet. While not an especially long route, the steep, 900 feet per mile gradient is compounded by high altitude, which is not a consideration on trails under 7000 feet.

Start early, go slow and allow more time than usual (presuming you don't have a heart condition or anything). Afterwards,

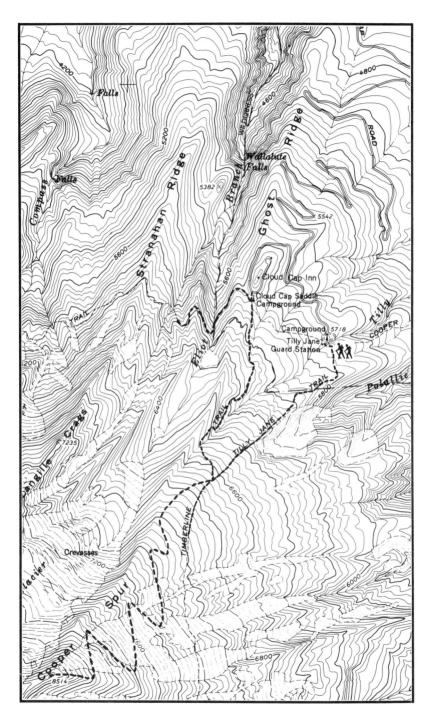

Cooper Spur

expect flashbacks for a few weeks as the beauty of the place is fairly haunting.

Your first task is to locate the trailhead. Here you have a choice. The trailhead at Cloud Cap Saddle, accessing the Cooper Spur Trail via the Timberline Trail, is located a half-mile from the Tilly Jane trailhead. The Cooper Spur Trail begins at Tilly Jane and crosses the Timberline Trail after a mile.

While I recommend a side trip to Cloud Cap Saddle and the old Cloud Cap Inn, the route from Tilly Jane is a tad shorter and more scenic. It is also a little steeper, beginning 200 feet lower. Cloud Cap Saddle offers a commanding view of Mount Hood and the valley of the Elliot Glacier. A way trail from the saddle leads up the Elliot Basin nearly to the snout of the glacier. To reach it, follow the Timberline Trail north (right), a short distance from Cloud Cap Saddle.

Should you commence your Cooper Spur ascent from Cloud Cap Saddle, take the Timberline Trail south (left) from the campground trailhead. Another path from the same trailhead leads back to the Tilly Jane Campground.

From Tilly Jane Campground, walk uphill and slightly to the right until you come to a trail sign. Various signs should steer you through a maze of converging trails. In the first 1/8 mile, we dropped down across a small creek, emerged near a campground amphitheater, made a hard right uphill just before the amphitheater, and hit the main Cooper Spur Trail soon after.

The first mile from Tilly Jane follows the rim of a tremendous eroded gorge, which drops hundreds of feet to Polallie Creek. The treeless chasm is surrounded on three sides by landslides and rock falls, with overhanging tree roots above.

It's a little discouraging, on first seeing the gorge, to realize that not only must you climb to the upper end, but that it is only the first 1/3 of your trip. The upper end looks more imposing than it really is, however, and lies less than a mile away.

The forest surrounding the gorge rim consists of lodgepole pine, mountain hemlock and Pacific silver fir, plus a few Western white pines. It puzzles me why I did not encounter noble fir or quaking aspen on Mount Hood.

Above the gorge, towards the end of mile one, things change dramatically. First, the trail breaks into the open. From there on up, the few remaining trees are limited to shrubby, stunted whitebark pines, nestled wherever they can find shelter in the bleak expanse.

Where the trail opens out, the main summit of Mount Hood comes into view, 2 1/2 miles away. The upper end of the Elliot Glacier can also be seen, tumbling down the mountain below an ominous rock face. To the left of the glacier lies a giant mound of loose rock and gravel. That, ladies and gentlemen, is Cooper Spur.

Shortly after leaving the comfort of the forest, the trail crosses the Timberline Trail, coming up from Cloud Cap. Since the Timberline Trail makes a complete loop around Mount Hood, it is also the trail from Wy'east Basin (Chapter 24), Ramona Falls (Chapter 23), Paradise Park (Chapter 19), and Newton Creek (Chapter 21). The Timberline Trail's highest elevation, 7300 feet, occurs a mile south of the Cooper Spur junction.

At the Timberline/Cooper Spur junction, continue straight ahead, on the Cooper Spur Trail. It follows a steep, barren field of ash, boulders and volcanic debris. It's a spooky and forbidding place, with ever improving views of Mount Hood, the Elliot Glacier, Cooper Spur and, across the valley of the Hood River's East Fork, Lookout Mountain in the Badger Creek Wilderness.

From here up, the entire trail can be seen to the Cooper Spur summit. So can everyone on the trail, all of whom appear to be moving in ghost-like slow motion in the thin air and steep gradient.

Shortly beyond the junction, you come to a stone shelter, which is fabulous place to stop for lunch. A half-mile beyond the shelter, the path finally approaches close enough to the rim of the Elliot Glacier gorge to warrant making the short side trip for a look.

The Elliot Glacier spills down the mountain in a series of ice falls and deep crevices. The valley below is a jumble of rock, gravel and debris which looks like somebody went crazy with a bulldozer. Vegetation is nil. From your perch on the rim of the basin's steep, slide scarred wall, the glacial snout lies less than a quarter-mile distant.

Noteworthy in the dirt piles below the glacier is an extremely long, narrow lateral moraine, with a trail along the top. Next to the lateral moraine, and perpendicular to it, a series of gravel piles are stacked row upon row. Each row constitutes a terminal moraine, representing a former end to the glacier as it retreated up the valley. You need only look at the dirt laden glacier to comprehend the vast amount of pulverized rock the moving ice sheet churns up and carries down the mountain.

As immense as Mount Hood is, it is extremely fragile and ephemeral in the geological scheme of things. The huge, rapidly eroding canyons eating away at the mountain's flanks stand in graphic testimony to this. Barring further eruptions, all that will be left of Mount Hood in a couple million years, will be the central lava conduit, much like at Table Rock (Chapter 46).

The last mile to the Cooper Spur summit inscribes a series of zig-zags up the side of the peak. The wilderness map shows it crossing and re-crossing a permanent snowfield. This is not entirely accurate. While the path does cross snowfields early in the season, most melt away by mid-August, except for a few small patches. The main snowfield, shown on the map, lies just south of the trail.

Eventually, you arrive at a small plateau just below the summit, on which some Japanese climbers carved their names on a rock in 1910. After that, it is a short trek to the 8500 foot overlook. The view includes all the landmarks mentioned previously, with the Newton Clark Glacier, immediately south, entering the picture just below the summit. All in all, it is not a bad day's work.

Gary Newbold at Cooper Spur Shelter.

23.

Ramona Falls

(Mount Hood Wilderness Area)

Length:	2 miles (4 mile loop)
Difficulty:	Easy to moderate
Elevation:	2800 to 3500 feet
Season:	June through November
Location:	T2S-R8E-Sec. 15
Water:	Always
USGS 7.5" Topo:	Bull Run Lake
Ownership:	Mount Hood NF
Phone:	(503) 622-5741
Camping:	Trailhead, Lost Creek
Use intensity:	Heavy

Directions*: From Highway 26 at Zig-Zag, take East Lolo Pass Road to road 1825 (paved), following signs to Ramona Falls. Just before Lost Creek campground, a gravel turnoff left says, "Ramona Falls Trailhead, 1/2 mile." The sign refers to a lower trailhead, 11/2 miles from the upper trailhead. The road to the upper trailhead is rather bumpy. The upper trailhead accommodates 20 cars.*

An easy trail, a great view of Mount Hood and one of Oregon's more unusual waterfalls outside the Columbia Gorge. What more could one want from a day-hike?

Before describing the Ramona Falls Trail, however, I feel compelled to discuss my night at Lost Creek Campground, near the trailhead. I hit the campground at 7:00 PM, exhausted from the Paradise Park Trail (Chapter 19). I found the facility well maintained, with wheelchair nature trails along Lost Creek.

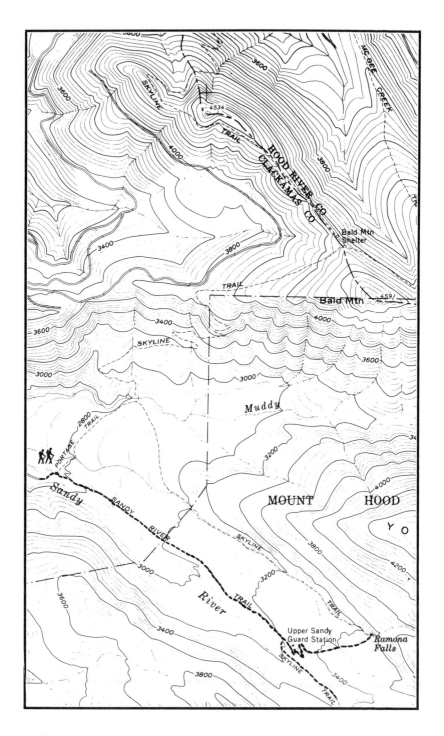

Ramona Falls

Shortly after my arrival, a family piled in with six kids, who proceeded to ride bicycles around and around, shrieking at the top of their lungs. When they didn't quiet down by 9:00 PM, I had a chat with their father; a soft spoken, educated man. He put forth the odd theory that since campground "quiet hours" didn't begin until 10:00 PM, he was "within his rights."

After a plying the man with a few conciliatory words, and some sharp ones, he agreed to settle his kids down.

All went well until 6:00 AM, when a whistlepunk across the road dashed any hope of further sleep. Such whistles, used in high lead logging to signal the movement of yarded logs up the hill, can be heard for miles. My only solace was that it disturbed the family with the kids.

Anyhow...Ramona Falls has an upper and a lower trailhead. The 1 1/2 mile path from the lower trailhead follows the Sandy River and closely parallels the road to the upper trailhead. Unless you fish or can't handle driving on bumpy roads, the path from the lower trailhead serves no purpose.

At the upper trailhead, a footbridge crosses the wide and rushing Sandy River, accessing both ends of a four mile loop trail on the other side. The bridge pylons obviously once supported an auto bridge. Since the river channel is reamed out and lined with huge slide scars, it is a good thing the bridge is fairly substantial. The Sandy Canyon is Mount Hood's largest and the river is prone to frequent rampages.

Note the glacial milk in the water and the view of Mount Hood and the Sandy and Reid Glaciers from the trailhead. It's the trail's only Mount Hood view. The Sandy River originates at the Reid, not the Sandy Glacier.

For the next 1 1/2 miles, the trail makes its way along the rim of the Sandy Canyon, above the slides forming its steep, treeless banks. The trend is slightly uphill as the elevation gains 400 feet.

Atop the canyon banks, the rolling terrain is treed with lodgepole pine, Western hemlock, Alaska cedar and rhododendron. Farther up, the forest evolves into a more typical, low elevation stand of Douglas-fir, Western hemlock and Western redcedar. Since lodgepole is an indicator of recent fires, it will eventually be crowded out by Douglas-fir and Western redcedar.

After 1 1/2 miles, the path meets the Pacific Crest Trail. Due to the immensity of the Sandy Canyon, the PCT has just dropped from 5800 feet, 31/2 miles way at Paradise Park, to a low of 3200 feet at the Sandy River. It's a worthwhile half-mile side trip (bear right), from the Ramona Falls/PCT junction to the Sandy River crossing.

Heading left at the junction, a half-mile jog, with a 300 foot rise (it didn't seem that steep), leads to Ramona Falls. The 150 foot waterfall tumbles over a wall of columnar basalt. It is best viewed from a footbridge, amid a towering cedar grove, at the base of the cliff. Since the bridge is the only decent place from which to photograph the falls, and the site receives little light, bring a wide angle lens and fast film.

The best way to describe Ramona Falls, aside from such generalities as "gorgeous" and "unusual," is to compare it to a champagne glass pyramid. You know...where they pour champagne into the top glass and it overflows into the glasses below, eventually filling all the glasses.

Suffice to say, it is one of the busiest waterfalls I've ever seen, made up of a thousand tiny waterfalls. I loved it, despite having seen nearly every waterfall in the Columbia Gorge and Yosemite.

I never did figure out the reason for the loop trail. The alternate route back to the trailhead parallels Ramona Creek along the base of a steep hillside. This route, a quarter-mile longer than the Sandy River route, is the only one permitting horses. Camping is not allowed at the falls due to a recovery project.

24.

Vista Ridge

(Mount Hood Wilderness Area)

Length:	21/2 miles
Difficulty:	Easy to moderate
Elevation:	4600 to 5700 feet
Season:	June through October
Location:	T1S-R9E-Sec. 31
Water:	No water
USGS 7.5" Topo:	Mont Hood North
Ownership:	Mount Hood NF
Phone:	(503) 352-6002 (666-0701 f/ Portland)
Camping:	Lost Lake, Wy'east Basin
Use intensity:	Moderate

Directions: From Highway 26 at Zig-Zag, take E. Lolo Pass Road to the pavement end at the summit. From there, turn left onto road 1810, which leads back to pavement of road 18. Leave road 18 for road 16, which is also blacktopped, following signs for Vista Ridge. The route becomes gravel when it turns onto road 1650. The last mile is a fairly rough spur road. There's parking for 15 cars at the trailhead.

𝄞𝄞𝄞

At least four trails, all outstanding, access Mount Hood's remote north side: Cathedral Ridge, Vista Ridge, Pinnacle and Elk Cove. Of these, Vista Ridge is the most central, shortest and easiest; which is why I've selected it to represent the other three. From the far end of the Vista Ridge Trail, at the Wy'east Basin, it is less than two miles in either direction, along the Timberline Trail, to the far ends of the three companion pathways.

The last couple miles of the trailhead drive offer some smash-

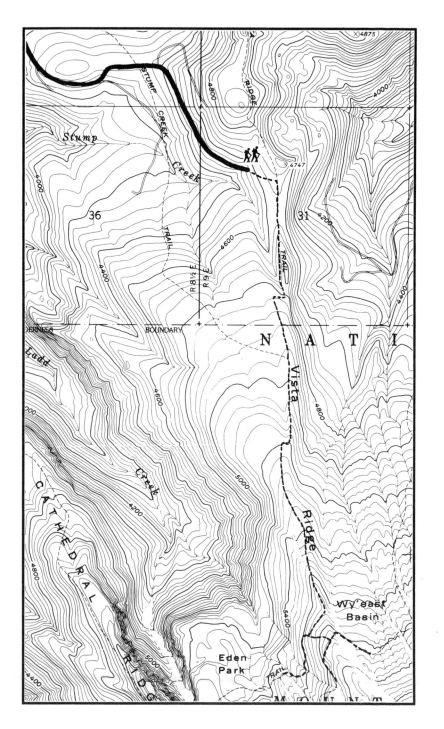

Vista Ridge

ing mountain panoramas across a series of clearcuts. From the trailhead at the road end, the Mount Hood summit is only 51/2 miles away. Views mainly reveal the Ladd and Coe Glaciers.

The trail is fairly uniform for the first two miles as it climbs gently but evenly along a broad, forested ridgetop. The entire route contains but a single switchback, 3/4 mile from the trailhead and just before the Wilderness boundary.

Until near the end of the route, vistas are blocked by airy stands of Mountain hemlock, Pacific silver fir, Western white pine and lodgepole pine. The forest floor is festooned with wildflowers, including Indian paintbrush and lupine.

While it is a pleasant and easy route, things don't get really good until just before the trail's end, when the path crosses a series of ridgetop meadows, with the Hood summit only 21/2 miles away. The main meadow species is heather, interspersed with daisy, paintbrush, lupine, and other wildflower species which come in and out of bloom as the season progresses.

After 21/2 miles, the Vista Ridge Trail joins the Timberline Trail amid the heather meadows of the Wy'east Basin. It's a gorgeous spot, with a handsome stand of stunted, windswept hemlocks sweeping up the ridgetop to the snowfields and rocky glacial basins just overhead.

From the Vista Ridge/Timberline Trail junction, a one mile hike west (right), will take you to Eden Park. Continuing west, it is 11/2 miles from the junction to the shelter at Cairn Basin and 21/4 miles to the upper end of the Cathedral Ridge Trail.

Travelling two miles east (left), from the VR/TT junction, lands you at Elk Cove, at the end of the Elk Cove Trail, a mile beyond the end of the Pinnacles Trail. Like the Wy'east Basin; Eden Park, Cairn Basin and Elk Cove are open, floral meadows at treeline. The trail east, out of Wy'east Basin, climbs steeply at first as it crosses loose areas of rock and scree. It then levels off.

Wy'east, is the Indian name for Mount Hood. Like many of the region's major peaks, Hood was named for an Englishman who never laid eyes on the mountain named in his honor.

25.

East Fork Hood River

Length:	4 miles
Difficulty:	Easy
Elevation:	500 to 3000 feet
Season:	May through November
Location:	R10E T2S Sec. 17 (Sherwood), R10E T3S Sec. 5 (Robinhood)
Water:	Yes
USGS 7.5" Topo:	Dog River, Badger Lake
Ownership:	Mount Hood NF
Phone:	(503) 352-6002; 666-0701 (f/ Portland)
Camping:	Sherwood, Robinhood Campgronds
Use intensity:	Light to moderate

Directions*: From Portland, follow US-26 to Highway 35, just past Government Camp. Take 35 towards Hood River. The first (southern) of the two trailheads lies along Highway 35, at the Robinhood Campground turnoff. The parking area, on the road shoulder, is signed "Gumjuwac Trail." Hike west, through the campground, for the East Fork Trail. The Gumjuwac Trail begins across the highway. There is space for a half dozen cars.*

The second trailhead is located immediately past the Sherwood Campground on Highway 35. The road sign says "trailheads" while the trailhead sign says "Tamanawas Falls." Fifteen cars can fit in the parking area.

🚶🚶🚶🚶🚶

I know what you're thinking. It's not like me to include a trail paralleling not just one but two roads, each never more than a quarter-mile away. Trust me, the roads are inobtrusive

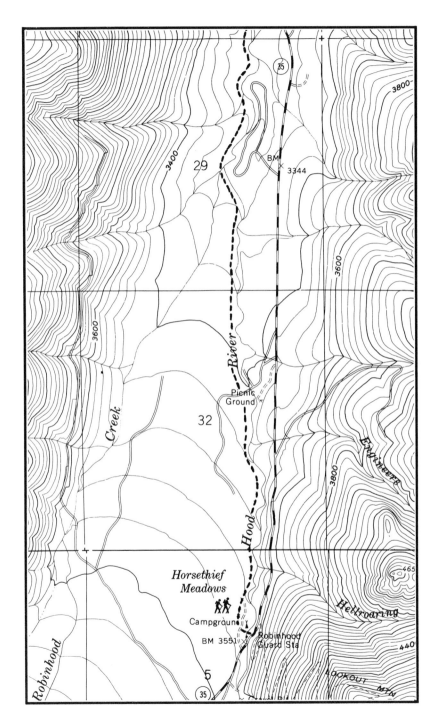

East Fork Hood River 131

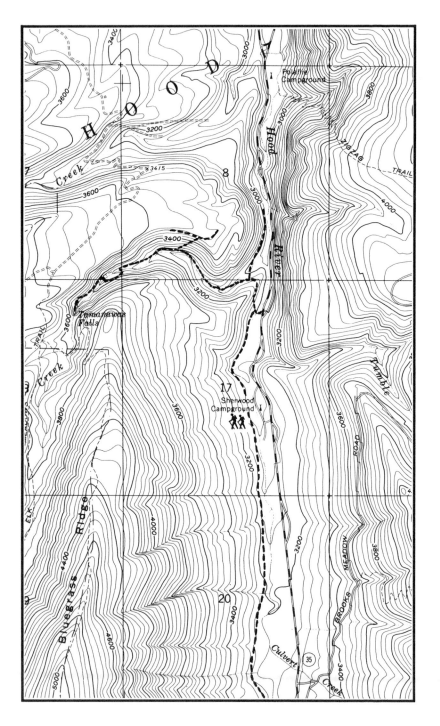

East Fork Hood River

and the path offers an experience unattainable via car. You will find the East Fork Trail quiet, lovely and charming with numerous choices and an easily reached trailhead on either end. To hike the entire four mile route, you'll want to arrange a pickup at the far end.

The trail's highest use, however, is not to hike the entire path. Rather, use it as after dinner exercise, or an excuse to get out of the car and stretch your legs when your spirit and psyche are in need of an easy, slow walk in the woods along a beautiful stream. My advice is to start at the trailhead of your choice, hike a mile or so, then return as you came.

The trail's south half differs slightly from the north half so take your pick as to which end appeals to you. From the Gumjuwac trailhead, the end with the higher elevation, the path cuts through the woods for a couple hundred feet, crosses the Robinhood Campground access road, then makes its way through some boggy, skunk cabbage areas on plank walkways. After that, it climbs a low hillside, still in the woods, as it circles around the campground. At the campground's far end, the path meets the river, which it follows for the next four miles.

The upper two miles run along the top of the bank on a level bench, passing Horsethief Meadows early on but remaining mostly in the cool shade of the low elevation forest. Look for all the old favorites; Douglas-fir, Western hemlock, Western red-cedar, red alder, bigleaf maple, black cottonwood, etc.

In the path's lower (north) half, the channel narrows considerably, the river speeds up (although it is pretty fast throughout), and the level bench gives way to a steep mountain slope. Still hugging the bank top, the trail ascends several high slide scars, dropping back down the other side. Things remain pretty level, however, as the entire route drops only 500 feet in four miles.

For the north trailhead, park at the Tamanawas Falls trailhead (Chapter 26), just past the Sherwood Campground. Follow the Tamanawas Falls Trail, briefly, down to the river and over the footbridge. Immediately over the bridge, turn left for the East Fork Trail and right for Tamanawas Falls.

26.

Tamanawas Falls

Length:	2 miles
Difficulty:	Easy to moderate
Elevation:	3000 to 3500 feet
Season:	May through November
Location:	R10E-T2S-Sec. 17
Water:	Plenty of water
USGS 7.5" Topo:	Dog River
Ownership:	Mount Hood NF
Phone:	(503) 352-6002; (666-0701 f/ Portland)
Camping:	Sherwood Campground
Use intensity:	Moderate

__Directions__: Follow Highway 26 from Portland to Mount Hood. Just past Government Camp, turn onto Highway 35, towards Hood River. Immediately north of Sherwood Campground, on 35, a sign on the left (west) of the highway says "trailheads." There's parking for 15 cars. A smaller sign says "Tamanawas Falls 2 miles."

🚶🚶🚶🚶

While Tamanawas Falls probably can't claim to be Oregon's highest waterfall outside the Columbia Gorge, the crashing, undercut, vertical plunge is nevertheless impressive. The easy walk along the wide, moss lined creek ain't bad, either.

The trail starts out in a parking area which also happens to be the trailhead for the East Fork Hood River Trail (Chapter 25). Follow a short path to the river and across a foot bridge. Once over the bridge, hang a left for the river trail and a right for the falls.

The first half-mile from the parking area tightly parallels

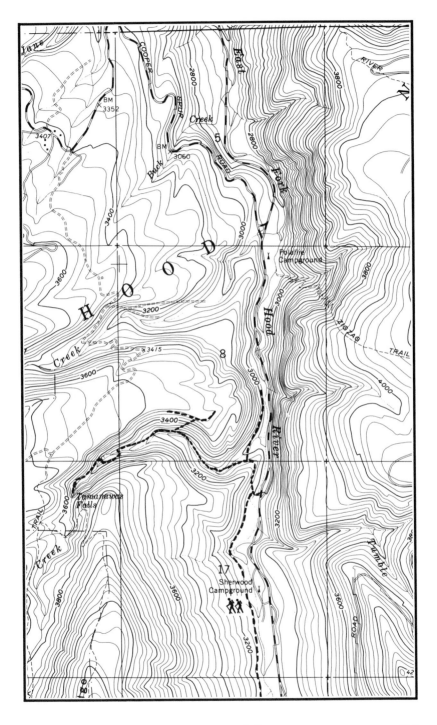

the East Fork and Highway 35. It climbs to the tops of a couple of low bluffs, then down again, but is mostly level.

Eventually, the route leaves the river and dips into the narrow, shaded gorge of Cold Springs Creek. The forest here is low elevation and dense (Douglas-fir, Western hemlock, Western red-cedar, red alder and bigleaf maple), and the creek is wide, fast and bountiful.

Shortly after entering the Cold Springs gorge, the path drops sharply to the creek, finds a second footbridge, and emerges at a little shaded flat. Just over the bridge, you come to a junction. Head left for Tamanawas Falls. A right continues along the East Fork to Polallie Falls, one mile away. You can also drive to Polallie Falls.

The next mile, on the Tamanawas Trail beyond the second bridge, is easy, peaceful and slightly uptrending as it hugs the moss and fern lined creek. It seemed longer than a mile but probably wasn't. You know you're getting somewhere when the creek steepens somewhat, into a series of low falls and cascades. It's all gorgeous.

Where the creek steepens, the gorge becomes narrower and the trail skirts a series of rock faces as it climbs to well above the creek. At the 1 1/2 mile mark, a side path breaks off to the right, leading to Elk Meadows in five miles. Check Chapter 21 for the preferred route to Elk Meadows.

Soon after the Elk Meadows junction, the trail abruptly drops back to the now bouldery creek, crosses a third footbridge, switches steeply up the far bank, drops to creek again and re-crosses it via a fourth bridge. Bolstered by wooden railings, the path then zig-zags up a steep, rocky slope to a small crest, where it levels off.

The falls come into view just beyond the crest. They're huge, about 150 feet high, with tremendous water volume, even in late season. The water drops in a sheer plunge, over an over-hanging cliff of basaltic lava. While the trail ends at the base of the falls, in a spectacular little grotto, it is possible to climb up to and under the overhang, behind the falls.

The Mount Hood Wilderness begins less than a quarter of a mile upstream from Tamanawas Falls.

27.

Mirror Lake

Length:	1 1/2 to 3 miles
Difficulty:	Moderate
Elevation:	3450 to 4050
Season:	May through November
Location:	T3S-R8E-Sec. 14
Water:	Yes
USGS7.5" Topo:	Government Camp
Ownership:	Mount Hood NF
Phone:	(503) 666-0704
Camping:	Camp Creek, Trillium Lk., Mirror Lk.
Use intensity:	Heavy

Directions*: Take US-26 to a mile west of Government Camp. Look for an unmarked turnout and parking area on the south side of the road. The Mirror Lake Trail begins one turnout east, after the turnout with an interpretive sign about pioneers. You'll see a waterfall (below the road) and a footbridge across a creek. The trailhead accommodates about 50 cars.*

One of the region's more popular trails, Mirror Lake offers a short, steep trek to a charming and fascinating spot. Views of Mount Hood, whose main flank begins just across the highway, are abundant and awesome.

The trail starts at a log bridge at the top of Yocum Falls. The bridge is an 18 by 18 inch wooden beam, with hand rails. Once across, the path enters a second growth forest dominated by low elevation species (Western hemlock, Douglas-fir and Western redcedar), despite the 3200 foot elevation. Numerous large, decaying stumps with springboard holes dot the landscape.

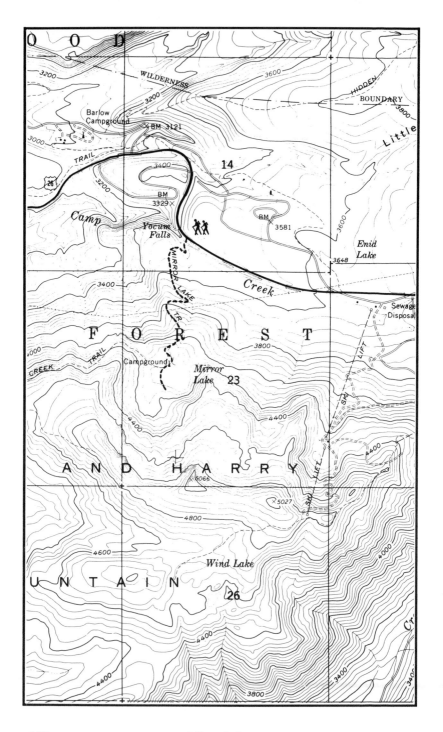

Mirror Lake

Only the abundance of lodgepole pine indicates that you're getting pretty far into the mountains. Once at the lakeshore, lodgepole pine and noble fir become dominant. Understory species include the ubiquitous but beautiful Pacific rhodo, along with vine maple, salal, alder brush, bunchberry, etc.

After crossing a moss lined creek via another foot bridge, 1/8 mile past the trailhead, the path meanders through the woods for a while, then begins a series of switchbacks up to the lake, with views of the Zig-Zag Valley and US-26. The latter is especially evident from where the path crosses and recrosses a lava rockfall. After that, it is back into the woods, and several more switchbacks, to the lake.

Mirror Lake sits at an elevation of 4050 feet. The shallow, eight-acre pool is stocked with brook and rainbow trout and surrounded on three sides by a treeless, rock walled cirque. The lake's outlet faces north, forming a "V" notch perfectly framing Mount Hood.

There are several campsites at the lake. At its north end, a boardwalk leads across a boggy area of grass, sedge, willow and skunk cabbage. This is part of a loop trail around the lake.

A number of interpretive signs at the lake explain peregrine falcon "hacking." This is a program in which birds hatched in captivity are reintroduced gradually into the wild from a site atop Tom Dick and Harry Mountain, the rock pyramid jutting from a high ridge just south of the lake. The trail beyond Mirror Lake is closed on certain dates in July, August and September because of this.

When not closed, the path above the lake wanders off into the woods, then works its way around to the southside ridgetop while rising another 1000 feet. After 1 1/2 miles, it breaks out of the forest, petering out near the top of the longer, slightly lower bluff immediately west of Tom Dick and Harry Mountain.

Climbing Tom Dick and Harry Mountain looked fairly do-able even without benefit of trail. You have to drop 100 feet or so from the bluff top, then scramble 300 feet up the rock pyramid to the summit. I did not try to climb it!

28.

Twin Lakes/Pacific Crest Trail

Length:	21/2 miles
Difficulty:	Moderate
Elevation:	3600 to 4300 feet
Season:	May through November
Location:	T4S-R9E-Sec. 17
Water:	None
USGS 7.5" Topo:	Wapinitia Pass
Ownership:	Mount Hood NF
Phone:	(503) 328-6211
Camping:	Frog Lake, Twin Lake
Use intensity:	Moderate

__Directions__: At Wapinitia Pass, four miles beyond Government Camp on US-26, pull into the parking area for the Pacific Crest Trail and Frog Lake Campground. The PCT trailhead is well marked at the far end of the 100 car parking lot. Head north for Twin Lakes.

𝀏𝀏𝀏𝀏𝀏

Aside from a pleasant hike to a secluded lake from this book's easiest to find trailhead, the Twin Lakes section of the Pacific Crest Trail is memorable as the site of my most boneheaded foul-up. I managed to hike three miles southbound, instead of northbound, before noticing my error. While my misguided efforts were rewarded, a mile down the trail, with a great view of Salmon Meadows, with Mount Hood in the background, it was scant compensation.

On returning to my car, I discovered I'd left my headlights on and my battery was dead. I had to push the vehicle out to Highway 26 and roll-start it down the hill.

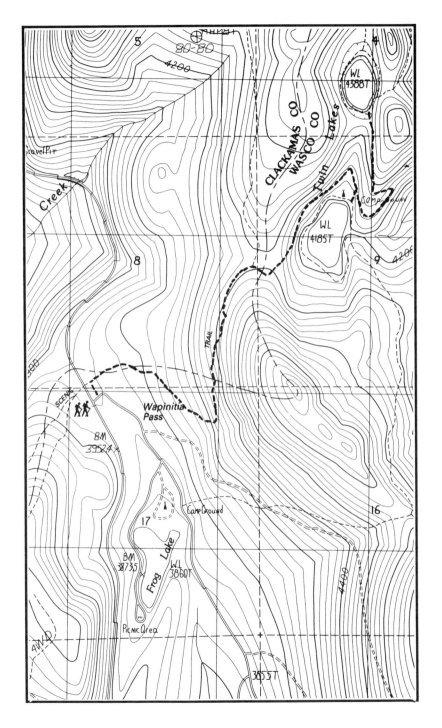

My luck didn't improve much on the correct trail, which reminded me of Inspector Gadget's arms. He's the cartoon character whose limbs can telescope to incredible lengths. Which is to say, the farther I hiked, the longer the path grew. On the map, it looked like a mile from trailhead to lake. When I reached the turnoff to Big Twin Lake, a sign claimed it was 11/2 miles back to the trailhead and a half-mile more to the lake. It was actually another mile to the lake, for a total of at least 21/2 miles.

Travelling northbound from the Frog Lake parking area (not southbound), the path winds through a monotonous woods, at an easy but steady upgrade, for 11/2 miles, sidehilling up a steep, uniform slope. The contour map claims a rise of 700 feet in 11/2 miles, but it didn't seem anywhere near that much.

The only thing breaking the monotony, and in fact the only reference point at all, was a switchback one-third of a mile from the trailhead.

Eventually, you meet a side trail leading to Big Twin Lake. Still in the woods, the side trail cuts across the top of the ridge for several hundred feet, then comes out 200 feet above the lake, atop a steep slope exactly like the one you just left. It's over a mile down the trail to the forested lakeshore.

The 4150 foot elevation lake covers eighteen acres and reaches a depth of eighteen feet. Like most area lakes, it is stocked with brook trout. A lovely campsite hides in the woods on the north shore.

If you stay on the trail past Big Twin Lake, you'll come to Little Twin Lake after a mile. Little Twin is similar to its neighbor but covers eleven acres and is only four feet deep. It's 100 feet higher in elevation. A mile past Little Twin Lake, the path rejoins the PCT, two miles north of where it branched off.

An alternate, somewhat more varied route to Twin Lakes begins at Barlow Pass and meets Big Twin Lake in five miles, crossing a series of meadows and passing the side trail to Palmateer Point after 11/2 miles. It's two mile down that side trail, past Palmateer Meadows, to Palmateer Point, where other side trails loop back to Twin Lakes, the PCT and Barlow Pass.

29.

Lookout Mountain

(Badger Creek Wilderness Area)

Length:	1 mile
Difficulty:	Moderate
Elevation:	5900 to 6525 feet
Season:	June through October
Location:	T2S-R10E-Sec. 34
Water:	None
USGS 7.5" Topo:	Badger Lake
Ownership:	Mount Hood NF
Phone:	(503) 467-2291
Camping:	High Prairie
Use intensity:	Moderate

Directions: From US-26 past Government Camp, take Highway 35 towards Hood River. Leave Highway 35 at road 44, where the sign says "Lookout Mountain 10 miles." Proceed three miles up the blacktop forest route to road 4410, whose turnoff says "High Prairie." The wide gravel road ends in five miles, at High Prairie. The High Prairie trailhead and campground are located a few hundred yards from the "T" junction where 4410 ends, down the primitive road to the left. There's parking for ten to 20 cars.

🚶🚶 🚶🚶 🚶🚶

This short hike may be one of the most scenic in this book, with a view of Mount Hood that will knock your socks off. Or at least your shoes. The highest point in the 24,000 acre Badger Creek Wilderness Area, 6525 foot Lookout Mountain offers a spectacular highlight even without Mount Hood looming one ridge away.

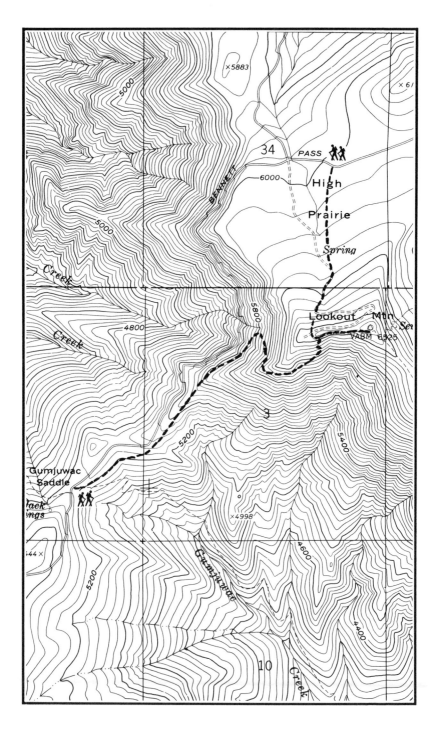

Lookout Mountain

The trailhead is magnificent by itself. High Prairie, at 5900 feet, is a series of wildflower carpeted meadows ringed in artistically placed clumps of alpine conifers. The meadows were full of shooting stars, one of my favorite flowers, when I visited but I suspect they undergo many changes during the season as different species come into bloom.

Conifers include Engelmann spruce, Pacific silver fir, lodgepole pine, subalpine fir and mountain hemlock near the trailhead. At the summit, 500 feet overhead, only the hemlock and subalpine fir remained. The narrow, snow adapted trees are considered high elevation but not quite treeline.

The Mount Hood view from High Prairie amply justifies the drive as Lookout Mountain plunges to the Hood River canyon and Highway 35, with Oregon's highest peak charging up the other side. As beautiful as the view is, Lookout Mountain's summit vista is much, much better.

Mount Hood disappears for a while as you depart the trailhead via a closed road and climb gently through more meadow and forest. Eventually, the path divides, with the old road curving left and a trail shooting straight uphill. Tree blazes and wear patterns suggest taking the steep route, which is slow going and exhausting but not very long.

The trail crests atop a flattop rimrock ledge, which drops 3000 feet southward in a nearly vertical tumble. The best Hood view may be had from the viewpoint just right of where the trail crests. The path from Gumjuwac Saddle and Badger Lake comes in on the other side of the viewpoint.

It's a quarter-mile along the crest of the rimrock to the true summit, with views into the Badger Creek drainage and the Central Oregon high desert. Vegetation in the Badger Creek Wilderness, consisting of open forest stands dominated by ponderosa pine and Oregon white oak, is much more "east side" than, say, that in the Salmon-Huckleberry Wilderness.

The level summit is about the size of a large living room. It offers a commanding, 360 degree view of the region, including numerous high peaks of the Oregon and Washington Cascades.

Many people prefer to climb Lookout Mountain from the bottom. A steep, 21/2 mile trail begins opposite Robinhood Campground on Highway 35 and ascends 1100 feet to Gumjuwac

Saddle. The latter is located three miles down the primitive road (3550) to Bennett Pass (on Highway 35), which takes off to the right at High Prairie.

Another 21/2 mile trail meets Gumjuwac Saddle from Badger Lake, at the core of the Badger Creek Wilderness, after an 800 foot rise. To drive to Badger Lake, follow 3550 to road 4860 to spur 140. Badger Lake sits in a glacial basin at 4400 feet. It covers 35 acres, hits a depth of 33 feet and is stocked with brook and rainbow trout.

From Gumjuwac Saddle, it is a 21/4 miles trail, and a 1300 foot rise, to the top of Lookout Mountain. None of these excellent alternate routes contain really killer gradients but all are much longer than the simple one mile route from High Prairie

Summit of Lookout Mt.. Badger Creek W.A.

30.

Salmon River

(Salmon-Huckleberry Wilderness Area)

Length:	3 miles
Difficulty:	Easy
Elevation:	600 to 2200 feet
Season:	All Seasons
Location:	T3S-R7E-Sec. 27
Water:	Oh yes!
USGS 7.5" Topo:	Rhododendron, High Rock
Ownership:	Mount Hood NF
Phone:	(503) 666-0704
Camping:	At trailhead
Use intensity:	Heavy

__Directions__: Take US-26 east from Portland to Zig-Zag. Just west of the Zig-Zag Ranger Station, a sign says "Salmon River Road." Follow this road to the pavement end at the bridge over the Salmon River. The Salmon River Trail begins at a well marked trailhead, east of the road, at the bridge's north end. At least 30 cars can fit along the shoulder at the bridge.

ⵉⵉ ⵉⵉ ⵉⵉ

If Idaho, California and Washington can have Salmon Rivers (Washington's is the White Salmon), why not Oregon? And if the Idaho and California entries can be nationally famous for their wilderness beauty, why can't Oregon's?

Oregon's version of the Salmon River begins high on Mount Hood, the state's loftiest peak. It flows south and west for forty miles, into the Sandy River. *En route*, it passes through the 44,000 acre Salmon-Huckleberry Wilderness, forming one of the

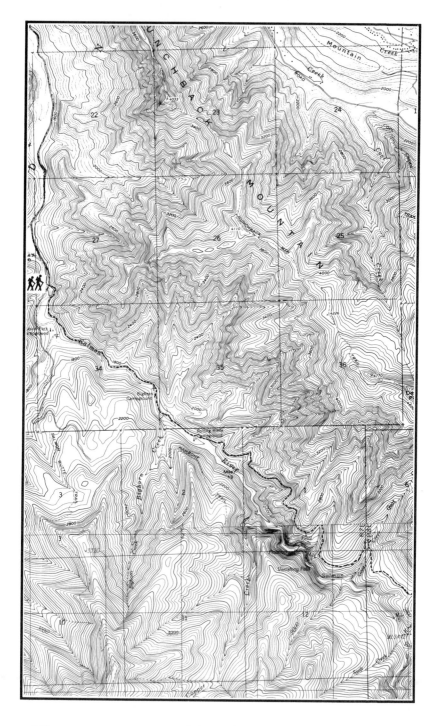

Salmon River

Northwest's most spectacular and least accessible river canyons.

The name "Salmon-Huckleberry," has always mystified me. The Forest Service normally does not name Wildernesses after two unrelated features, such as a fish and a berry, or a river and a berry. Naming a Wilderness for two berries makes a little more sense, since the area abounds with both salmonberry and huckleberry.

In fact, the Wilderness is named for the Salmon River and Huckleberry Mountain. It also contains a Salmon Mountain and a Salmon Butte. Salmon Butte, the area's 4800 foot high point, rises just south of the river.

Early on, the Salmon River Trail provides intimate access to the river's more placid areas. Farther up, the route parallels the best of the canyon's cliffs, waterfalls and whitewater rapids. It offers few if any views of them, however. Despite bypassing the canyon's main highlights, the upper trail is rugged and highly scenic.

Unfortunately, many people hike the trail's upper section only because the National Forest map lists places like Final Falls, Frustration Falls, Little Niagara Falls, Vanishing Falls, Split Falls and Stein Falls. None are visible from the trail and hikers are warned not to attempt to climb down to them. Such attempts have occasionally proved fatal. From the trailhead, the path climbs briefly over a rock face, then drops to a forested flat. The first two miles run through low elevation old growth with trees up to five feet in diameter. The forest consists of Douglas-fir, Western hemlock and Western redcedar, along with bigleaf maple and red alder. The understory is a sea of bunchberry, dwarf Oregon-grape, sorrel, trillium, swordfern and moss. Not to mention salmonberry and huckleberry.

Beyond the flat, a quarter-mile from the trailhead, the path hits the river. It meets it several more times in the next mile, following twenty to 50 feet uphill while making its way around several rock outcroppings.

The second mile runs through a rolling area a bit farther inland, although never far from the water. Numerous side paths lead to secluded riverside camps. It's 1 1/2 miles from the trailhead to the Wilderness boundary.

After two miles, the path begins a marked climb, rising 400 feet in 1 1/2 miles after having risen only 200 the first two miles.

The forest becomes a little younger and smaller as the path moves still farther inland.

The uphill pitch means you've entered the canyon, although you would not guess it from the trail. 21/2 miles from the trailhead, the path swings into a small side canyon and across a pretty step-across creek. It repeats the process a half-mile later, at mile 3, and again at mile 31/2. Between miles 21/2 and 3, an impressive "almost" view of the canyon is blocked by trees. Final Falls lies out of sight, 500 feet down.

I suggest the creek crossing at mile 3, where the path makes an extended detour into a side canyon, as a day-hike turnaround. For what it is worth, the creek in the side canyon hits the river at Frustration Falls.

Should you continue, it is a half-mile farther to Goat Creek, 11/2 to Kinzel Creek and four miles to the Linney Creek trailhead. The total trail covers thirteen miles, seven to the Linney Creek trailhead and six more to the Trillium Lake trailhead. A beautiful canyon view comes near Kinzel Creek, 41/2 miles from the Salmon River Road.

The Forest Service map shows an enticing trailhead just past the canyon's far end, at Linney Creek. I spent a frustrating morning trying to locate it. A sign on road 58, at the turnoff to road 5850, says "Linney Creek Trailhead 5 miles." I drove clear to the road's end, at a bridge over Linney Creek, and found nary a trace of a trailhead. The extra driving was not a complete loss—I saw three cougars on the road!

The real Linney Creek trailhead is hidden at the end of spur 240, off road 58 a few miles north of road 5850. After 21/2 miles, 240 jogs to the left, at a small sign denoting the Linney Creek Trailhead. From there on, the road is rocky and of extremely low quality.

I made it five miles down 240 before being halted by a deeply rutted mud puddle. According to the Forest Service, there is a trailhead at the end of 240, with a 1/8 mile connecting link to the far end of the Salmon River Trail. Go west on the Salmon River Trail, downriver, for the canyon and the Salmon River bridge.

Salmon Butte, highest point in the Salmon-Huckleberry Wilderness, is accessed by a trail beginning 11/2 miles past the Salmon River bridge. Look for a spur on the right, a half-mile before the road end. This path rises 2600 feet in three miles, offering an outstanding view of the region.

There is also supposed to be a 11/2 mile trail up Salmon Butte from the other direction, which rises only 800 feet. Its trailhead is located on road 4610, from High Rock.

Road 4610 is miserably bumpy and, when I drove it, frought with bottomless mud puddles. One nearly swallowed my car. It's five miles from High Rock to the trailhead, with spectacular views of the Roaring River canyon.

Actually, I never did reach the trailhead. I turned back at a dubious looking mud puddle just past the five mile mark.

31

Indian Ridge/Shining Lake

Length:	51/2 miles
Difficulty:	Easy
Elevation:	4600 to 4000 feet
Season:	May though. November
Location:	T5S-R7E-Sec. 9
Water:	At the lake
USGS 7.5" Topo:	High Rock, Three Lynx
Ownership:	Mount Hood NF
Phone:	(503) 630-6861
Camping:	Frazier Fork, Hideaway Lake
Use intensity:	Light

Directions: *Leave US-26, beyond Government Camp and just prior to Blue Box Pass, turning onto road 2660 (seven miles gravel, one mile blacktop). Where 2660 ends, turn right onto road 58 and proceed to the High Rock turnoff (road 4610). Road 4610 is paved for 11/2 miles. Watch carefully for road 240, Frazier Turnaround Road, on the left where road 4610 crests. If you hit the end of the blacktop, you have gone too far.*

It's four miles down the bumpy but driveable road 240 to the Shining Lake trailhead. Take the high road at mile 4 for the Frazier Fork Campground (and the low road for Frazier Turnaround). The Shining Lake Trail lies immediately past the Frazier Fork Campground, following the closed road.

🚶🚶🚶🚶

This long, somewhat monotonous path is redeemed by a lovely lake and vista at the end, extreme remoteness considering it is outside the Wilderness Areas, and an elevation varying less

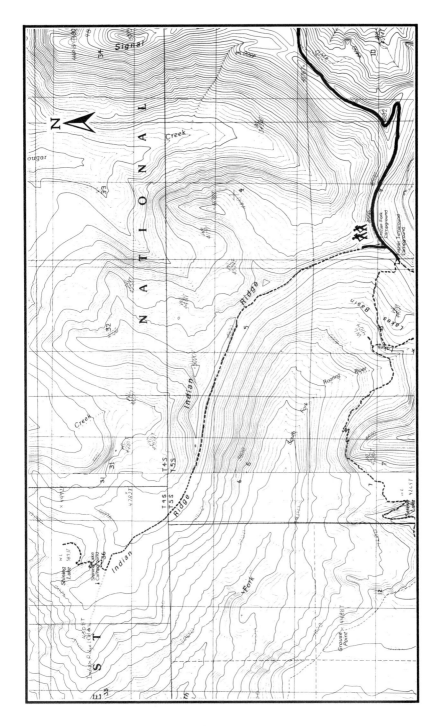

Indian Ridge/Shining Lake   153

than 100 feet in five miles. Being non-wilderness, fewer use restrictions are in effect.

Just finding the trailhead, at a place called Frazier Turnaround, is an accomplishment. To reach this lonely spot, leave the security of road 58 at High Rock, a huge volcanic plug rising from the ridge between the Roaring River, the Salmon River and Shellrock Creek. It's a short, fairly easy drive/walk to the top of High Rock, with great views of the Cascades.

I should note that on the Mount Hood National Forest Map, it appears as though Road 240 to Frazier Turnaround can be reached via spur road 130 from Hideaway Lake, lopping two miles off 240's four miles length. I camped (in the rain) at Hideaway Lake for this very reason.

In fact, spur 140 comes within 1/8 mile of 240 but does not connect. The Hideaway Lake Campground is, however, only a quarter-mile from the well marked and roomy Shellrock Lake trailhead. The Shellrock Lake Trail begins in a rhododendron choked clearcut. It meets Shellrock Lake after a level, brushy half-mile and emerges at Frazier Turnaround a fairly steep 1 1/2 miles later. The shallow (eight feet deep) lake covers 20 acres and is stocked with brook and rainbow trout.

Hideaway Lake is reached via road 5830, a turnoff four miles past High Rock on road 58. It's three miles up 5830's blacktop to the campground. The lake covers 12 acres in a wooded basin. It is thirty feet deep and stocked with brookies and rain-bowies.

The map indicates that the Shining Lake Trail follows a gated road. While there's no gate, it may be the most "closed" road I've ever seen. No less than seven pits and mounds make the first quarter-mile impassable to any four-wheeled vehicle. Even getting through on foot is a nuisance.

Beyond the trailhead, the path follows a level course for 4 1/2 miles, through dense middle elevation forests. According to the Mount Hood National Forest map, it parallels the tops of a series of cliffs. Actually, although the trail brushes the heads of a couple fairly deep glacial basins, the topography and vistas are, for the most part, obscured by timber.

After 4 1/4 miles, the route finally breaks out into the open and things get interesting. Soon after emerging from the woods, the path hits the top of a headwall, 600 feet above Shining Lake. The view of the lake and the Roaring River valley is superb. The trail's last half-mile drops 300 feet to a little crest with an even better view.

A brushy side trail to Shining Lake descends 600 feet in a mile, via a series of tight switchbacks, to the open lake basin. The 12 acre lake is 20 feet deep and stocked with brook and rainbow trout. It's very, very secluded.

32.

Rock Lake/Serene Lake Loop

Length:	3 miles (81/2 mile loop)
Difficulty:	Moderate
Elevation:	4000 to 5000 feet
Season:	May though November
Location:	T5S-R7E-Sec. 9
Water:	Plenty of water
USGS 7.5" Topo:	High Rock, Three Lynx
Ownership:	Mount Hood NF
Phone:	(503) 630-6861
Camping:	Frazier Turnaround, Hideaway Lake
Use intensity:	Moderate

Directions: *Leave US-26 beyond Government Camp, just prior to Blue Box Pass, turning onto road 2660 (seven miles gravel, one mile blacktop). Where 2660 ends, turn right onto road 58 and proceed nine miles to the High Rock turnoff (road 4610). Road 4610 is paved for 11/2 miles. Watch carefully for road 240, to Frazier Turnaround, on the left where 4610 crests. If you hit the end of the blacktop, you've gone too far.*

It's four bumpy but level and driveable miles down 240 to the Rock Lake trailhead. Take the low road at mile 4 for the Frazier Turnaround Campground (and the high road for Frazier Fork Campground). The Rock Lake Trail begins at Frazier Turnaround Campground.

𝅓𝅓𝅓 𝅓𝅓 𝅓𝅓

This beautiful loop rises and falls through old growth forests and charming floral meadows as it visits four major lakes. And it is not even wilderness, although the Frazier Turnaround trailhead may be among the Mount Hood region's more remote locations.

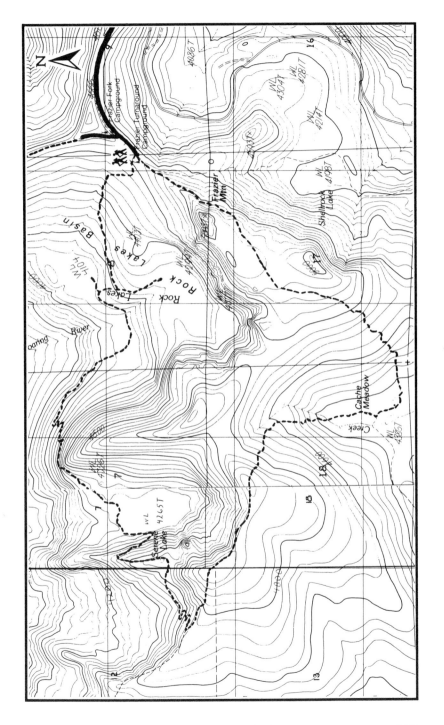

Rock Lake/Serene Lake Loop   157

The Frazier Turnaround trailhead is nestled on a heavily wooded ridge, at a spot marked by an eerie and overwhelming sense of isolation. From the well signed trailhead, two paths and a road take off. The middle one, uphill, marks the end of the Rock Lake/Cripple Creek Lake loop while the less obvious trailhead on the extreme right is the preferred beginning.

The sign at the trailhead says, "Rock Lake 1/2, Serene Lake three miles." After walking awhile, you come to a sign saying, "Trailhead one mile, Rock Lake a 1/4, Serene Lake two miles." Obviously, everything has been measured in Forest Service distance, where consistency is not required.

My only beef with the Serene Lake loop is that I don't like to begin with long downhill pitches. If I'm going to expend major hill climbing energy, I'd rather do it while motivated by the glow of anticipation, not on the way back. However, since the loop crests in the middle, there is no ideal direction.

Topographically, the path drops 600 feet in the first two miles, bottoming at 4000 feet, beyond Lower Rock Lake. Passing Serene Lake and coming around the loop's far end, it rises 1000 feet in three miles, cresting at 5000 feet a mile before Cache Meadows. The last three miles return to the trailhead elevation of 4600 feet, with a major dip at Cripple Creek Lake. Despite the ups and downs and brief steep spots, the overall gradient rarely exceeds 300 feet per mile, placing the trail in the "easy to moderate" category.

From the trailhead, the path meanders gradually down through a vast, even aged, old growth stand, with a forest floor carpeted by such diminutive and shade loving species as bunchberry, vanillaleaf and trillium. After a mile, you arrive at the junction with the Middle Rock Lake Trail.

Middle Rock Lake lies a quarter-mile up a side trail to the left, in a steep walled cirque surrounded by brushy cliffs. The narrow, 15 acre pool is 35 feet deep and stocked with brook and rainbow trout. Upper Rock Lake occupies the same basin just above the middle lake. It covers three acres, is twenty two feet deep and is also stocked with brook and rainbow trout.

For Lower Rock Lake, continue down the main path for a quarter-mile. The nine acre, thirteen foot deep lake sits in a wooded flat, not a basin. Like every other lake in the region, it is stocked with brook and rainbow trout. Its outlet is the South Fork of Roaring River.

As much as I savor brook and rainbow trout, I get a little tired of running into these same species in every lake (plus an occassional brown or cutthroat trout). In Northern California, the Fish and Game folks get creative once in a while. For every 50 lakes stocked with brook and rainbow trout, there's one where they've experimented with Arctic grayling, golden trout or white-fish. I stumbled across a lake there where brown and rainbow trout had hybridized.

Since few northern Oregon lakes contain native fish popu-lations, or even naturally reproducing introduced populations, the Fish and Wildlife Department could stock them with octopus if they wanted to. Not that I advocate such a thing.

Anyhow, the trail bottoms out a mile beyond Lower Rock Lake, below an ancient rock slide. After holding a level contour for a half-mile, it ascends 400 feet in a quarter-mile, via a series of tight switchbacks, pulling level with the Serene Lake outlet, which it enters a half-mile later.

Serene Lake is the loop's largest and prettiest. Like Middle Rock Lake, it occupies a steep walled, north facing glacial cirque with excellent campsites. The 20 acre lake sits at 4400 feet. Its 46 foot depth places it among the area's deeper. And of course, it is stocked with rainbow and brook trout.

For those in a hurry, Serene Lake makes a fine turnaround. You'll save 21/2 miles and much climbing by doubling back instead of completing the loop. Although most people continue on, I won't think any less of you if you don't.

Past Serene Lake, the trail holds a contour for a while, then chugs steeply up to the ridgetop marking the loop's far end, four miles from the trailhead. Here, the Rock Lake/Serene Lake Trail ends at the junction with the Grouse Point/Cache Meadows Trail. Grouse Point, a mile to the right, offers a panorama of the Roaring River Valley. The trail in that direction emerges on Highway 224, on the Clackamas River, after ten miles.

A left turn at the ridgetop junction takes you gradually to the path's 5000 foot crest, with views of Serene Lake and Cache Lake far below. Past a helipad, the route plunges sharply to the series of floral meadows and ponds comprising Cache Meadows.

Soon after, an old shelter and two trail junctions appears. It's 1/3 mile down a side path to Cripple Creek Lake (15 acres, four feet deep, brook trout, 4300 feet elevation).

Past the shelter and the Cripple Creek Lake turnoff, the trail makes its way uphill and back into the forest, reaching another crest, at 4900 feet, after a mile. Here the path meets an abandoned road, which it follows along a level ridgetop for a considerable distance before dropping off just before the Frazier Turnaround trailhead.

Bath House at Badgy Hot Springs.

33

Bagby Hot Springs

Length:	11/2 miles
Difficulty:	Easy
Elevation:	
Season:	May through November
Location:	T7S-R5W-Sec. 14
Water:	No
USGS 7.5" Topo:	Bagby Hot Springs
Ownership:	Hood River NF
Phone:	(503) 630-6861
Camping:	Kingfisher Campground
Use intensity:	Heavy

Directions*: From Estacada, twenty-five miles southeast of Portland, take Highway 224 to the Ripplebrook Ranger Station. From there, follow the signs to Bagby Hot Springs, via routes 46, 63 and 70, all paved. There's a restroom and large parking area at the trailhead. Kingfisher Campground is located on route 70, four miles prior to the trailhead.*

🚶🚶🚶

For kids, young lovers or those interested in capping off a scenic Sunday drive with a bit of unstrenuous exercise, Bagby Hot Springs makes an ideal destination. The twenty five mile road up the Clackamas River canyon, from Estacada to Ripplebrook, ranks among the region's loveliest drives, with waterfalls and towering rock formations. The last few miles, up the Collawash and Hot Springs Fork Rivers, are also beautiful.

From the well marked and busy trailhead, the trail to Bagby Hot Springs follows a level course through a lichen draped, low elevation forest. It crosses the Hot Springs Fork just beyond the

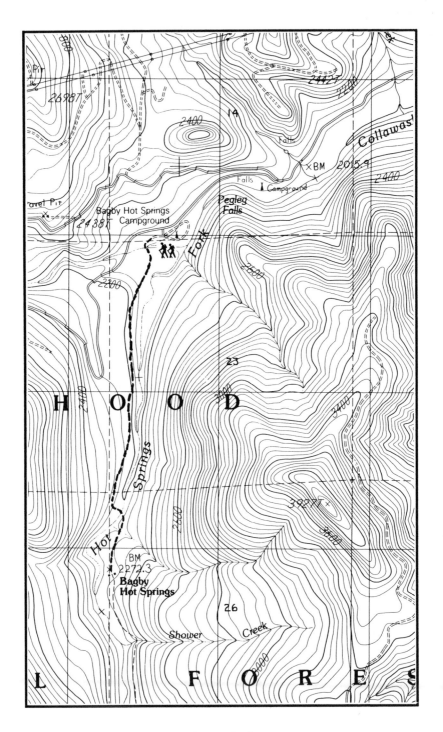

Bagby Hot Springs

trailhead, via an elaborate wooden bridge, and again via another bridge, 11/4 miles later.

Views of the river are frequent and the trail ranks among the best maintained I've ever seen. Be aware however, that some users don't quite fit the typical "outdoors" image and one tends to encounter a higher than normal incidence of smoking and alcohol use. But everyone is pretty friendly.

The second bridge crosses at a lovely configuration of low waterfalls and rock formations. The path then steepens slightly for the last quarter-mile to the springs.

Bagby Hot Springs was discovered in 1876 by a miner named Bagby, although the local native Americans had been using it as a ritual bath for generations. These days, it is maintained by a group called the Friends of Bagby. They do a commendable job keeping the trail and facilities beautiful and free.

The hot springs area occupies a hillside with a ranger house, a historic cabin and bathhouses. The latter, rustic log structures, contain numerous little booths, each with a wooden tub. The booths provide enough privacy to avoid embarrassment but enough exposure to give a sense of being outdoors, not locked in a booth. Use is limited to an hour and you may have to wait two or three hours for a booth on summer weekends.

If you continue up the trail past the hot springs, it is a half-mile to Shower Creek Camp and seven to Twin Lakes. See Chapter 36 for the preferred route to Twin Lakes.

34.

Bull of the Woods Mountain

(Bull of the Woods Wilderness Area)

Length:	31/2 miles
Difficulty:	Moderate
Elevation:	4800 to 5530 feet
Season:	June through October
Location:	T7S-R6E-Sec. 32
Water:	No water
USGS 7.5" Topo:	Bull of the Woods
Ownership:	Mount Hood NF
Phone:	(503) 630-6861
Camping:	Big Slide Lake
Use intensity:	Moderate

Directions*: From Estacada, 25 miles southeast of Portland, follow Highway 224 to the Ripplebrook Guard Station. From there, take routes 46 and 63 to road 340. It's ten well signed, gravel miles from the 63/6340 junction to the trailhead, which accommodates at least 30 cars.*

☆☆ ☆☆ ☆☆

Bull of the Woods Mountain, at 5530 feet, is the highest point in the 35,000 acre Bull of the Woods Wilderness. While that's not particularly high, the surrounding glacial valleys, jagged peaks and alpine lakes make this area a hidden gem.

The Bull of the Woods Trail reaches the top of Bull of the Woods Mountain in 31/2 miles, of which the first three are nearly level. Just beyond the rocky summit, a series of steep connecting paths lead to several of the area's most spectacular high lakes in two to four miles.

The Bull of the Woods Trail begins at the end of a scenic

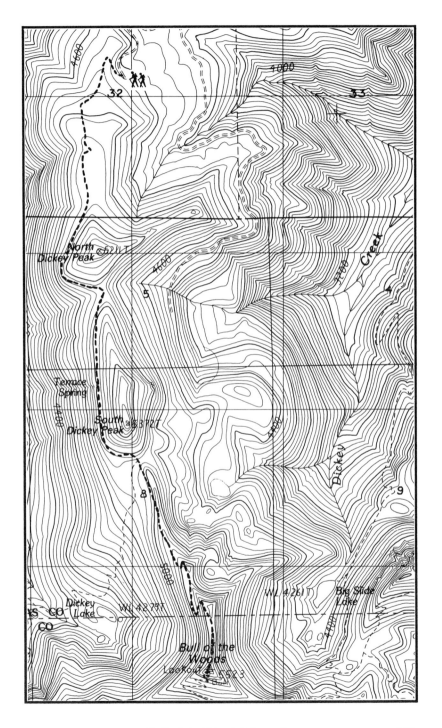

Bull of the Woods Mountain   165

access road, amid logging clearcuts overgrown with rhododendron, beargrass, Indian paintbrush, lupine and several other wildflower species. Vistas abound of Mount Hood, Mount Jefferson and the valley of the Hot Springs Fork River.

The view from the trailhead unveils an enticing glimpse into the heart of the Wilderness Area's high country. The full panorama is not revealed until near the trail's end, however.

For its first 21/2 miles, the path hides beneath a canopy of mountain hemlock, Alaska cedar, Pacific silver fir and noble fir, hugging the 5000 foot contour and jumping between the ridgetop, the east slope and the west slope. After 21/2 miles, it breaks out into the open and the rocky summit, capped by an operational lookout, comes into view.

Actually, the lookout is occupied by a wilderness ranger, not a fire spotter. As a non-conforming structure, it will probably be dismantled within the next few years.

The final half-mile to the lookout ascends 500 feet up the rock outcropping to a 360 degree vista of high crags, lake basins and converging glacial valleys, with Mount Hood and Mount Jefferson overseeing the proceedings. This segment tends to hold snow until fairly late in the season.

In the half-mile beyond the summit, the path drops 500 feet to a saddle between Big Slide Lake and Pansy Lake. From it, most of the best lakes in the Wilderness can be reached, although the route is steep. I'd start with Big Slide Lake, tucked beneath a soaring headwall at the base of Bull of the Woods Mountain, a mile from the saddle at 4200 feet elevation (five miles from the trailhead). The four acre lake is ten feet deep and stocked with Eastern brook trout. Also nearby are West Lake, Welcome Lake, Lake Lenore and Pansy Lake.

It's miles from the Bull of the Woods Trailhead to West Lake and 51/2 to Welcome Lake. Shallow West Lake sits at 4300 feet, covers 31/2 acres and is stocked with Eastern brook trout. At six acres, Lower Welcome Lake boasts about the same depth and elevation.

Because of their relatively low elevations, the glaciers which formed these lakes retreated early and the lakes have been silting in longer than those at higher elevations. That is the reason for their shallow depth and green water.

To avoid having to reclimb Bull of the Woods Mountain, and if you happen to have two vehicles, you might exit via the Pansy Lake, Dickey Creek or Elk Lake Creek Trails.

The Dickey Creek trailhead is located on the same road as the Bull of the Woods trail. It's five miles from there to Big Slide Lake, about the same as the Bull of the Woods route. Except the Dickey Creek Trail begins at 2600 feet instead of 4800 feet.

The Elk Lake Creek trailhead takes off a few miles down route 63. It offers the shortest route to Welcome Lake, 41/2 miles (51/2 to West Lake) but begins at about the same elevation as Dickey Creek.

See Chapter 35 for an explanation of how to reach the Bull of the Woods Trail from Pansy Lake.

35.

Pansy Lake

(Bull of the Woods Wilderness Area)

Length: 1 mile
Difficulty: Moderate
Elevation: 3600 to 4000 feet
Season: May through November
Location: T8S-R6E-Sec. 7
Water: Lots
USGS 7.5" Topo: Bull of the Woods
Ownership: Mount Hood NF
Phone: (503) 630-6861
Camping: Pansy Lake, Pansy Basin
Use intensity: Moderate

Directions: *From Estacada, 25 miles southeast of Portland, follow Highway 224 to the Ripplebrook Ranger Station. From there, take routes 46 and 63 to road 6340 and 6341. It's 13 well signed, partly paved, partly gravel miles from the 63/6340 junction to the trailhead, which accommodates 20 cars.*

🚶🚶🚶

Bull of the Woods is one of several small, newer Wilderness Areas between Mount Hood and Mount Jefferson. Although it covers less than 35,000 acres and tops out at only 5523 feet, it is a hidden gem, cut by deep glacial cirques and richly deserving of its protected status.

The shortest, easiest entry to the heart of the area is the Pansy Lake Trail. From Pansy Lake, connecting trails lead to most of the area's other high lakes within three or four miles.

The drive along road 6341, from the Bull of the Woods trailhead (Chapter 34) to the Pansy Lake trailhead, provides ample

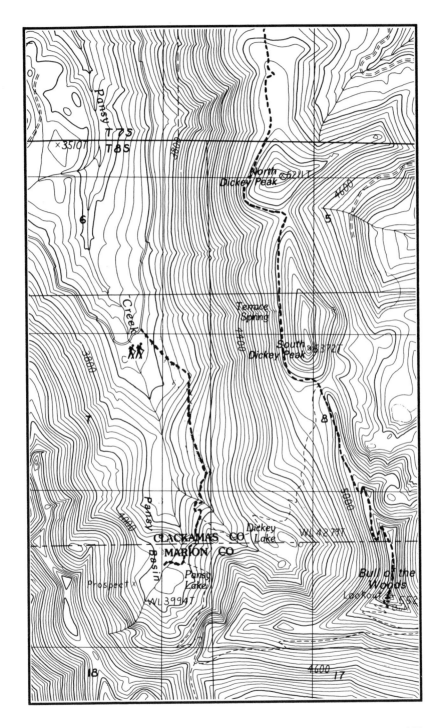

Pansy Lake 169

justification for leaving home. It affords a spectacular panorama high above the Hot Springs Fork River, with outstanding views of Mount Hood and Mount Jefferson.

As a logging road, 6340/6341 passes many miles of clearcuts, most of which are overgrown with rhododendron and beargrass, two of the Northwest's showiest wildflowers. Other clearcuts are carpeted with Indian paintbrush, lupine and myriad other floral species. Better that than poison oak.

The Bull of the Woods trailhead elevation is 1200 feet higher than the Pansy Lake trailhead. Thus, beyond the Bull of the Woods turnoff, the road drops sharply as it heads into Pansy Basin. The latter can be seen as a large, north facing glacial valley surrounded by high, rocky peaks and sheer cliffs.

The trail begins in the woods, where it remains as it contours high above and out of sight of Pansy Lake Creek. The middle elevation forest consists of mountain hemlock, Pacific silver fir and Alaska cedar. Contrast this with the Bull of the Woods Trail, a mile away, where noble fir dominates. Rhododendron seems to be the predominant understory species throughout the region.

I should mention that in my July visit, mosquitoes were swarming everywhere and very aggressive. Normally, mosquitoes don't find me very tasty. That didn't seem to bother these guys, though. Bring insect repellant.

The trail passes a couple luscious side creeks before meeting the Pansy Basin turnoff after 3/4 mile. The side trail to Pansy Basin drops 250 feet in a quarter-mile, passing a marvelous waterfall halfway down and bottoming out at a secluded campsite, in the woods near a rushing creek.

Pansy Basin itself, just past the campsite, is a floral meadow choked with Indian paintbrush, columbine, delphinium, etc. On its far side, it is bordered with rockfalls and high cliffs. Be sure to visit Pansy Basin but don't try to reach the lake from there. It's a half-mile farther than on the main trail, and the side trail is very faint and rocky beyond the meadow.

Pansy Lake emerges on the main trail an easy quarter-mile past the Pansy Basin turnoff. The seven acre pool occupies a wide bowl surrounded by mostly forested peaks. None of the Wilderness Area's main summits are visible.

Fishing for Eastern brook trout is excellent in the shallow, green water lake. I saw fly fishermen wading in its very center and the water was barely above their waists.

As noted, several major trails lead out of Pansy Basin. I made the mistake of attempting Trail #549, which on the map connects with the Bull of the Woods Trail in one mile, rising 1000 feet. Theoretically, this is a shorter route by one mile to Bull of the Woods Mountain than via the Bull of the Woods Trail. Except the map is wrong. I hiked for nearly two miles, at an unrelenting upgrade, and never did reach the end. I gave up when the path disappeared into a morass of blowdown and snowbanks.

The latter was a big surprise, at 4900 feet in mid-July. I'm told there are several sheltered pockets in the area which retain snow far into summer. Suffice to say, Trail #549 is not a good shortcut to Bull of the Woods Mountain.

If you continue past Pansy Lake on the main trail, you'll come to Trail # 558 after a steep half-mile. Trail # 558 climbs out of Pansy Basin, then contours across Bull of the Woods Mountain's south face to a 5000 foot saddle between Pansy Basin and West Lake. This is a 1000 foot rise from Pansy Lake, in two miles. From the saddle, numerous trails, all steep, lead to Bull of the Woods Mountain, West Lake, Big Slide Lake, Lake Lenore, Welcome Lake, etc.

These lakes fit the image of an alpine glacial cirque lake far better than Pansy Lake. They are higher and deeper, with distinct rock headwalls shooting up from the water. Whether they are best reached via Pansy Lake, Bull of the Woods or some other trail, is a tossup.

The Pansy Lake Trail also leads to Twin Lakes (Chapter 36) after eight miles. Beyond Pansy Lake, the path climbs and drops 500 feet over a ridge, then makes a broad, level loop around the head of Mother Lode Creek. A side trail, which rises 800 feet then descends the same distance, takes you around Mother Lode Mountain to Twin Lakes. Twin Lakes are much more easily reached from the trailhead at Elk Lake, on the other side of the Wilderness.

36.

Twin Lakes

(Bull of the Woods Wilderness)

Length:	41/2 miles
Difficulty:	Moderate
Elevation:	4000 to 4755 feet
Season:	May through November
Location:	T9S-R6E-Sec. 6
Water:	Lots
USGS 7.5" Topo:	Mother Lode Mt.
Ownership:	Mount Hood/Willamette NF
Phone:	(503)630-6861(Hood); 854-3366 (Will.)
Camping:	Elk Lake, Twin Lakes
Use intensity:	Moderate

Directions: Leave I-5 at Highway 22 east, in Salem, and pro-ceed 50 miles to Detroit. From Detroit, take route 46 for four miles to road 4696. It's one mile on 4696 to road 4697. Follow the signs to Elk Lake. Road 4697 is steep and washboarded its first five miles. The final two miles to Elk Lake are extremely rough, though level. Once at the lake, the road improves a little.

To reach the trailhead, continue past Elk Lake to the junction and bear right, uphill a quarter-mile for Twin Lakes Trail #544. Parking is limited at the trailhead, with room for only a few cars along the shoulder. Many more can fit at the junction.

𝅉𝅉 𝅉𝅉 𝅉𝅉

For a challenging Wilderness excursion within minutes of the Detroit Lake resort area, Twin Lakes is ideal. Elk Lake, where the trail begins, ranks among the largest of the region's natural

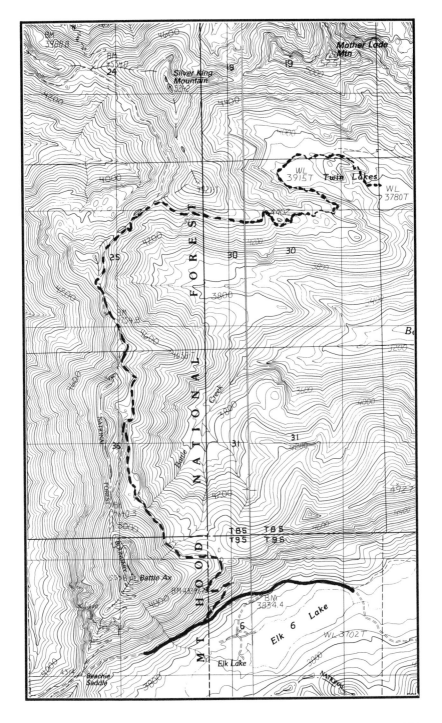

Twin Lakes

lakes, covering at least 100 acres, while West (upper) Twin is the largest in the Bull of the Woods Wilderness Area.

The last two miles of road to Elk Lake are notorious. It's level but extremely bumpy. I'd never seen eight inch road aggregate before. Many visitors park at the turnoff and walk in. This increases the distance to Twin Lake by three miles, making it almost as long as the Pansy Lake route to Twin Lake (Chapter 35).

If you drive slowly and your car has fair ground clearance, the road is passable. Conditions improve on reaching the lake. According to the Forest Service, the heavy usage of the roads at Elk Lake is due to the proximity to Detroit Lake. The neglected maintenance of the roads is a way to control traffic and reduce usage.

The trail's first 3/4 mile rises 600 feet, not 300 feet, in a series of tight switchbacks. It's a great beginning, with ever improving views of Elk Lake and Mount Jefferson. The mountain hemlock, silver fir and Alaska cedar forest contains many thin spots and clearings, most clogged with wildflowers such as rhododendron, pentstemon and Indian paintbrush.

After a mile, the path levels off and crosses from the Elk Lake drainage to the Battle Creek drainage. Again, it passes numerous openings around meadows and steep rock falls, with views of Battle Creek, Mother Lode Mountain and Mount Jefferson. Tumbling side creeks are plentiful.

Two miles from the trailhead, you meet the junction with the Battle Ax Mountain Trail. The Battle Ax summit lies a mile south and 1000 feet up. It can also be reached from Elk Lake via a trailhead 3/4 mile beyond the Twin Lakes trailhead.

Three miles from the Twin Lakes trailhead, the path crests at 4754 feet, near a forested summit on the ridge between Battle Ax and Mother Lode Mountains. The trail makes a tight loop around the summit, crossing briefly and for the only time, to the ridge's west side and the Battle Ax Creek drainage.

And yes, it is true. Battle Creek lies on one side of the ridge and Battle Ax Creek on the other.

Don't miss the junction a half-mile beyond the summit, or you'll end up at Bagby Hot Springs after eight miles (Chapter 33). From the junction, it is a mile to West Twin and 11/2 miles to East Twin, with a 500 foot drop to an elevation of 4100 feet.

While most Forest Service handouts and the Hood River National Forest maps list the lakes at 4150 and 4100 feet, the Bull of the Woods Wilderness map shows them at 3915 and 3780. Carry a magnifying glass if you use this most accurate of all maps.

At 15 acres, West Twin is the largest and deepest (50 feet) in the Wilderness. East Twin runs a close second in both categories, covering 15 acres at a depth of 40 feet. The lakes occupy a wide, forested cirque basin with no obvious headwall. Both contain naturally reproducing Eastern brook trout.

If you continue past Twin Lakes, you'll arrive at Pansy Lake in seven miles. Also, it is 1 1/2 miles to Silver King Lake from the Bagby/Twin Lakes junction, passed at mile 3 1/2 on the Twin Lakes Trail. That route follows a level contour over a saddle, then drops 500 feet into a deep basin to a four acre pond.

37.

Fish Lake/Lower Lake

(Olallie Lake Scenic Area)

Length:	3 miles
Difficulty:	Easy
Elevation:	4250 to 4950 feet
Season:	May through November
Location:	T8S-R8E-Sec. 28 (Fish Lake TH)
	T9S-R8E-Sec. 2 (Lower Lake TH)
Water:	Lots and lots of water
USGS 7.5" Topo:	Olallie Butte
Ownership:	Mount Hood NF
Phone:	(503) 630-4256
Camping:	Lower Lake camp grounds, lakes
Use intensity:	Moderate

Directions: For the Fish Lake trailhead, take Highway 22 from Salem to Detroit and road 46 from Detroit. Continue on 46 to road 4690. Proceed on 4690 to 4691 to spur 120, following signs for Fish Lake. Road 46 is paved, 4690 is blacktopped, 4691 and 120 are wide gravel roads. The trail-head is well marked at a small clearcut, with parking for three or four cars along the shoulder.

For the Lower Lake trailhead, continue on 4690, which eventually becomes gravel. Where it meets 4220, also gravel, turn towards Olallie Lake. The trailhead is in the Lower Lake Campground, with parking for about ten cars.

🚶🚶 🚶🚶 🚶🚶

For a short, easy hike across the heart of the Olallie Lake Scenic Area, this four-lake tour is ideal. With a trailhead on

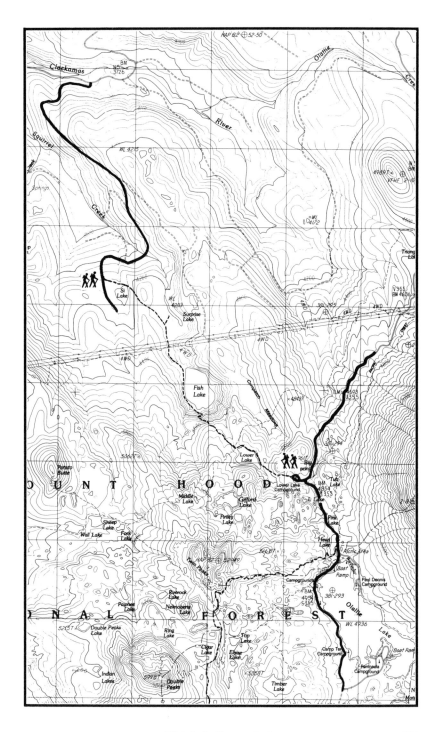

Fish Lake/Lower Lake   177

each end, clever vehicle juggling will eliminate the need for a return hike.

Since I prefer to start low and end high, I'll describe the path beginning at the Fish Lake trailhead.

From the Fish Lake trailhead, the absolutely level path winds through a forest of Western hemlock, Douglas-fir, lodgepole pine and Pacific silver fir, meeting Si Lake in a quarter-mile. At three acres and ten feet deep, Si Lake is hidden in the dense woods and contains brook and rainbow trout. Its main role is as a precursor of the much more impressive lakes to come.

It is a half-mile, with a slight upgrade and downgrade, from Si Lake to Surprise Lake, at the end of a short side trail. Surprisingly, Surprise Lake sits 200 feet lower than Si lake, at 4050 feet versus 4250. It covers five acres in a pretty little basin but is only four feet deep. Brook and rainbow trout are there for the taking.

Shortly beyond Surprise Lake, the trail emerges from the woods at a cleared powerline right of way at the foot of a rocky cliff. The spot is also accessed by a jeep road. Look for lodgepole pine and Engelmann spruce beginning to fill in the clearcut. To pick up the trail where it re-enters the woods, continue in a straight line across the maze or jeep roads. Or just follow the creek.

Fish Lake appears 3/4 mile past Surprise Lake, in a steep walled basin with brush and tree covered cliffs on two sides. Fish Lake is the largest in the Olallie Lakes area without road access, at 24 acres (Olallie Lake, the main attraction, covers 240 acres while Monon Lake, next to Olallie Lake, takes up 91 acres).

From Fish Lake, the trail, which had been virtually level, begins rising, gaining 300 feet in a mile and emerging at 15 acre Lower Lake. Note the vegetation change as mountain hemlock replaces Western hemlock, Douglas-fir fades away and lodgepole pine becomes the dominant species on this fire prone, volcanic plateau.

Of all the lakes on this particular path, I liked Lower Lake best, probably because it was only a half-mile from the trailhead on the Olallie Lake side. At 4750 feet, it occupies a basin similar to Fish Lake but with steeper, more exposed walls.

The last half-mile to the trailhead rises a couple hundred feet but hey, it is not very far. Were it me, I'd forget the far trailhead, return to my car from Lower Lake, and drive around to Olallie Lake, which has a boat rental, a store and a Ranger Station, plus at least seven campgrounds.

38.

Upper Lake/PCT

(Olallie Lake Scenic Area)

Length:	21/2 to 6 miles
Difficulty:	Easy to moderate
Elevation:	5850 to 4950
Season:	June through November
Location:	T9S-R8E-Sec. 11 (Olallie)
	T9S-R8E-Sec. 26 (Breitenbush)
Water:	Scads
USGS 7.5" Topo:	Olallie Butte
Ownership:	Mount Hood NF
Phone:	(503) 630-4256
Camping:	Olallie Lake
Use intensity:	Moderate

Directions: *For the Pacific Crest Trail trailhead at Olallie Lake, take Highway 22 from Salem to Detroit and road 46 from Detroit. Continue on 46, which is paved, to road 4690, blacktopped all but the last mile. Where 4690 meets 4220, turn south on the gravel towards Olallie Lake. The PCT crossing is well marked just before the Olallie Lake Guard Station. Park on the shoulder or at Head Lake. Head south for Upper Lake.*

While the Breitenbush trailhead, at the other end of this six mile PCT segment, is only a few miles south of the Olallie Lake trailhead on 4220, the route is impassible for many vehicles beyond Horseshoe Lake. To reach the spectacular Breitenbush trailhead, follow the directions in Chapter 39 (Jefferson Park). Head north on the PCT instead of south.

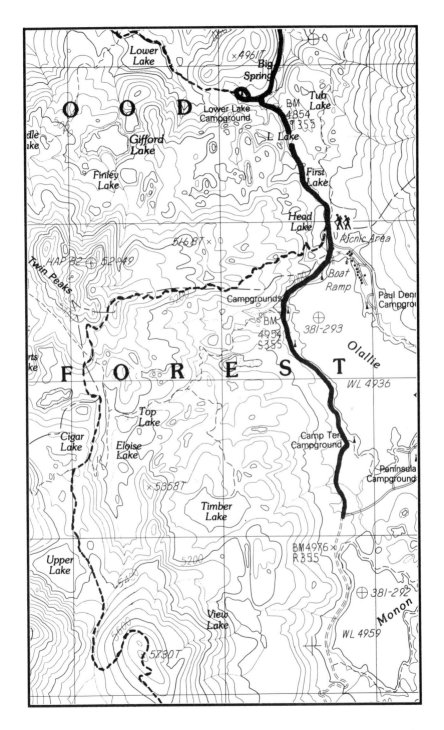

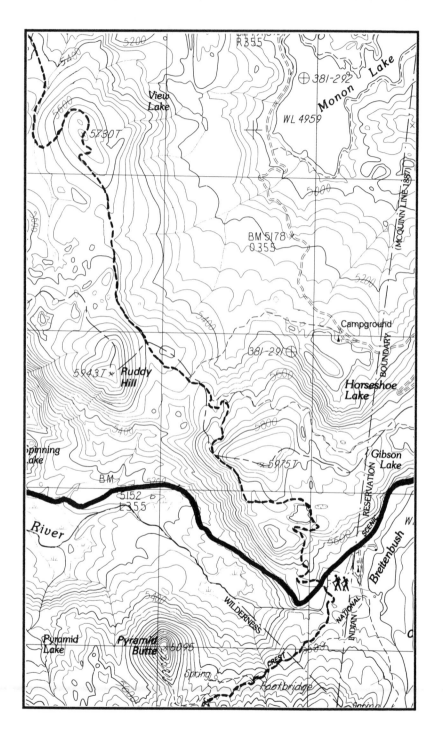

Upper Lake/PCT

亣 亣 亣

This chapter may seem like a lot of work just to reach a shallow, eight acre pool amid dozens of similar lakes. However, the Upper Lake's location in the dead center of the unroaded portion of the Olallie Lake Scenic Area, and its accessibility from two vastly differing trailheads, makes it a compelling destination.

The most scenic approach would be to follow the PCT from the Breitenbush trailhead to the Olallie Lake trailhead, going from higher to lower elevations and juggling cars so you won't have to hike back. The route is six miles long. To cut it down, it is 21/2 miles from Olallie Lake to Upper Lake and 31/2 miles from the Breitenbush trailhead to Upper Lake.

The PCT trailhead, just before Breitenbush Lake, offers a stunning panorama of Mount Jefferson, Pyramid Butte and the meadows near the Breitenbush River headwaters. The area receives heavy use, however, and the seven-mile access road is narrow and of poor quality. Avoid it on summer weekends.

From the 5500 foot elevation Breitenbush trailhead, the path winds steeply uphill through a mixed, young and open forest of mountain hemlock, lodgepole pine, Alaska cedar, Pacific silver fir and subalpine fir, with lots of wildflowers and rhododendrons. Zigzagging just east of a large escarpment, it levels off briefly after a half-mile, on a ledge occupied by a shallow, nameless pond.

Soon after, the trail makes a bouldery contour around the escarpment, hitting the 5800 foot crest marking the trail's high point. It then drops to a saddle above Horseshoe Lake. A half-mile side trail leads down to Horseshoe Lake, which is also accessible from road 4220.

Contouring around Ruddy Hill, the path reenters the woods, descends to a series of ponds, then climbs View Hill to a place called Many Lakes Viewpoint, elevation 5730. The nearest visible lake, not surprisingly, is View Lake. Huge Olallie Lake (240 acres) is the chief landmark, along with Olallie Butte, a perfect cinder cone topping off at 7222 feet.

From View Hill, the path wends its way down to a steep creek, which it follows into the main lake basin. Upper Lake is the next stop, in the woods at the base of a 5900 foot crest.

The lake covers eight acres at 5150 feet elevation, reaches a depth of 15 feet, and is stocked with brook trout.

Beyond Upper Lake, the trail wends and winds through the woods, past several more ponds and lakes. The largest are Cigar Lake (five acres, eight feet deep, brook trout) and Top Lake (three acres, six feet deep, brook trout).

It's a mile from Upper Lake to the junction with the Red Lake Trail. The last 11/2 PCT miles to Olallie Lake follows a low divide through the woods and past several more ponds, before emerging at Head Lake, opposite Olallie Lake on road 4220. Head Lake covers six acres at 4950 feet elevation. It is a whopping nine feet deep and stocked with cutthroat trout.

39.

Jefferson Park/PCT

(Mount Jefferson Wilderness Area)

Length:	51/2 miles
Difficulty:	Moderate to difficult
Elevation:	5500 to 7015 feet
Season:	July through October
Location:	T9S-R8E-Sec. 25
Water:	Aplenty
USGS 7.5" Topo:	Olallie Butte, Mount Jefferson
Ownership:	Mount Hood NF, Willamette NF
Phone:	(503) 630-4256, 854-3366
Camping:	Breitenbush Lake
Use intensity:	Heavy

__Directions__: Take Highway 22 from Salem to Detroit. At Detroit, follow road 46, which is paved, to road 4220, the Skyline Road. It's seven miles down the Skyline Road to the Pacific Crest Trail trailhead at Breitenbush Lake. Road 4220 is wide and graveled the first mile, then surfaced with rough aggregate for a couple of miles. The rest is narrow and a little bumpy but driveable. Bear right at the PCT crossing for the 50 car parking lot. A short connecting path links the parking area to the southbound PCT (northbound is across the road).

When I attempted to approach from the other end of 4220, via Olallie Lake, I found the road to Breitenbush Lake impassable for my two wheel drive car, beyond Horseshoe Lake. I'm told this is true for most vehicles.

🚶🚶🚶🚶

This world class route, through the upper reaches of Mount

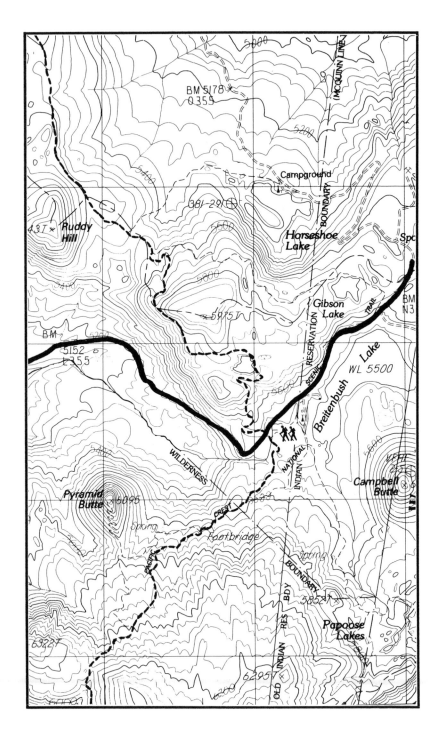

Jefferson Park/PCT

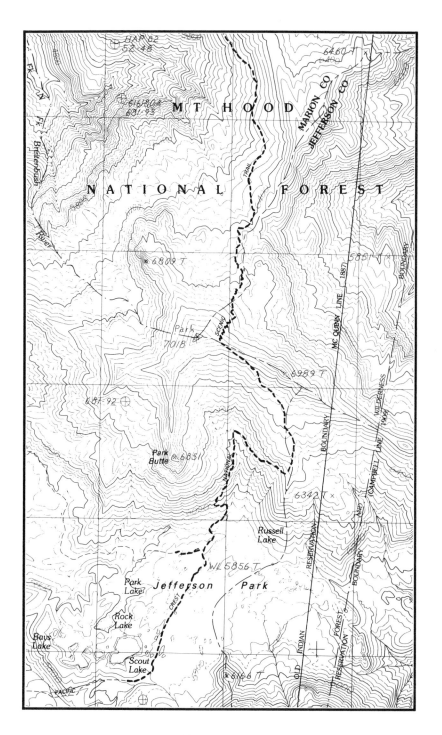

Jefferson, ranks among the most splendid trail chunks you're likely to find. While the path rises 1500 feet in three miles, then drops 1200 feet in two miles, every inch is awesome.

Mount Jefferson, Oregon's second highest peak at 10,497 feet, is a composite volcano pocked with lava flows and cinder cones. Jefferson Park, the trail's destination, lies within three miles of the rocky pinnacles and active glaciers of the Mount Jefferson crest, particularly the Russell and Jefferson Park Glaciers.

Before beginning your hike, be aware of a few things. First, since the Breitenbush Lake/PCT route to Jefferson Park climbs a steep, 7000 foot north slope, it usually doesn't open until mid-July. When I visited on July 25 of an unusually snowy year, it was impassable after 11/2 miles.

It was also totally fogged in. While this obliterated any view of Mount Jefferson, it only minimally impacted my enjoyment of the area, which was still gorgeous.

The equidistant but less scenic Whitewater Trail to Jefferson Park opens much earlier. It will be described shortly.

Be aware also that the Skyline Road (4220) from road 46 is narrow and of low quality. Although the sign says it is unmaintained, some work was done in 1991. It is subject to very heavy use. People haul boats up it (at 10 mph), to Breitenbush Lake and there's a 50 car parking lot at the PCT trailhead.

Breitenbush Lake covers 60 acres, at 5500 feet, and is stocked with brook trout. Immediately beyond the PCT trailhead, it lies entirely within the Warm Springs Indian Reservation, although its campground is managed by the Forest Service.

I suggest a mid-week, late or early season visit, or the Whitewater Trail, to Jefferson Park because the area is extremely fragile and suffers from overuse. These measures will also help avoid the traffic on 4220.

🏃🏃🏃🏃

The PCT trailhead offers closeup views of Pyramid Butte, Mount Jefferson and the meadows of the upper Breitenbush River. Hiking south, the path is fairly level at first, traversing an open subalpine forest with a surprising variety of tree species, none very big. I especially liked the droopy clumps of Alaska cedar.

While these trees grow straight and tall at lower elevations, the stunted, treeline version has a special charm.

After a mile, most tree species fade away, except for mountain hemlock, which at this elevation is dwarfed, bent over, narrow and built to withstand tons of snow. Mountain heather is the principal ground cover, a tiny plant whose leaves look like those of a juniper but which produces masses of pink belly flowers.

Look for areas that have just come out from under the snow. You'll be amazed at how adept treeline wildflowers are at taking advantage of a little warm weather.

It's a mile from the trailhead to the top of the ridge connecting to Pyramid Butte, a steep cinder cone just west of the trail. The ridge crests at 5800 feet while a one mile side trail to Pyramid Butte drops 100 feet, then zig-zags to a 6100 foot summit.

Beyond Pyramid Butte, the forest thins as the steepening path makes its way across creeks, rock outcroppings and meadows. At mile 1 1/2, it crosses a second crest, then contours around high above the South Breitenbush River. A mile later, it levels off on a beautiful ridgetop, offering the trail's only views eastward. The ridgetop, also the Marion/Jefferson County line, is dotted with meadows and ponds.

2 1/2 miles from the trailhead, the way steepens into a series of switchbacks as it chugs upward to Park Ridge, the trail's height at 7015 feet. Park Ridge marks the boundary between the Willamette and Mount Hood National Forests.

On Park Ridge, a short way trail leads to the route's best vista, with panoramas of Russell Lake, Mount Jefferson and other High Cascades peaks. Since the next 1 1/2 miles drops 1000 feet, you may wish to turn around here if you don't relish a hefty climb on the return trip.

Should you continue, the trail inscribes a wide loop back into the woods and over a couple more creeks, down to Russell Lake, source of the South Breitenbush River. The lake sits at the foot of some high slopes marking the Jefferson Park basin's northeast corner. At 5856 feet elevation, Russell Lake covers 12 acres, reaches a depth of 27 feet deep and is stocked with cutthroat trout.

A half-mile past Russell Lake, through a rolling expanse of meadow and forest clumps, you come to the main Jefferson Park lake group, accessed by a side trail from the PCT. Note the glacial milk (certain times of year), caused by ice-pulverized rock particles, in the creeks feeding Jefferson Park. Such glacially fed creeks tend to rise markedly on warm afternoons early in the season.

The main lakes are Bays Lake (6000 feet, 12 acres, 20 feet deep), Scout Lake (6000 feet, seven acres, 31 feet deep), Rock Lake (5850 feet, two acres, ten feet deep), and Park Lake (5800 feet, two acres, eight feet deep). All are stocked with brook trout. Look also for Pacific giant salamander.

ᛗᛗ ᛗᛗ ᛗᛗ

Since Jefferson Park lies 1000 to 1200 feet below Park Ridge, it becomes snow free much earlier. There are other trails to Jefferson Park which don't have to surmount high ridges and therefore open much earlier than the PCT. Shortest of these is the Whitewater Creek Trail. While it reaches Jefferson Park in the same distance as the PCT, it is less scenic, although not hideous by any means. Much of its 1800 foot elevation gain occurs in the first 11/2 miles.

To reach the Whitewater Creek trailhead, continue on Highway 22 past Detroit, to road 4243. Follow it to the 4100 foot elevation trailhead at the end. The trail mostly follows the ridge high above Whitewater Creek, largely in the woods but with occasional openings. It's four miles from the trailhead to the PCT junction, then 11/2 miles north on the PCT to Jefferson Park.

40.

Pamelia Lake

(Mount Jefferson Wilderness Area)

Length:	21/2 miles
Difficulty:	Easy
Elevation:	3100 to 3884 feet
Season:	May through November
Location:	T10S-R7E-Sec. 36
Water:	Fairly gushing
USGS 7.5" Topo:	Mount Jefferson
Ownership:	Willamette NF
Phone:	(503) 854-3366
Camping:	Trailhead, lake
Use intensity:	Heavy

Directions: From Salem, take Highway 22 past Detroit to road 2246. Road 2246 is one lane paved, with turnouts, except the last mile, which is gravel. The well developed trailhead has a restroom, campsites and accommodates 30 cars.

𝕏𝕏 𝕏𝕏 𝕏𝕏

Not only does Pamelia Lake boast a lovely name, its trail has all the attributes of a perfect day-hike. It is wide, easy, short, close to a main highway, beautiful throughout and ends at a large lake with a spectacular mountain view.

The only drawbacks are overuse, lack of noteworthy landmarks along the trail and the fact that the trailhead is, yes, slightly more than 100 miles from Portland. So sue me.

Actually, while it is 115 miles from Burnside and Broadway to the trailhead, it is exactly 100 miles from Portland's south city limits.

From the very first step, the route makes its way through

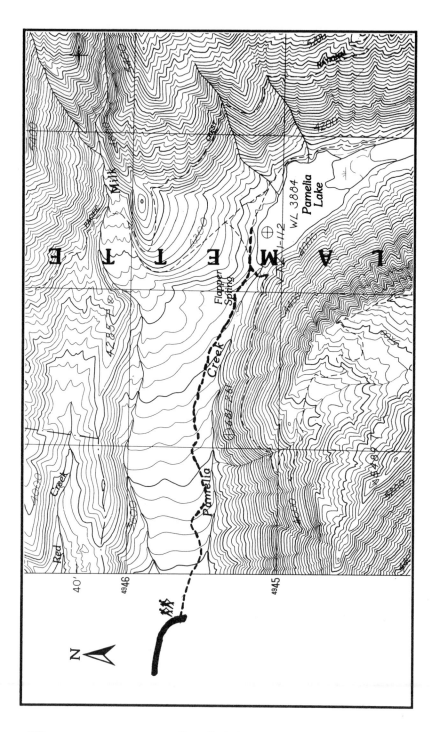

Pamelia Lake

a forest of old growth giants, although their size diminishes some-what in the path's second half. The understory consists mostly of green moss, which covers everything in sight. The entire route runs alongside Pamelia Creek, a wide, fast rushing stream.

While the trail rises nearly 800 feet in 2 1/2 miles, putting it in the "moderate" category of difficulty, I rated it "easy" because it just didn't feel that steep. The gradient is unvarying and the trail is wide and even.

As noted, my only complaint was the lack of landmarks. Except for a small waterfall a mile up, there's nothing to let you know how close you are to the trailhead on the way back. But I'd be hard pressed to label an area so lovely as "monotonous."

You know you're approaching the lake when you see a steep wall rising from the opposite side of the creek. The lake itself, second largest in the Mount Jefferson Wilderness after Marion Lake, sits in the lower end of a large glacial valley. The valley is bounded on two sides by steep, forested slopes.

Farther up the trail, the valley culminates, after 2 1/2 miles, in a cirque basin called Hunt's Cove, containing Hunt's Lake and Hanks Lake. Above rises a row of alpine spires called Cathedral Rocks, also visible from Pamelia Lake.

To reach the ridgetop paralleling the valley's north side, a short, steep side trail from the Pamelia Lake outlet meets the Pacific Crest Trail in one half-mile. From there, it is three miles to Cathedral Rocks.

Pamelia Lake's lower shore is riddled with campsites and crowds up on weekends. While the lake covers 45 acres, it attains a depth of only 12 feet. It contains a naturally reproducing population of trout.

41.

Crown Lake

(Mount Jefferson Wilderness Area)

Length:	11/2 miles
Difficulty:	Easy to moderate
Elevation:	4600 to 4900 to 4700 feet
Season:	June through October
Location:	T9S-R7E-Sec. 25
Water:	At lakes
USGS 7.5" Topo:	Breitenbush Hot Springs
Ownership:	Willamette NF
Phone:	(503) 854-3366
Camping:	Breitenbush
Use intensity:	Moderate

__Directions__: From Salem, take Highway 22 east to Detroit, then follow road 46 past Breitenbush Hot Springs to road 4685. The trailhead is located at the end of road 4685, a wide, gravel route. It holds a dozen cars. While the spot is clearly marked as a trailhead, no signs give the name of the trail.

ᛜᛜ ᛜᛜ ᛜᛜ

This short route climbs through a varied and interesting forest stand, over a hilltop, to a secluded basin housing three beautiful lakes in the Mount Jefferson Wilderness. The access road is the same one taken to the South Breitenbush Gorge Trail (Chapter 42). The road also passes the South Breitenbush Trail, which leads to Jefferson Park in six miles. See Chapter 39 for other routes to Jefferson Park.

Note a couple things while driving drive road 4685. At Lake Creek, be aware that Crown Lake, your destination, is the source of this stream. Also, the area around the road's far end has

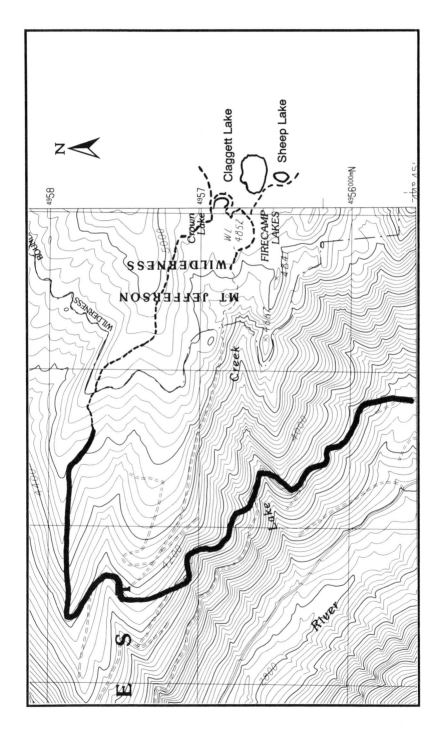

Crown Lake

been selectively logged rather than clearcut and look excellent. One stand appears to have recently suffered a spectacular wind shear, with the tops of many large trees blown out 60 feet up. I've seen wind shear which has blown the top off every tree in the stand, all at the exact same height.

The trail's initial quarter-mile, by far the steepest and rockiest pitch, begins in an old clearcut which has regenerated to a surprisingly diverse meadow. Look for rhododendron, manzanita, evergreen chinkapin, abundant beargrass and numerous other brush and herbaceous species. There is also quite a variety of conifer species, mostly young and small. I noted Douglas-fir, mountain hemlock, noble fir, Pacific silver fir, lodgepole pine and Western white pine. Alaska cedar lines the shore of Crown Lake.

The clearcut ends, and the path mostly levels off, at the wilderness boundary. After a pleasant, 3/4 mile stroll through the woods, the trail emerges at an overlook high above the lake basin. Crown Lake can be seen below, well in the distance. The two neighboring lakes, Claggett and Sheep, are not visible from the overlook.

Collectively, the three lakes are called the Firecamp Lakes. The basin they occupy is a rare, south facing glacial cirque basin. Most cirque basins face north because north slopes receive less direct sunlight and are thus cooler and more prone to glaciation. The scree strewn cirque headwall can be seen, briefly, far to the left (north), well away from the lakes.

The dominant feature of the overlook above the Firecamp Lakes basin is Mount Jefferson, rising to the southeast behind Bear Point. Jefferson is Oregon's second highest peak at 10,497 feet. The snowfield on its flank is the Jefferson Park Glacier.

From the overlook, the trail drops steadily for a half-mile to the basin floor and thence through an airy, youthful woods to the lake. Crown Lake's 12 acre pool is clear, green and beautiful, with a fairly solid bottom, but only six feet deep. It is stocked with rainbow trout. Large meadows border the lake in two places and a peninsula juts into the middle.

From Crown Lake, the trail you entered on continues across the basin and up the far slopes to the north and east. If there's an established path to neighboring Claggett and Sheep Lakes, I couldn't find it. To reach Claggett Lake, make your way southward, around the west side of Crown Lake, then head off through the woods to the south-southeast. Hopefully, you'll bump into the trail to Claggett Lake shown on the wilderness map.

Claggett Lake, less than a quarter-mile from Crown Lake, covers six acres, reaches a depth of ten feet and teems with brook trout. Sheep Lake sits a few hundred feet south of Claggett Lake. It covers two acres, at a depth of six feet, and also contains brook trout.

42

South Breitenbush Gorge

Length:	11/2 to 2 miles
Difficulty:	Easy
Elevation:	2600 feet
Season:	May through November
Location:	T9S-R7E-Secs. 21 & 26
Water:	Plentiful
USGS 7.5" Topo:	Breitenbush Hot Springs
Ownership:	Willamette NF
Phone:	(503) 854-3366
Camping:	Breitenbush
Use intensity:	Moderate

Directions: From Salem, follow Highway 22 east to Detroit, then take road 46 for ten miles. The trail has three main trailheads (plus a couple of others).

The first trailhead is located between Breitenbush Hot Springs and the Breitenbush Guard Station. Turn off 46 onto a gravel side road, where a sign says "Guard Station." Park either at the guard station, on the shoulder, or at the Hot Springs (guests only). The trailhead sign faces the hot springs but is easy to find.

For the second trailhead, turn right onto road 4685 (gravel), just past the guard station. The trailhead is well marked near a gravel pit, a quarter-mile from road 46. It holds seven or eight cars. The third trailhead lies 11/2 miles beyond the second, immediately past Roaring Creek. It also accommodates seven or eight cars.

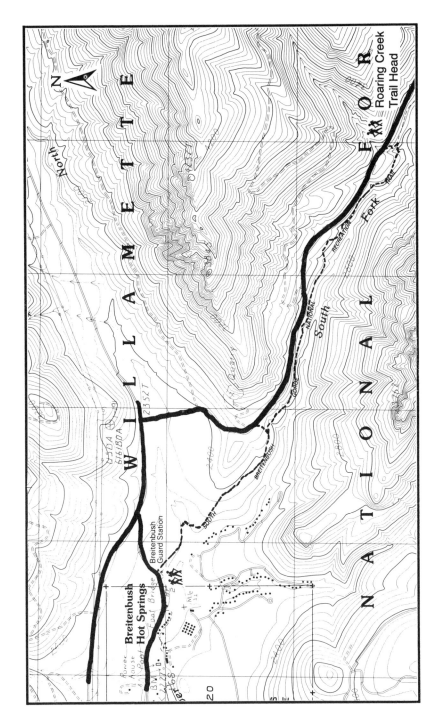

South Breitenbush Gorge   199

This short, easy trail is spectacular enough to have been featured on the cover of Ray Atkison's book *Oregon II*. Unfortunately, that book is now out of print. The latest in the series, *Oregon III*, has Elowah Falls (Chapter 14) on the cover.

While road 4685 parallels the trail a little too closely, and the South Breitenbush Gorge, its main highlight, can be visited by walking only a half-mile, I included the South Breitenbush Gorge Trail for a number of reasons.

First, the path is significantly downhill from the road in this densely forested canyon. The road offers neither views of the river nor the gorge and is an entirely separate universe.

Second, you're missing a lot if you start at the Roaring Creek trailhead and make the easy, a half-mile trek to the gorge without taking in the rest of the trail. Most visitors hike to the gorge from Breitenbush Guard Station (two miles), or the Gravel Pit trailhead (11/2 miles), rather than from the shorter Roaring Creek trailhead.

For the purpose of this narrative, however, I will begin at Roaring Creek. From that trailhead, a connecting path scoots sharply downward, levelling off 100 feet above the South Breitenbush River. Soon after hanging a right, the path takes a steep switchback down to beautiful Roaring Creek, spanned by a wooden footbridge.

Roaring Creek is a fast moving series of cascades and small waterfalls careening down a maze of moss covered boulders. Venita Mills, at the Detroit Ranger Station, who is unusually attuned to the sounds of nature, claims there's a special magic to the roar of Roaring Creek. She also has an affection for the gorge's echoing waters.

Before describing the South Breitenbush Gorge, which turns up five to ten minutes beyond Roaring Creek, I must tell you about the marvelous old growth forest blanketing the steep hillsides on either side of the river. As for species composition, of course, there's nothing remarkable. It's the same old Pacific Northwest trio of Douglas-fir, Western Hemlock and Western red cedar.

Old growth forests along isolated rivers tend to be serene

and restful places, rejuvenating to the spirit and evoking all manner of poetic hyperbole. And much of the forest along the South Breitenbush more than meets that description.

Large areas are not so serene, however, as the forest seems unusually susceptible to blowdown. In two places, old growth giants are scattered like toothpicks from an intense 1989 storm, creating what looks like logging clearcuts. You can tell it isn't logging debris because the huge, high quality logs haven't been removed and because there's a giant, upended root wad on the end of each tree.

This clearly is not a place to hang out during a winter storm.

The gorge itself is accessed by a short, very steep side trail. Unfortunately for those starting at Roaring Creek, the sign at the turnoff can only be seen from the other direction. For you Roaring Creekers, look for the turnoff near the beginning of the first blowdown area. You'll see a large root wad, then two parallel, peeled logs with flat upper surfaces, leading downhill. The double logs are supposed to be a walkway.

From the main trail above the gorge, the river appears to disappear at this point and the canyon bottom is strewn with jackstrawed trees. Many trees actually span the gorge.

The South Breitenbush Gorge is a narrow slit of basalt lava, averaging ten to 15 feet in width but narrowing to four feet at one point. It's 20 to 30 feet down to the river, which churns through the crevice over several small waterfalls. While the gorge is no more than 500 feet long, it is certainly worth a look. Just don't fall in. And watch small children carefully.

The remainder of the hike runs through the woods well up from the river. While it passes a second blowdown area, most of the trail falls into the "serene old growth" category. Beyond the turnoff to the Gravel Pit trailhead, the path follows the South Breitenbush to its mouth, then crosses the main Breitenbush River over a low-water footbridge before emerging at the hot springs. The footbridge has a tendency to become submerged.

On completing the hike, a visit to Breitenbush Hot Springs is just the thing to cap your day. The privately owned facility offers not only hot tub baths but cabins, massage, meals, a conference center, special events, etc.

43.

Little North Santiam

Length:	41/4 miles
Difficulty:	Easy
Elevation:	1500 feet
Season:	Any season
Location:	T8S-R4E-Sections 26 and 32
Water:	Plentiful
USGS 7.5" Topo:	Elkhorn
Ownership:	Willamette NF
Phone:	(503) 854-3366
Camping:	Elkhorn Valley, Shady Cove
Use intensity:	Light

**Directions**: From Salem, follow Highway 22 east to Little North Fork Road, also marked, "Little North Santiam Recreation Area." Little North Fork Road, a paved highway, eventually becomes road 2209. For the near trailhead, turn right onto Elkhorn Drive SE (road 201), a gravel route crossing the Little North Santiam River. The trailhead is marked by a wooden post, a half-mile beyond the crossing. There's parking for five cars.

For the far trailhead, continue on 2209 beyond the pavement end, to the junction with road 2207. Follow 2207 (gravel), down to the Shady Cove Campground and bridge. The trailhead is well marked on the right, where the guard rail ends on the bridge's far side. A parking lot on the bridge's near side accommodates eight cars.

This unpretentious, pleasant path along a creek is the focal point of a spectacular scenic area around the Little North Fork

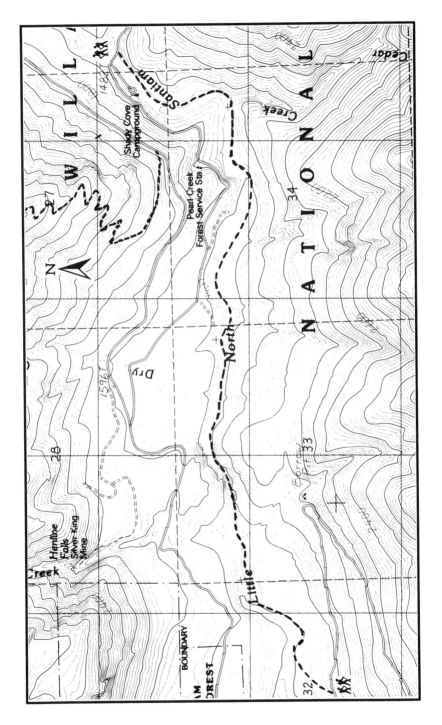

Little North Santiam

of the Santiam River. Myriad alternate hikes in the immediate vicinity include the Opal Creek Trail, Opal Lake, Phantom Natural Bridge (all in Chapter 45), Henline Falls and Henline Lookout (both in Chapter 44).

Since the 41/2 mile Little North Santiam Trail has a trailhead at both ends, much redundancy can be eliminated by arranging a pickup at the far end. Were it me, I'd start at the more scenic eastern (Shady Cove) trailhead, hike as far as the spirit moved me, then double back.

Between the western (Elkhorn) and eastern trailheads, the Little North Fork of the Santiam evolves from a broad valley to an impressive canyon, whose heavily timbered slopes soar upwards to a series of craggy mountaintops.

Where road 2207 meets the eastern trailhead at Shady Cove Campground, the river is wide and unusually clear, with rock formations jutting from the turquoise water. According to a Forest Service flyer, the Shady Cove Bridge, at the campground, is closed. Not so. The road beyond the bridge leads to the Opal Lake and Phantom Natural Bridge trailheads.

For the Little North Santiam Trail, park at the campground and walk over the bridge. You'll find a trailhead marker on the right, where the guard rail ends.

The trail is fairly uniform, threading a needle between steep, forested slopes and the wide creek bed. The magnificent, quiet forest is typically Northwest, consisting of Douglas-fir, Western hemlock and Western redcedar. Redcedar, the most beautiful of the trio, tends to proliferate near water, alongside red alder and bigleaf maple.

Since the trail has no particular highlights (albeit few lowlights, either), let me say only that fishing is excellent and several deep pools offer marvelous swimming for both fish and humans. Three of the pools, near the Shady Cove trailhead, are called Three Pools. They can be also reached from road 2207. The trail's last half-mile cuts away from the river and slightly uphill to avoid some buildings.

44.

Henline Lookout Site

Length:	3 miles
Difficulty:	Difficult
Elevation:	2000 to 4100 feet
Season:	June through October
Location:	T8S-R4E-Sec. 27
Water:	No water available
USGS 7.5" Topo:	Elkhorn
Ownership:	Willamette NF
Phone:	(503) 854-3366
Camping:	Shady Cove
Use intensity:	Moderate

Directions: Take Highway 22 east from Salem to Little North Fork Road, following signs to the Little North Santiam Recreation Area. Little North Fork Road becomes road 2209. Proceed past the pavement end, onto the gravel, to the junction with road 2207. The trailhead is on 2209, 1.1 miles past the 2207 junction. It can be a little difficult to locate because the trail's initial pitch climbs a road cutbank where one doesn't expect trailheads. The sign is embedded in the cutbank and easy to miss. There's parking for a dozen cars along the shoulder.

As you approach the Little North Santiam Recreation Area from Little North Fork Road, you see in the distance a series of treeless cliffs and spires, forming a portion of the canyon's north face. The challenging and exciting Henline Lookout Trail climbs to the top of these cliffs, and beyond, for a majestic view of the Little North Santiam, Mount Jefferson and Table Rock.

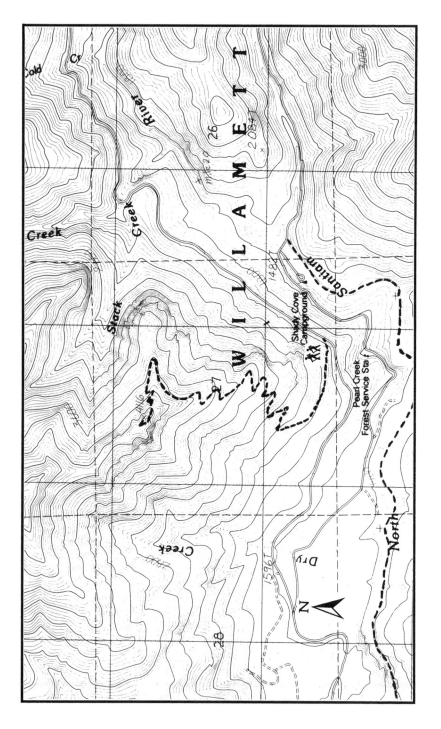

206   Henline Lookout Site

Beginning at 2000 feet elevation, the path rises 2100 feet at a gradient of 763 feet per mile. While I've been on steeper trails, the ascent is unrelenting, with virtually no level spots as it makes its way up a series of short switchbacks. On the map, the trail resembles a seismograph readout after an earthquake.

As noted, the trail begins by climbing a road cutbank. At the top of the gravel slope, it enters a second growth Douglas-fir forest, where it pretty much remains until near the end.

The trail's lower 2/3's are fairly uneventful. The path emerges from the woods every once in a while, to make its way across small rockfalls and scree slopes. Views look westward, towards a mountainscape retreating to an ever broadening horizon.

Two points of rock are passed and surmounted *en route*, the second dropping off a couple hundred feet. Both offer scenic aeries from which to take a breather and survey the countryside.

Not quite 2/3's of the way up, the lookout site, and your destination, appears for the first time, briefly, as a large outcropping jutting from the forested ridge crest, 3/4 mile to the north.

Soon after, the trail crosses the ridge for its first eastward look. This is an outstanding view, with nearly vertical cliffs dropping off hundreds of feet. The cliffs sweep around to the north, forming a large ampitheater. The ampitheater's far end, a mile away, culminates in a flattopped point, with sheer cliffs similar to the one you're standing on. The road far below, running up a wooded canyon across the Little North Santiam, is 2207, on its way up Cedar Creek to Opal Lake.

Eventually, the path will make its way halfway around the rim of the ampitheater, before reversing directions and beginning the final ascent to the lookout site.

After the initial eastward glimpse of the ampitheater, the trail swings back to the west side. Amid a stunted forest of Douglas-fir, hardwoods and brush, it takes its longest, straightest uphill pitch.

When the path finally hits the ridgetop, revealing the first views of Mount Jefferson on the eastern horizon, it levels off only briefly. It quickly starts climbing again as it swings east, breaks out of the woods, then swings back west to surmount the imposing rock pinnacle that is its destination.

And yes, you'll be glad you hung in to the end. You'll probably want to linger awhile, to catch your breath and admire the view. Going down is much, much easier.

The lookout site lies 11/2 mile from, and 500 feet below, the true summit of Henline Mountain. It is accessed by a primitive way trail from the lookout site. Unlike the lookout site, Henline Mountain is heavily forested and offers few vistas.

𝍫𝍫𝍫𝍫

A quarter-mile beyond the 2207/2209 junction, on 2207, a narrow spur called road 301 takes off to the right. If you follow it to the end, bearing left, you'll come to the short Henline Falls Trail. The cascading waterfall measures 120 feet, top to bottom. Look for 1000 foot long mining tunnel nearby.

45.

Opal Creek

Length:	51/2 miles
Difficulty:	Moderate
Elevation:	1900 to 3000 feet
Season:	May through November
Location:	T8S-R5E-Sec. 19
Water:	Plentiful
USGS 7.5" Topo:	Battle Ax
Ownership:	Willamette NF
Phone:	(503) 854-3366
Camping:	Shady Cove
Use intensity:	Heavy

**Directions**: From Salem, follow Highway 22 east to Little North Fork Road, where the sign says, "Little North Santiam Recreation Area." Little North Fork Road, a paved highway, becomes road 2209. Continue on 2209, past the pavement end, to where a locked gate blocks the road. There's parking for 30 cars.

𐰾𐰾 𐰾𐰾 𐰾𐰾

The Opal Creek Trail, a few miles upstream from the Little North Santiam Trail (chapter 43), is far more scenic and infinitely more popular than its sister route. It is also quite long, at 51/2 miles, and a bit of a hassle to reach.

While this is unquestionably an exceptional trail, its popularity is a bit disproportionate, in my opinion. Opal Creek has become the focus of a controversy over old growth preservation and received much nationwide publicity. Ironically, overuse may pose more of a threat to this fragile area than logging.

While the old growth Douglas-fir stands along Opal Creek

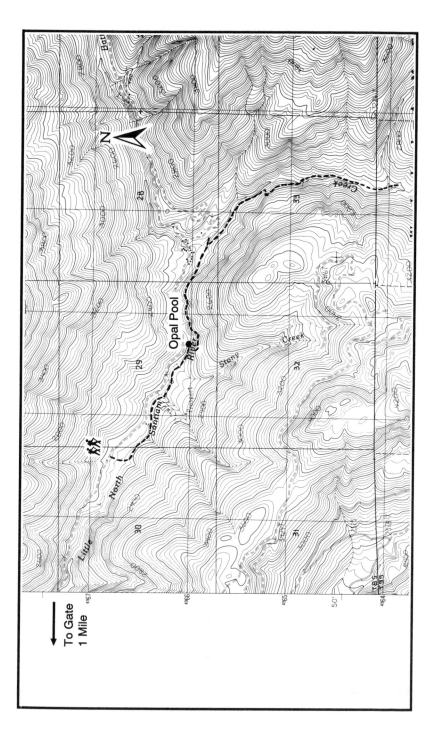

Opal Creek

and the upper Little North Santiam are lovely, the trail passes much second growth. If anything, the area testifies to the fact that harvested or burned forests can grow back vigorously.

Reaching the Opal Creek trailhead involves a 21/2 mile walk along road 2209, from a locked gate. It's not bad going as it closely hugs the river. The route's most impressive old growth surrounds portions of the road. The trees are larger than the old growth along Opal Creek.

The trailhead is well marked on the closed road. After crossing the river via a wooden footbridge, the path follows the opposite bank of the Little North Santiam for a mile before finally turning into the Opal Creek drainage.

Soon after turning up Opal Creek, a short side trail leads to Opal Pool, the area's highlight. The rock lined pool is amazingly deep and clear, with luxuriant vegetation all around.

The final two miles, along Opal Creek, has become a major highlight of the Detroit Ranger District. This fairyland gorge boasts sheer rock faces, narrow clefts, countless small waterfalls and some of the deepest, clearest pools anywhere.

The trail's moderate gradient is exacerbated by a rocky tread. Portions of the trail are narrow and precarious, with cutbanks above and vertical drops below. The path fords the creek halfway up. Presently it is a step across, although the Forest Service plans to build a bridge.

A pool similar to Opal pool, but much less visited, lies near the trail end at Beachie Creek. My friend Venita Mills, at the Detroit Ranger Station, claims it reminds her of the movie "Blue Lagoon," except with vine maple instead of palm trees. The deep pool is surrounded by fantastic rock formations, rushing water and lush jungle.

Be aware that the Opal Creek Trail is under construction as of 1993. Visitors may thus find things a little different than described. For this and other reasons, there's some advantage to following the old route to Opal Creek, or making a loop between the new trail and the old route.

For the old route, stay on the road instead of turning onto the trail. Continue through Jawbone Flat, an area of mining artifacts three miles from the gate, to a spur road right. This leads, shortly, to a path down to Opal Pool and, soon after, a way trail up Opal Creek. The way trail ends at the creek crossing on the new trail, where they're building the footbridge.

A couple final facts I couldn't work in elsewhere: (*1*) Road 2209 marks the southern boundary of the Bull of the Woods Wilderness. (*2*) The Little North Santiam River officially begins at Jawbone Flat, with the confluence of Opal and Battle Ax Creeks.

🚶🚶 🚶🚶 🚶🚶

To visit to Opal Lake, source of Opal Creek, backtrack on 2209 to the junction with road 2207. Follow 2207 over the Shady Cove Bridge and continue for eight miles. The trailhead is well marked, with a small parking area. It's a steep, rocky half-mile hike to the lake. The 11 acre pool is 40 feet deep and stocked with brook trout. The shore tends to be a little brushy and the water isn't as clear as that in its namesake creek. The elevation at Opal Lake is 3200 feet.

🚶🚶 🚶🚶 🚶🚶

Opal Lake lies very near Phantom Natural Bridge. The Phantom Natural Bridge/Elkhorn Ridge Trail begins a quarter-mile beyond the Opal Lake trailhead, (although the preferred route to Phantom Bridge is off road 2223, French Creek Road out of Detroit). The trail from 2207 crosses 2223 after a mile and reaches the natural bridge a quarter-mile beyond that. The arch spans 40 feet and offers excellent vistas of Opal Lake and Mount Jefferson.

46.

Table Rock

(Table Rock Wilderness Area)

Length:	21/2 miles
Difficulty:	Moderate to difficult
Elevation:	3600 to 4881
Season:	June through November
Location:	T7S-R4E-Sec. 13
Water:	Absolutely no water
USGS 7.5" Topo:	Rooster Rock
Ownership:	Salem Dist. BLM
Phone:	(503) 375-5646
Camping:	None
Use intensity:	Moderate

Directions: Leave I-5 at the Highway 214/Woodburn exit. Proceed east, through Woodburn, to Highway 211. Follow 211 to Mathias Road, just past Mollala. Turn right on Mathias, left on S. Feyrer Park Road and right on South Dickey Prairie Road. Follow Dickey Prairie to the bridge at Glen Avon, the start of South Mollala Road (6-3E-6) and the Mollala River Recreation Area. The south Mollala Road ends after 12 miles, at the junction of Middle Fork and Copper Creek Roads. Bear left, onto Middle Fork Road (7-3E-14) and continue to Table Rock Road (7-4E-7). It's five miles up Table Rock Road to the trailhead, accommodating 20 cars along the shoulder.

🚶🚶🚶🚶🚶

Unlike the Forest Service, the U.S. Bureau of Land Management is not known for its wilderness areas. In fact, the Table Rock Wilderness, near Mollala, is Oregon's only entirely BLM managed wilderness (they also manage a portion of the Wild

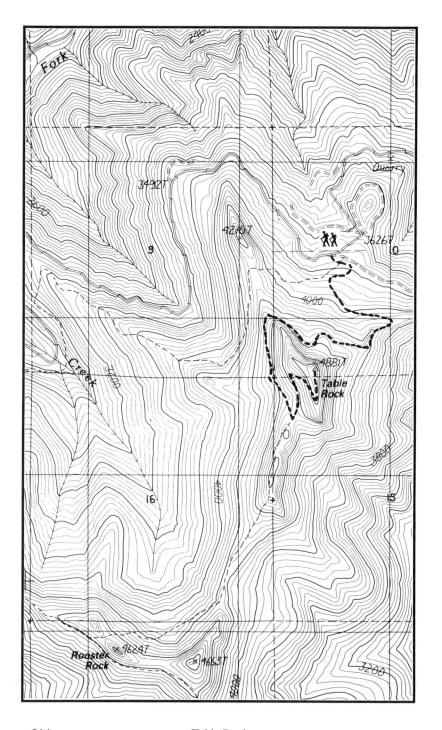

Table Rock

Rogue Wilderness, near Grants Pass). Although minuscule at 5750 acres, the Table Rock Wilderness more than holds its own as a compact, challenging and scenic destination.

While the Table Rock trailhead is not difficult to find, given adequate directions, getting there is complicated. The fact that the most popular map of the region, Mount Hood National Forest, labels only roads within its jurisdiction, adds to the difficulty. While the Mount Hood map shows the entire route from Mollala to Table Rock, and the entire Wilderness Area, it gives no road names.

Furthermore, the 1993 Mount Hood map, while improved over earlier editions, shows Table Rock Road incorrectly (it is closed beyond the trailhead and does not go through to Camp Creek). Also, it places the trailhead in the wrong place.

I located the trailhead by driving over the mountains on Forest Service back roads from Bagby Hot Springs (Chapter 33). I figured it would be easier to trace a route back to Mollala than to try to reach the trailhead from Mollala using a map without road names.

Had I first visited the BLM office in Salem, they would have provided a handout with excellent directions.

My back door route, long and dusty as it was, afforded vistas of Table Rock unavailable from the Mollala River direction. It revealed Table Rock as an almost flat-topped mesa, surrounded by perpendicular cliffs and perched atop one of the region's many steep sided, forested peaks. While the formation has a distinctly Southwestern look, it is made of lava, not sandstone.

Table Rock is the last vestige of an ancient volcano in a range called the Western Cascades. The Western Cascades are considerably older and much more eroded than the High Cascades, immediately east. Unlike the High Cascades, which boasts such dramatic summits as Mount Hood and Mount Jefferson, the peaks of the Western Cascades have long since worn away, leaving only their innermost lava conduits. Table Rock is such a conduit, also known as a "volcanic plug."

From the parking area high above the Table Rock Fork of the Mollala River, amid clearcuts and brush fields, it is 10 steps into a dense, beautiful stand of middle-sized Pacific silver fir and Douglas-fir. My only complaint about the trailhead was the arrows spray painted on rocks, pointing to the trail.

You'd think the sign would suffice.

From the trailhead, the path climbs to an old jeep road, then takes off a little more steeply. A half-mile later, it passes a vertical, 200 foot cliff, barely visible through the woods. If you think the summit lies at the top of this cliff, think again.

After wandering through the woods for another half-mile, the path steepens as it approaches the base of a second cliff, this one only 100 feet high but much longer than the first. The trail makes its way along the cliff base, then cuts around behind it and up to the top, passing a short side trail to a point of rock. You're still nowhere near the summit. Sorry.

The path then wanders through the woods for yet another half-mile, rounding a bend near a small creek. Here the main rise of Table Rock appears. A vertical cliff of columnar basalt, 500 feet high and a half-mile long, blocks your path.

The trail makes its way up a rocky talus slope, overgrown with brush, to the base of the cliff, which it then follows across boulder fields around the western point. Beyond the point, the overhead cliff gradually grows less steep while the path ascends a low ridge.

Atop the ridge, the side trail leading to the summit breaks off north while the main path follows the ridge south for two miles to Rooster Rock (elevation 4663), and two more to the Peachuck trailhead.

Although the half-mile side trail to the summit zig-zags up Table Rock's least steep facet, it still gains another 400 feet. Once on top, visitors are greeted with wildflower meadows, stunted tree clumps and precarious dropoffs. Look for Indian paintbrush and phlox at the highest elevations, along with such sensitive species as Gorman's aster, smooth-leaved Douglasia and Shasta lily.

The summit offers a stunning view of the Willamette Valley and the Cascade Mountains, both Western and High. They say that on an exceptionally clear day, you can see Mount Shasta, in California. On normally clear days, you can at least see Mount Hood and Mount Jefferson.

Washington

The Middle Falls. Lewis River.

47.

Beacon Rock

(Beacon Rock State Park)

Length: 1 mile
Difficulty: Difficult but short
Elevation: 200 to 850
Season: Any season
Location: T2N-R6E-Sec. 25
Water: No water
USGS 7.5" Topo: Beacon Rock
Ownership: Beacon Rock State Park
Phone: (509) 427-8265
Camping: At park
Use intensity: Heavy

_Directions__: Take I-84 to Bridge of the Gods (75 cents) and cross the Columbia into Washington. Turn left on Highway 14 and proceed five miles to the Beacon Rock Rest Area. Park at the rest area or at the picnic area immediately after. The trailhead is between the two areas, which are only a couple hundred feet apart._

𝌀𝌀 𝌀𝌀 𝌀𝌀

One of the main landmarks from the overlook at Vista House, on the Columbia River Scenic Drive, looking east up the river, is a huge, flattop rock which appears to rise out of the middle of the river. You're looking at Beacon Rock.

Up close, one sees that the formation is not in the middle of the river but adjacent to the Washington shore. Also, Vista House catches the rock from its wide side. When you turn the rock 90 degrees, it is much narrower. However, the thing is unquestionably huge, towering a spectacular 750 feet above the Columbia.

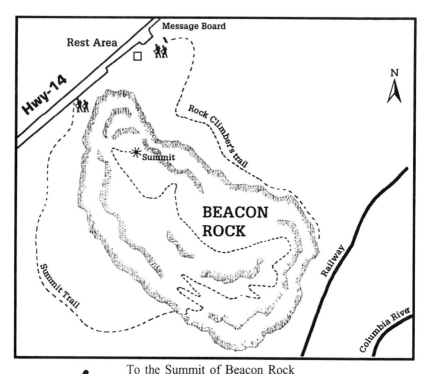

To the Summit of Beacon Rock

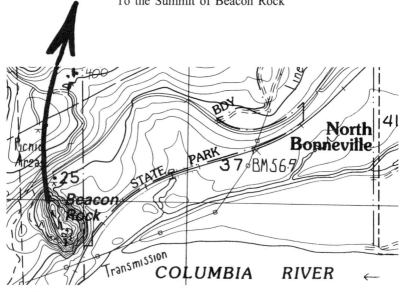

Beacon Rock

Most literature on Beacon Rock claims it is 848 feet high. More precisely, it is 650 feet base to summit, 750 feet above the river and 848 feet above sea level.

Beacon Rock is actually a volcanic plug, the central lava conduit of a once massive volcanic mountain whose entire superstructure has eroded away. Such plugs are common in the Western Cascades, which are much older than the adjacent High Cascades, immediately east. The High Cascades are noted for such landmarks as Mount Hood and Mount Rainier. The Western Cascades, while covering more area, offers nothing better than Beacon and Table Rocks (Chapter 46).

There's not much to describe along the trail, except to say that it is one of the more unusual pathways around. While it rises 650 feet in a mile, placing it in the "difficult" category, it is short enough so that nearly anybody can make it if they take their time.

The only thing I could not figure out is why, when there's a parking lot on either side of the trailhead, you need to practically walk out into the highway to reach the start of the path itself. Be very careful of traffic on Highway 14.

From the trailhead, the wide walkway climbs a rubble slope, though a small wooded area. After 1/8 mile, it comes to the base of the rock, on the river side. Here's where it gets interesting. If the gate is opened, an impossible tangle of switchbacks within switchbacks greets the hiker, as the trail makes its way from narrow ledge to narrow ledge. The entire route is protected by heavy metal railings.

This is not a place for someone with a fear of heights.

Eventually, the path finds the summit, and a little patch of forest. The high point is an outcropping with one of the better views up and down the Columbia. On a clear day, you can see from the Pacific Ocean to Montana. Or at least from just east of Portland to just west of Hood River.

Beacon Rock is an outstanding rock climbing site, with solid surfaces and many sheer walls and overhangs. There's a sign-in sheet, in the rest area, for climbers, and a designated rock climbing area.

48.

Hamilton Mountain

(Beacon Rock State Park)

Length:	4 miles
Difficulty:	Difficult
Elevation:	400 to 2436 feet
Season:	Any season
Location:	T2N-R6E-Sec. 25
Water:	At Hardy Falls
USGS 7.5" Topo:	Beacon Rock
Ownership:	Beacon Rock State Park
Phone:	(509) 427-8265
Camping:	At trailhead
Use intensity:	Heavy

___

**Directions**: Take I-84 to Bridge of the Gods (75¢) and cross the Columbia into Washington. Turn left on Highway 14 and proceed five miles west to the Beacon Rock Rest Area. Turn right, opposite the rest area, towards Beacon Rock Campground. A paved trailhead parking lot, a half-mile up the access road, holds 25 cars. The trail begins between the restroom and picnic shelter.

The campground is closed November 1 to March 31. If so, walk up the access road from the gate. It's ten minutes to the trailhead.

🚶🚶 🚶🚶 🚶🚶

Yes, Virginia, there is a Washington side to the Columbia Gorge. And as the Hamilton Mountain Trail amply affirms, it has its moments, even though the Oregon side is far more popular.

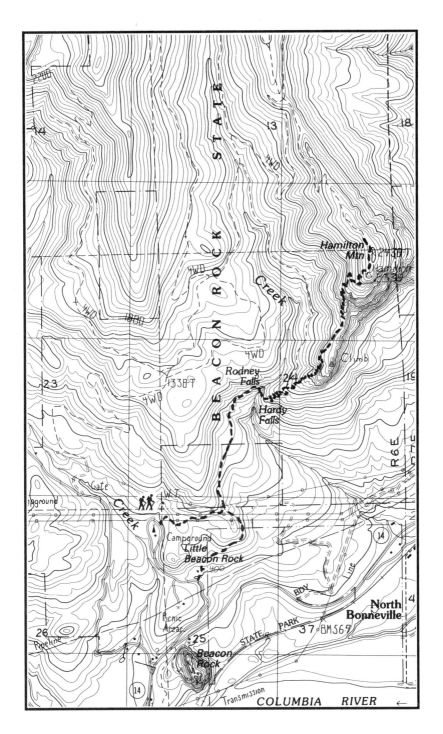

Hamilton Mountain

There are significant differences between the Washington and Oregon sides of the gorge. While the cliffs in Washington are just as steep and high as those in Oregon, the line is more broken up. The Hamilton Mountain Trail scales one such Washington cliff.

While the gorge's Oregon side is famous for numerous high waterfalls, including Multnomah Falls (Chapter 12), the Washington side languishes in obscurity. The Oregon side boasts these waterfalls for a simple reason: It faces north. In the Northern Hemisphere, north facing slopes receive less direct sunlight than south slopes. With less sunlight, there is less evaporation and therefore more water running off.

The Hamilton Mountain Trail visits one of the Columbia Gorge's few Washington waterfalls, and an impressive one at that.

A glance at the Washington side's many barren slopes confirms that it is drier than its Oregon counterpart. Forests on the Washington side of the gorge, (things change farther inland), consist almost entirely of Douglas-fir. On the Oregon side, Douglas-fir is joined by hemlock and redcedar, two very shade loving species.

Hamilton Mountain is located in Beacon Rock State Park. As noted in Chapter 47, Beacon Rock juts 750 feet above the Columbia's Washington shore and is a major gorge landmark, visible for miles up and down river.

From I-84, Hamilton Mountain can be seen as the high cliff immediately east of Beacon Rock. The four mile trail ascends 2000 feet, to a vantage point similar to Angel's Rest on the Oregon Side (Chapter 11). In contrast to the Angel's Rest Trail, Hamilton Mountain has many more open areas and more hours of direct sunlight. So carry lots of water. Also, the Hamilton Mountain Trail is longer and a little more difficult.

In winter, the added sunshine can be a real blessing. In summer, it is far less of a blessing.

From the trailhead, the path climbs steeply through the woods for 3/4 mile, rising 1000 feet. After a quarter-mile, it crosses a wide powerline clearing overgrown with brush. It reenters the woods on the far side.

The clearing affords an excellent view of Hamilton Mountain and the trail route. The path makes its way around the forested upper end of the Hardy Creek drainage, scaling the mostly barren slopes of Hamilton Mountain on the far side. The best vista from Hamilton Mountain occurs at the lower summit, atop the main cliff, three miles from the trailhead. The path also climbs the main summit, immediately behind the lower summit.

At the 3/4 mile mark, well beyond the powerline clearing, the path levels off as it passes several small feeder creeks. A half-mile later, Hardy Creek comes into view. The trail crosses Hardy Creek below Rodney Falls and above Hardy Falls.

Just before dropping briefly but steeply to the densely forested creek, a 500 foot side path, with a sign reading "Pool of the Winds," leads to Rodney Falls. Although only 50 feet high, Rodney Falls are impressive and unusual.

The narrow, cylindrical grotto into which Rodney Falls tumbles appears to be some sort of volcanic shaft or vertical tube, fifteen feet in diameter. A narrow slit, two to three feet wide, allows the water to spill out of the eerie collecting pool inside the shaft. The slit also allows hikers to peer in from a railed vantage point. For all I know, the collecting pool is 500 feet deep, although it appeared only three or four feet deep.

From the slit outlet, the creek tumbles down a convoluted rock slope, flows under the footbridge and drops over Hardy Falls.

Beyond Hardy Creek, the trail's last water, the route begins an infinite series of short switchbacks, gaining 600 feet in the next 1 1/2 miles. It leaves forest behind as it makes its way to the grassy, 1700 foot lower summit. Approaching the lower summit, the switchbacks end for half-mile and the path levels considerably. This is the best unimpeded vista of the Columbia Gorge.

Beyond the lower summit, the switchbacks start anew as the trail negotiates the final mile, rising 700 feet. The actual top of Hamilton Mountain is wooded and the view obscured, although there are some fine intermediate vantage points. Beyond, the path follows the ridge north, connecting with jeep roads and other trails.

49.

Goat Mountain

(Mount Saint Helens Nat. Volcanic Monument)

Length:	3 to 8 miles
Difficulty:	Difficult, then easy
Elevation:	3200 to 5100 feet
Season:	July through October
Water:	Absolutely none, except at the lakes
Location:	T10N-R6E-Sec. 16
USGS 7.5" topo:	Spirit Lake East, Vanson Peak
Ownership:	Mount Saint Helens NVM
Phone:	(206) 274-4038
Camping:	Bear Meadows Campground
Use intensity:	Medium

Directions: Take I-5 north to Woodland, Washington. Head east from there on Highway 503 to Cougar, where 503 becomes Forest Road 90. Continue to road 25, following signs north towards Windy Ridge. Road 25 leads to road 99 (at MP-19), which leads to road 26. Follow 26 north (right) to road 2612, near Ryan Lake. The trail begins a short distance up 2612, at a pullout with room for eight cars.

🚶🚶🚶

The Goat Mountain Trail, offering one of the better overviews of the denuded blast zone from the May 18, 1980, Mount Saint Helens eruption, begins in a huge clearcut, fanning up the hillside in over 1000 feet of elevation gain. From there, the path climbs to the elongated, east-west summit of Goat Mountain, amid panoramas of the blast zone and the Mount Saint Helens crater. The ridgetop is marked by standing deadwood, live old growth forests, alpine meadows and high lakes.

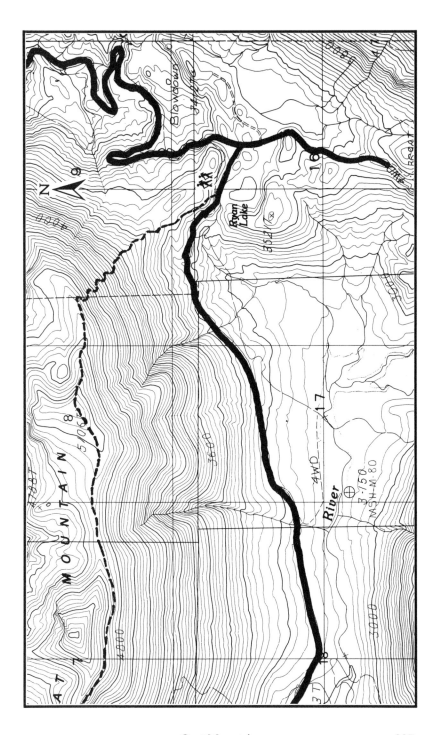

Goat Mountain   227

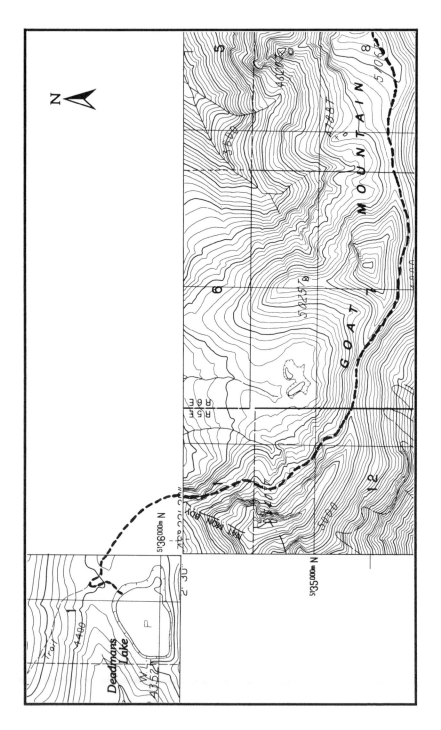

Be sure to carry water as the first two miles are extremely steep, with many exposed areas. Even after the path levels off at the ridgetop, there are many open stretches.

The trail begins as an old salvage logging road but quickly becomes a foot path. The tread consists of compacted pumice, ash and sand, laid down by the eruptions of 1980.

As you hike, the view looks south into the Green River valley. The area has been designated as "Timber Production Priority" within the monument. After the 1980 eruption, the surrounding forest was killed but most of its trees remained standing. Almost the entire valley was salvage logged, with up to 500 truck loads a day being hauled away.

The price paid for this timber was reportedly 15 dollars per 1000 board-feet. Normally, Douglas-fir and Pacific silver fir sells for 400 to 800 dollars per 1000 board-feet.

A short distance up the path, the tread cuts through a stand of dead, standing, unsalvaged trees. The contrast between the salvaged and unsalvaged stands is fascinating. The understory in the unsalvaged stand is composed of huckleberry, bracken fern, thimbleberry, fireweed, wild strawberry and Western princess pine. Natural conifer regeneration is uneven, ranging from nil to positively lush.

Although Douglas-fir was planted in the salvage areas, several other species are regenerating naturally. They include alder, willow, dwarf Oregon grape, salal and dewberry. Oddly enough, these species are more shade loving than the understory species in the unsalvaged areas. I have no explanation for this.

The trail rises easily for the initial half-mile as it crosses an old logging road and disappears into the live forest. After that, it scoots up a precipitous goat slope, around the top of the clearcut and back into the old growth, in a series of short switchbacks. It gains 1400 feet in two miles as it snakes between live forest and the gray skeletons of the blast zone.

In the live stands, little undergrowth is found beneath the dense canopy of Douglas-fir, Pacific silver fir and hemlock, except for wild rose, false salal and fern. Where the trail breaks into the open, huckleberry, thimbleberry and lupine appear.

Approaching the ridgetop, the surrounding high peaks come into view. Mount Hood and Mount Adams are seen first. Then Mount Saint Helens emerges with a view into the blast crater, with its growing lava dome. Atop the ridge, the view looks north to Mount Rainier.

The panorama of the blast zone is fascinating. On the periphery, some stands were virtually unharmed, while a few yards away, miles of dead snags, some standing, many blown over, begin. The direction of the blowdown indicates the flow of the pyroclastic blast wave, pushing the trees over in a domino effect. The mountains seem much more angular where they have been denuded. A forest canopy softens the steep slopes into a smoother, more undulating landscape.

On the ridge, the trail becomes nearly level as it heads west toward Deadmans Lake. Scattered along the ridge are clusters of trees including subalpine fir, lodgepole pine and silver fir. Numerous meadows are lined with huckleberry, yarrow and lupine, with an occasional patch of sedum growing from exposed rock.

It is eight miles to Deadmans Lake so you may choose to content yourself with exploring the ridgetop. If you make it to Deadmans Lake, you'll find the 34 acre pool teeming with eastern brook trout. Beyond the lake, you must hike four more miles, along the Vanson Ridge Trail, to Vanson Lake and Vanson Peak, which have their own trailhead.

From Vanson Lake, a very steep trail drops down to the Green River, following it back to the end of Road 2612, two miles beyond the Goat Mountain trailhead. If you're dying to check out the Green River, drive down 2612 to the Green River trailhead and follow the easy trail for a mile or so. The river's lower portions are supposedly green and shaded, although things look pretty bleak at the trailhead. I'm told fishing is excellent.

You're talking about an overnight stay if you venture beyond Deadman's Lake.

50.

Norway Pass/Mount Margaret

(Mount Saint Helens Nat. Volcanic Mon.)

Length:	2¼ miles (Norway Pass) 5¼ miles (Mount Margaret)
Difficulty:	Moderate
Elevation:	3600 to 4600 to 5858 feet
Season:	July through October
Location:	T10N-R6E-Sec. 32
Water:	None
USGS 7.5" Topo:	Spirit Lake East, Spirit Lake West
Ownership:	Gifford Pinchot NF
Phone:	(206) 247-5473
Camping:	Bear Meadow
Use intensity:	Medium

Directions: *Take I-5 north to Woodland, Washington. From there, head east on Highway 503 to Cougar, where 503 becomes Forest Road 90. Continue to road 25, following signs north towards Windy Ridge. Road 25 leads to road 99 (at MP-19), which leads to road 26. Follow 26 north (right), one mile, to the paved trailhead parking area, with restroom, near Meta Lake. There is room for 15 cars*

𝄪𝄪 𝄪𝄪 𝄪𝄪

Prior to May 18, 1980, Norway Pass looked very much like a small slice of Norway. On that day, a blast of hot wind and ash from Mount Saint Helens, seven miles south, reduced the site to something reminiscent of Saudi Arabia.

Before hiking this amazing trail, through the Saint Helens blast zone to the ridge above Spirit Lake, you should know a few things about the 1980 eruption and the ecology of trees.

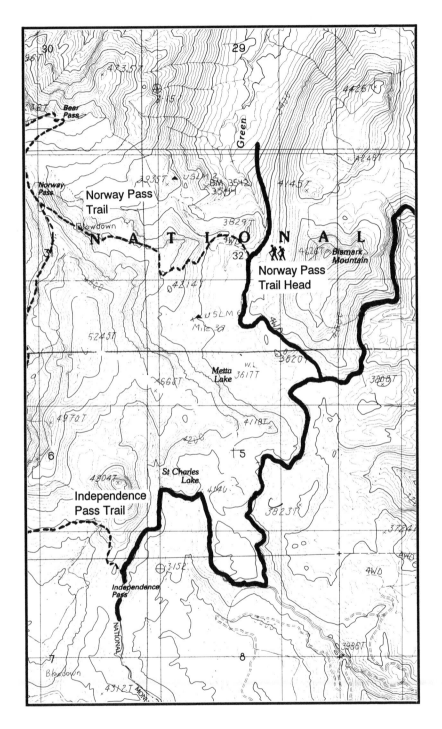

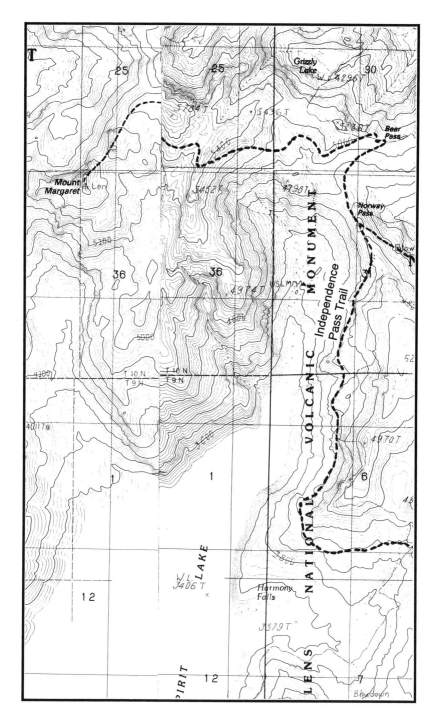

First of all, a mystery: During the 1980 blast, every tree for miles was killed and instantly defoliated, even those left standing. Yet walking the Norway Pass Trail, one observes no fire charring on the thousands of tree skeletons lining the route. After a normal forest fire, charred black scars can be seen for up to 50 years. How then, did the trees die?

It is estimated that air temperatures during the 1980 blast reached 200 degrees, but that the temperature of the ash and rock carried by it was much higher. To kill a tree, the living tissue in the main trunk must be heated to 130 degrees for a sustained period of time, or to 150 degrees for a brief period. The foliage won't catch fire, however, until at least 300 degrees.

In addition to having their trunks heated to near or above lethal levels, the trees did in fact, have their leaves and fine branches burned off.

While there was much fire, it didn't spread because falling ash smothered it. The fine fuels required for a sustained blaze were all instantly burned or buried. No scorched tree trunks are seen because unlike a sustained fire, the scorching was brief, shallow and has since weathered away.

Winds in the 1980 blast were estimated at 200 to 650 MPH, which equals or exceeds the most severe weather systems and approaches the speed of sound. On the Norway Pass Trail, 80% of the trees were blown over, some up to 40 inches diameter. These larger trees are more rigid, with greater mass to catch the wind. Trees left standing are smaller and nearly all had their tops sheared off. Such wind shear is common on steep mountain slopes, where the lower trunk is sheltered from storms by the slope. Many trees were pushed over by other trees.

Finally, note the patterns of natural conifer regeneration. On some sites, the ground beneath the dead trees is positively green with baby trees. On other sites, there's nothing. While reproduction is sporadic along the Norway Pass Trail, some green conifers have grown to 15 feet (as of 1993), and are doing very well.

Volcanic ash is a poor planting medium and I suspect conifer seedlings must struggle until their roots reach the buried, nutrient rich duff soil layer. In some replanted areas, workers dug down to the duff around each tree. Ash varies in depth from a couple inches to 20 feet. With no vegetation to hold it in place, it is quickly eroding away in many places.

The main conifer along the Norway Pass Trail is Pacific silver fir, plus scattered few Douglas-firs and Alaska cedars. There is also much willow, which loves both moisture and sunlight, and fireweed, that has similar requirements. Plant diversity increases on the trail's shaded north slope.

The Norway Pass Trail is extremely exposed, with only a little respite on the north slope approaching the pass. So carry water and/or delay your hike until the off-season. Hiking on a warm mid-November day, I managed to get a little sunburned. Two days later, a foot of snow blanketed Norway Pass.

From the trailhead, the ash and pumice tread of the Norway Pass Trail swings north up a barren hillock. Views of a red stained creek and waterfall, with Mount Rainier peeking through a notch on the horizon, quickly greets hikers. To your left, a nearly vertical bluff rises several hundred feet. Behind it lies a row of higher, foreboding peaks.

The trail's initial objective is to work its way to the top of the bluff so it can swing around to the ridge's north side. Thus, the path rises 900 feet in the first 11/2 miles, in a series of switchbacks with improving views of Meta Lake and Mount Adams.

The trail soon emerges on the north slope, with the narrow notch of Norway Pass visible 3/4 miles away, at the base of Mount Margaret. The trail gains only another 100 feet in reaching the pass.

Norway Pass, 21/4 miles from the trailhead, offers a frightening closeup of the Saint Helens blast crater above Spirit Lake. Unlike Mount Adams and Mount Rainier, with their white glacial mantles and green forests, Mount Saint Helens appears stark and evil. Occasionally, a wisp of steam emerges from the lava dome inside the blast crater.

Spirit Lake, by far the largest natural lake in Gifford Pinchot National Forest, has no shoreline vegetation. Although the water is extremely clear, 1/3 of the lake is covered by a massive log raft. Originally a glacial valley, Spirit Lake has undergone several incarnations in the last few thousand years, most recently when it emptied and refilled following the 1980 eruption. At the monument, it has no outlet. Eventually, it will cut through the massive debris dam to once again become the source of the Toutle River.

At Norway Pass, a 31/2 mile trail takes off along the ridgetop to the left, ending at Independence Pass, two miles down the Windy Ridge Road from the 99-26 junction. Views of Spirit Lake and Mount Saint Helens are spectacular from the Independence Pass Trail.

Also at Norway Pass, the Mount Margaret Trail begins with a tremendous switchback, gaining 600 feet in a mile. It then follows a ridgetop for two miles, past Bear Lake to Mount Margaret's 5858 foot summit.

Beyond Mount Margaret, the trail continues along the ridgetop, with views of Saint Helens Lake and several other lakes. Ultimately, it forms a 16 mile loop around Spirit Lake, ending at Windy Ridge.

51.

Lava Canyon

(Mount Saint Helens National Volcanic Monument)

Length:	31/2 miles
Difficulty:	Easy to difficult
Elevation:	2900 feet
Season:	All seasons
Water:	Plenty of water
Location:	T8N-R6E-Sec. 15
USGS 7.5" topo:	Smith Creek Butte
Ownership:	Mount Saint Helens NVM
Phone:	(206) 274-9344
Camping:	Swift Reservoir
Use intensity:	Moderate to Light

__Directions__: From Portland, take I-5 north to Highway 503, then to road 83, just past Swift Dam. The Lava Canyon trailhead is eleven miles up road 83, at the end of the road, on the south end of Mount Saint Helens NVM. There is a paved parking lot with solar bathrooms, picnic tables and room for two dozen cars.

For the Smith Creek trailhead, turn right onto road 8322 a mile before the Lava Canyon trailhead and proceed to the end of the road.

🚶🚶 🚶🚶 🚶🚶

The rugged, multi-tiered, waterfall laden Lava Canyon Trail consists of three separate segments. They range in difficulty from very easy and paved to quite difficult, with poor footing and steep cliffs. The canyon itself was scoured clean of vegetation by mud flows resulting from the May 18, 1980, Mount Saint

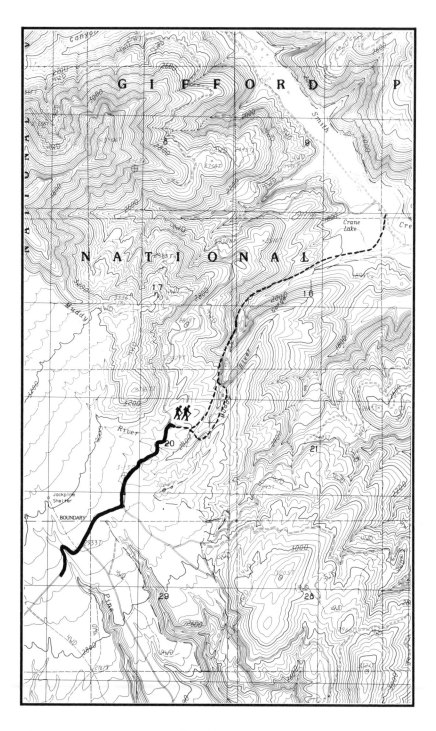

Helens explosion. While most of the debris has washed away, the trail offers a closeup lesson in how ecosystems recover from such devastation.

The path begins as a combination of pavement and boardwalk. This segment covers a half-mile and offers wheelchair access. In addition to easy hiking, there are benches and developed overlooks with interpretive signs.

At the end of the initial paved a half-mile, a more difficult, 11/2 mile loop takes off which drops down to the canyon floor and explores the Muddy River drainage. The loop crosses the river, runs for 3/4 mile on the far bank, recrosses the river and returns to the paved trail along the near bank.

When I visited in 1993, the suspension bridge which will complete the loop had not been finished, so one still must now double back to the starting point. The segment presently constitutes a one mile side trail.

The final segment, taking off from the loop trail's far end, a mile from the trailhead, is much less developed. The faint, difficult path winds among giant boulders as it tries to make its way down to the Muddy River. It then follows the river up Lava Canyon for 21/2 miles, connecting with the Lower Smith Creek Trail.

This portion of the trail is by far the most difficult. While the path never strays far from the Muddy River, river access is impossible over much of the route. There are no guard rails in this precarious segment so I caution against bringing younger children. Being a low elevation canyon, it tends to get quite warm, so carry plenty of water.

Shortly after leaving the paved trail, one encounters a beautiful waterfall which plunges over an abrupt columnar basalt rock face. This waterfall can also be accessed from the upper end of the loop trail. The path then continues along the base of the canyon wall, through some youngish stands of Douglas-fir and red alder and across several side creeks. The forest floor here is covered with dewberry, one of several blackberry varieties native to the Pacific Northwest.

Some interesting rock formations have been exposed by the river. A thick layer of black basalt overlays a deep red rock with some light colored intrusions.

As the trail continues to descend, each time you think you've lost enough elevation to reach the Muddy River, the river drops over another basalt rock face. Eventually, the path enters a grove of old growth Douglas-fir jutting oddly from the canyon wall at nearly right angles and providing much appreciated shade.

This is the only trail I recall, outside of caves or cliff dwellings, which includes a ladder as part of the route. At the ladder (or latter), the path is separated from the Muddy River by a 60 foot basalt wall. The ladder accesses an alder grove containing several interesting plant species, including equisetum and maidenhair fern.

Equisetum is also called horsetail or scouring brush. It represents a plant family, now somewhat rare, which dominated the earth during the Carboniferous age. It has several medicinal and practical uses.

The black stemmed maidenhair fern can be used as a hair rinse or conditioner (only by maidens, of course). Steep a half-cup of the plant in a cup of boiling water until cool, then pour the strained liquid through the hair as a final rinse. Of course, no gathering of materials, plants or artifacts is allowed in the monument.

There are several spots where a waterfall or spectacular view of the canyon makes a suitable turnaround site. Should you elect to follow the canyon to the junction with the Smith Creek Trail, you could then hike out to the road, which offers a much easier, if a little longer, return route. Turning left on the Smith Creek Trail, there are only two miles to go, to the mouth of Ape Canyon. Turning right, it is half a mile to the Smith Creek trailhead.

52.

Ape Cave

(Mount St. Helens Nat. Volcanic Mon.)

Length:	3/4 (Lower Cave) 11/4 miles (Upper Cave) 1 mile (Surface trail)
Difficulty:	Easy to moderate
Elevation:	2100 to 2400 feet
Season:	All seasons
Location:	T7N-R5E Sec. 5
Water:	None
USGS 7.5" Topo:	Mount Mitchell
Ownership:	Mount Saint. Helens NVM
Phone:	(206) 274-4038
Camping:	Cougar Camp
Use intensity:	Heavy

Directions*: From I-5 at Woodland, Washington, take Highway 503 east, which becomes Forest Road 90 at Cougar. Soon after, the paved road 83 takes off left, towards Lava Canyon, Climber's Bivouac and Ape Cave. Follow 83 to road 8303, branching left and also paved. The Ape Cave trailhead, site of the Lower Cave and the lower entrance to the Upper Cave, is a mile up 8303. The trailhead is well developed with a paved, 50 car parking lot.*

For the Upper Cave's upper entrance, continue on 83 to road 81 and proceed a mile to the well marked site.

🚶🚶 🚶🚶

The Ape Cave Trail provides an opportunity to hike into the earth as well as upon it. It also offers a fabulous chance to cool off in summer. Upper Ape Cave is the longest intact lava tube in the United States outside Hawaii, just over 11/4 miles

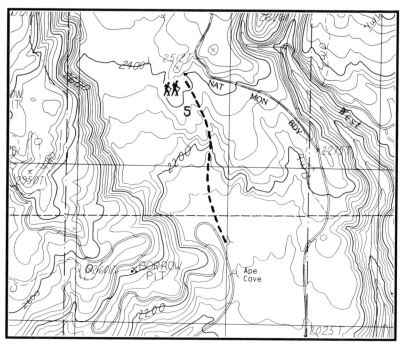

Ape Cave (Surface Trail)

Ape Cave

in length. The Lower Cave extends 3/4 mile in the opposite direction, from the same trailhead, before dead ending.

A one mile surface trail connects the Upper Cave's twin entrances. It offers some unique highlights for an easy and interesting return trip.

Although Ape Cave is unusual for its length, such tubes are common in many volcanic areas. They form because molten lava hardens from the outside in. In a flow of highly fluid, fast moving magma (called "pahoehoe lava"), the liquid continues flowing after the outside has hardened into a tubular shell. Volcanic areas are sometimes honeycombed with multiple layers of lava tubes, which may have permanent ice formations at the bottom.

Pahoehoe flows and lava tubes are rare around Mount Saint Helens, however, because it tends more towards explosive eruptions, with pasty and blocky ("aa lava") flows. The Ape Cave flow was laid down 1900 years ago.

While Ape Cave makes a fascinating outing, cave hiking is not for everyone. Visitors must climb in and out of the cave; stoop, crawl and bend while inside and walk over the highly broken lava floors. Claustrophobia can be a real problem. The lower cave is much wider and easier, with a level floor of compacted silt.

Before going cave exploring, be aware that caves tend to be cool no matter what the season (in this case, 42 degrees), so dress accordingly. Also, the jagged lava rock tends to be rough on knees, hands, head and feet, so wear long pants and sturdy shoes. You may wish to bring extra protection such as gloves and a hat. Some sort of hardhat or helmet wouldn't hurt, either.

Above all, always carry at least two light sources per person (the Forest Service recommends three). This is a prime rule among cave explorers. Although the Visitor Center at the trailhead will rent you a flashlight, backup light sources are up to you. Remember that if your flashlight fails or falls where you can not retrieve it, you may be hard pressed to find your way out, especially in the Upper Cave. Footing is treacherous there and it is often difficult to walk using someone else's light.

Those who have never explored a lava tube should begin with the Lower Cave. This will allow a feel for caving and test your equipment. The level floor was laid down during an ash eruption 450 years ago. Look for a seasonal stream and obvious flow marks on the wall. The latter marks successive stages of retreating lava.

Hot gasses from continuing lava movement remelted the upper and side surfaces of the tube, forming "stalactites," glazes and ripples. Most stalactites have been vandalized in both the Lower and Upper Caves.

A Lower Cave highlight is the Lava Ball, a chunk of hardened material swept along by the flows until becoming wedged in a crevice.

The Upper Cave, ending at a metal ladder, is much more difficult than the Lower Cave and in no way resembles a stroll through the woods, so allow plenty of time. To begin with, it gains 300 feet in elevation. The route is a maze of jagged rock piles, pits, crevices, step-ups and step downs. At one point, the trail climbs an eight foot lava fall. The first glimpse of light, streaming in the Upper Entrance, can be a thrilling relief. It may or may not comfort you to know that at no point will you ever be more than 30 feet below the surface.

Ape Cave was named for the "Saint Helens Apes," an early youth outdoors group. I've read, but have not seen mentioned in park literature, that the frequent use of the name "Ape" (as in Ape Cave and Ape Canyon), relates to bigfoot sightings.

𓀂𓀂 𓀂𓀂 𓀂𓀂

The surface trail is paved for a short distance near the lower entrance, but soon changes to a more natural tread as it wanders through stands of young Western hemlock, Pacific silver fir, Douglas-fir and Western redcedar. Alder, black cottonwood, salal, beargrass and huckleberry also line the path.

Several side trails lead to a variety of geologic sites. The path skirts a large boulder field which appears to have been piled up by a bulldozer but wasn't. Maidenhair fern grows within small collapses along the route.

An interesting wildlife assortment inhabits the area. Aside from the usual birds, such as ravens and juncos, I spotted a pika storing greenery near the upper entrance.

Pika's are unique, wary and rarely observed. The best (and only) place to peek at a pika, is in alpine boulder fields, where they nest and forage for food. North America's only representative of their family, pikas belong to the same order as rabbits (Lagomorpha). Like rabbits, and unlike rodents, they have four upper incisors, not two.

Pikas are active during daylight hours and make easy prey if caught outside their rock crevice homes. They tend to scurry from location to location, holding very still when they stop, to avoid detection. Since they do not hibernate, they often venture fairly far from home in quest of enough food to last the winter.

53.

Big Creek Falls

Length: 1 mile
Difficulty: Easy
Elevation: 1900 to 2100 feet
Season: Any season
Location: T8N-R7E-Sec. 14
Water: Enuff
USGS 7.5" Topo: Burnt Peak
Ownership: Gifford Pinchot NF
Phone: (206) 247-5473
Camping: Swift Reservoir
Use intensity: Heavy

Directions: From Portland, head north on I-5 to Highway 503 at Woodland. At Cougar, 503 becomes road 90. Continue six miles on 90, which is paved but narrow, to the Big Creek Falls trailhead. The gravel parking lot holds ten cars.

🚶🚶🚶

This easy trek is perfect for hikers desiring a minimum of exertion, who have small children in tow, or who wish to combine a hike with sightseeing or car camping. The trail is easily accessed by a paved road and runs through a beautiful forest stand. After visiting the waterfalls, it ends at a marvelous overlook of the Lewis River Valley.

From the trailhead, the Big Creek Falls Trail wanders through a dense stand of second growth Douglas-fir and alder. Look for a very large, upended root wad on a giant tree which blew over not too long ago. Douglas-fir is surprisingly shallow rooted for a species which reaches heights of well over 200 in this rainy, coastal region.

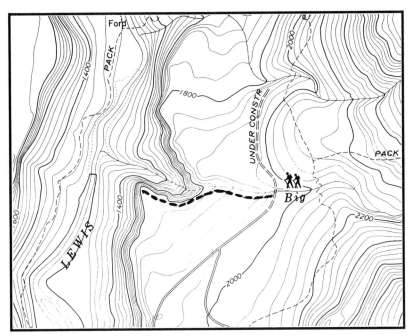
Big Creek Falls trail

As you walk, notice the young trees growing out of the downed, decaying logs on the forest floor amid the huckleberry. These downed "nurse logs," give rise to a huge array of new growth. As the nurse log decomposes, the bases of the trees on top, which had wrapped around it, end up with a characteristic flared look. This is evident on many trees in the vicinity.

Big Creek Falls lie fairly near the trailhead, at the far end of a loop trail. Approaching them, you first come to a fence along a cliff top, with the falls in view but not easily seen. A little further down, a side spur leads to the ultimate view of the falls. Big Creek Falls plunge 110 feet over an overhanging rim into a deep, mist shrouded pool. Hanging ferns, mosses and lichens cover the basalt cliff.

After viewing the falls, either complete the loop and return to the parking lot, or continue along the gorge rim toward the Lewis River overlook. Beyond the falls, the trail's second portion is a little more challenging but boasts fine vistas into the deep, rocky chasm. Shafts of light filter through the branches of the trees above, giving a cathedral affect to the forest, lighting up the mosses and creating a tapestry of foliage.

Amid the Douglas-fir and vine maple, I noted an impressive collection of Western redcedars, many with large buttressed bases. Where light permits, a variety of shrubs and herbaceous plants have taken hold. Most evident are Oregongrape, salal, wild rose and a variety of ferns and mosses.

A mile from the parking lot, the trail reaches the Lewis River overlook. From here, you can see panoramas of the upper Lewis River drainage, neighboring Hemlock Creek and Big Creek Gorge, with its huge basalt outcrops and dense forests. The view is especially pleasing in autumn, when the bright yellows and oranges of the deciduous trees contrast with the deep greens of the evergreen forests.

54.

Three Falls

Length:	3 miles
Difficulty:	Easy
Elevation:	1300 to 1600 feet
Season:	All Seasons
Water:	Oh my! Yes
Location:	T8N-R7E-Sec. 24
USGS 7.5" topo:	Quartz Creek Butte, Spencer Butte
Ownership:	Gifford Pinchot NF
Phone:	(509) 395-2501
Camping:	Lower Falls Recreational Area
Use intensity:	Moderate

<u>Directions</u>: Take I-5 to Highway 503, the Lewis River Road from Woodland, which becomes road 90 at Cougar. Beyond Big Creek Falls (Chapter 53), continue to the Lower Falls Recreation Area and the Lewis River Trail. Head west (right) for Lower Falls and east (left), for Middle and Upper Falls.

Lower Falls may also be reached from the trail at the far end of the bridge over the Lewis River, a mile before the Recreation Area. The bridge trailhead is unmarked and has room for only a couple cars.

𪤦𪤦𪤦𪤦𪤦

This hike along the Lewis River visits three unique and beautiful waterfalls. Each fall is separated from its neighbor by 1 1/2 miles of river, making the overall trek from Lower Falls to Upper Falls just over three miles. The nicely groomed trail follows the river as it meanders through extensive old growth stands.

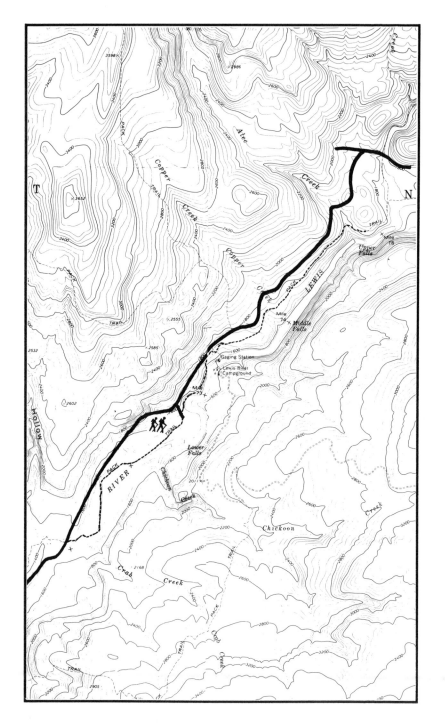

Three Falls

While each of the falls can be reached by its own short trail from road 90, such a strategy misses the full potential of the experience, with its secluded river walk, wildlife, forest communities, etc.

The Lower Falls can be approached either from the Lewis River bridge or the Lower Falls Recreation Area. You will hike the same distance no matter where you start, since the falls are halfway between the two trailheads.

The trail offers a marvelous opportunity to observe old growth understory vegetation. Look for Oregongrape, salal, huckleberry, vine maple, trillium, gooseberry and several representatives of the Wintergreen family, including Western princess pine. There are also many fern species.

Oregongrape is named for its grape-like, clustered berries. It is a member of the Barberry family, not the Grape family. The berries are a favorite among several mammal and bird species but too bitter for the human palate. The fruit's natural yeast bloom (a gray, waxy substance), has been used in wine fermentation. Oregongrape can be used for a variety of ailments, primarily relating to liver disorders. The roots make a natural yellow dye.

As it continues up the Lewis River, the trail offers many outstanding vistas, as well as some interesting historical features. Many spur trails branch from the main path to secluded spots along the riverbank.

One historical feature is an abandoned bridge used for logging operations. Another is a leftover frame from a steam logging mule. Steam mules were used to yard logs to the landing. Such skids are common because when old time loggers finished an area, they would remove the mule from its skid and build a new skid at the new site.

The ever-changing river alternates between rapids, deep pools and the waterfalls for which the area is famous. Just before Middle Falls, the trail crosses Copper Creek, which contains some enticing, swimmable pools. There are also beautiful emerald pools just below Middle Falls, with an abundance of potential picnic sites.

While Middle Falls only drops 20 feet, they are exquisite. The river spills over a wide, bowl shaped formation to a series of rock shelves. I spotted some merganser ducks diving for fish near Middle Falls.

Leaving Middle Falls, the trail follows the base of a steep canyon wall which overhangs the trail. The wall is home to several species of lichen, moss and fern. If you look closely, you can see roots poking out of cracks in the rock.

The Upper Falls are completely different from Lower and Middle Falls. The wide, double tiered tumble makes a right angle turn between tiers.

A short ways above Upper Falls, the path splits into the Quartz Creek and the Lewis River Trails, both of which continue for several miles, visiting still more waterfalls and old growth forest.

Quartz Creek.

55.

Trapper Creek

(Trapper Creek Wilderness)

Length:	31/2 miles
Difficulty:	Easy to moderate
Elevation:	1200 to 1800 to 3800 feet
Season:	May through November
Water:	Plenty of water
Location:	T5N-R6E-Sec. 25
USGS 7.5" topo:	Bare Mountain, Termination Point
Ownership:	Gifford Pinchot NF
Phone:	(206) 696-7500
Camping:	Gov't Mineral Springs CG
Use intensity:	Light

Directions: *From I-84, take Exit 44 to Bridge of the Gods (75¢ toll), at Cascade Locks. Across the bridge, head east on Highway 14, toward Carson. Turn left onto the Wind River Road and proceed through Carson. Where the Wind River Road becomes road 30 and veers right, continue straight on the pavement towards Government Mineral Springs. Take a right onto road 5401 (or continue straight for Government Mineral Springs Campground). The Trapper Creek trailhead is located a half-mile up 5401, at a well signed parking area with room for 15 cars.*

𝆐𝆐𝆐𝆐𝆐

The Trapper Creek Trail has all the trappings of an easy and fascinating wilderness excursion. Better yet, the quiet hike along a secluded creek is easily reached from Portland on paved roads. The 6000 acre Trapper Creek Wilderness offers several

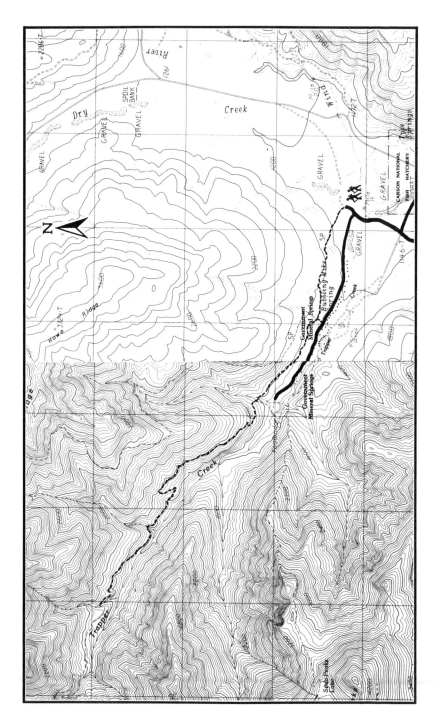

Trapper Creek

hiking opportunities besides the Trapper Creek Trail, with an interesting historical site near the main trailhead.

To shave a mile off the recommended 31/2 mile route, proceed up 5401 from the main trailhead to an unmarked but obvious crossing where a way trail from Government Mineral Springs Campground connects to the Trapper Creek Trail. Park on the shoulder or in the campground and be aware that the lost mile runs well above the road through some outstanding old growth.

Basically, the Trapper Creek Trail follows Trapper Creek. The path runs parallel to Forest Road 5401 for the first two miles (or one mile). Soon after, it meets the far end of the Soda Peaks Lakes Trail (Chapter 56), which quickly drops 200 feet to Trapper Creek and crosses it via a footbridge.

For the Trapper Creek route's initial three miles (or two miles), you're well above the creek, making your way upstream and around several side creeks. Finally, the path drops to the water's edge in a large switchback. I made this the turnaround spot, although the route follows the creek for another two miles. It connects with the Observation Peak Trail (Chapter 57), after seven miles.

The trail's Douglas-fir and Western redcedar overstory, with patches of red alder, is accented by an understory of vine maple, red huckleberry, salal and fern. The lush understory is remarkably diverse so bring your botanical books along. I spotted many unusual specimens, including mushrooms, saprophytes (without green chlorophyll) and orchids. Trillium, saxifrages, tall Oregon-grape, vanillaleaf, etc., also inhabit the deep humus beneath the old growth conifers.

Saprophytes include pine-drops and a member of the Wintergreen family called Indian pipe. I encountered several unusually large clusters of Indian pipe, some more the ten inches across.

The wildflower display made this a very worthwhile day-hike. Observing the many species together makes one appreciate the complexity of Washington's west side old growth forests.

Between miles three and four, the trail pretty much hugs the creek. In mile five and six, the interest level picks up when the path hits an outstanding rimrock viewpoint at Cliff Creek, crosses the creek, then passes Trapper Falls, a 100 foot cascade over bedrock with a pool in the middle. At mile six, the trail begins climbing seriously towards Observation Peak.

𝕩𝕩𝕩𝕩

Government Mineral Springs, a half-mile past the trailhead on road 5401, is also of some interest. Apparently, there used to be a fancy hotel at the site, between 1910 and 1935. The hotel advertised the mineral waters (which they heated), as a cure for numerous ailments including rheumatism, diabetes and nervous disorders. While I'll grant them the latter, the water's main mineral is salt, along with much dissolved calcium.

These days, only a well remains at the hotel site, from which cold mineral water may be taken. The Government Mineral Springs Campground, a mile away, was built in 1920.

56.

Soda Peaks Lake

(Trapper Creek Wilderness)

Length:	21/2 miles
Difficulty:	Moderate
Elevation:	3700 to 4400 feet
Season:	July through October
Water:	At lake
Location:	T5N-R6E-Sec. 28
USGS 7.5" topo:	Bare Mountain
Ownership:	Gifford Pinchot NF
Phone:	(206) 696-7500
Camping:	Beaver Campground
Use intensity:	Moderate

Directions: From I-84, take Exit 44 to the Bridge of the Gods (75¢), at Cascade Locks. Across the bridge, head east on Highway 14, toward Carson. Turn left where the sign says "Wind River Recreation Area" and proceed north via the paved Wind River Road.

Turn left, from the Wind River Road, towards the Wind River Ranger Station. Once across the river, turn right onto road 54, Szydlo Road, a paved route which parallels the Wind River's west bank, then climbs towards the Soda Peaks. The well signed trailhead is located 13 miles up Szydlo Road, near the pavement end. Look for a fork in the road with a small parking area, at the edge of a recent clearcut.

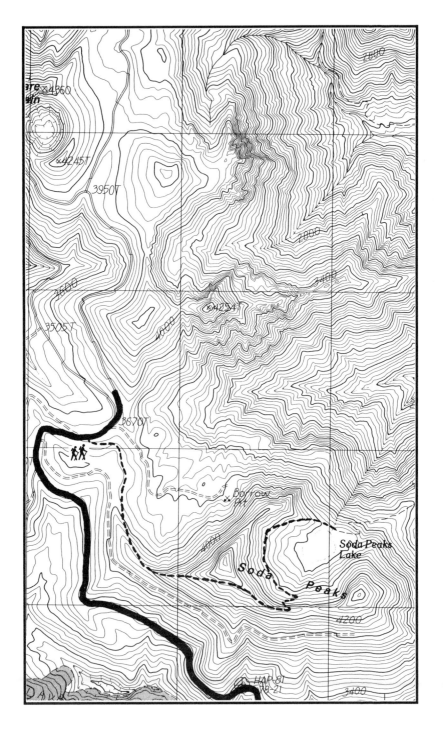

This rugged, 21/2 mile hike offers outstanding vistas between Mount Hood and Mount Saint Helens from a charming and lesser visited wilderness area. It traverses dense forest, ascends to a rugged saddle with a 700 foot elevation gain, then drops 400 feet in the last half-mile, to visit the Trapper Creek Wilderness Area's only lake.

Even the trailhead drive, along the west bank of the Wind River, offers outstanding scenery as it passes some impressive second growth forests. Three miles up Szydlo Road, where it narrows from two to one lane, you'll find a meadow with an outstanding display of digitalis (foxglove), lupine, hypericum, thistle, daisy and fern. Look for vistas of Mount Hood here.

There are three main access routes to the 6000 acre Trapper Creek Wilderness. The Government Mineral Springs and Observation Peak trailheads are discussed in Chapters 54 and 55. The Soda Peaks Lake Trail connects with the Trapper Creek Trail after 51/2 miles.

From the trailhead, the path winds through a relatively level clearcut for half-mile, then begins climbing as it enters some older stands of Douglas-fir. Trees here tend to have large side branches which reduces their market value as timber.

The trail tread becomes rather faint as it crosses the clearcut and it may take a bit of searching to find your way. If you remain north of the harvest boundary, you should pick up the route. The path is scheduled for maintenance in 1994.

The trail continues up the ridge on the south facing slope, crossing meadows and talus slopes and getting quite steep as the saddle is approached. The Wilderness boundary is crossed just before the saddle. Abundant mosquitoes are offset by abundant wildflowers. Do not forget your mosquito repellent.

Although the saddle lies mostly in the woods, I spotted Indian paintbrush, catchfly and trillium in my late August visit. There was also a spectacular vista of the surrounding peaks, with Soda Peaks Lake below.

The last quarter-mile to the lake, dropping 400 feet from a switchback atop the saddle, presents a difficult but short climb on the return trip. The green water lake, with its heavily wooded shore, covers ten acres, reaches a depth of 22 feet and is stocked with Eastern brook and German brown trout. The lake lies in a deep depression and thus could use some cheering up.

From Soda Peaks Lake, it is an easy three mile miles to Trapper Creek and Government Mineral Springs.

View of Soda Peaks Lake.

57.

Observation Peak

(Trapper Creek Wilderness)

Length:	31/2 miles
Difficulty:	Moderate
Elevation:	3600 to 4200 feet
Season:	June through November
Water:	None
Location:	T5N-R6E-Sec. 10
USGS 7.5" topo:	Bare Mountain
Ownership:	Gifford Pinchot NF
Phone:	(206) 696-7500
Camping:	Beaver Campground
Use intensity:	Light

__Directions__: From I-84, take Exit 44 to Bridge of the Gods (75¢ toll), at Cascade Locks. Across the bridge, head east on Highway 14, toward Carson. Just before Carson, turn left (north) on the paved Wind River Road. Follow the Wind River Road past where it turns right and becomes road 30, to the junction with road 64, a paved road left. Road 64 eventually runs into road 58, a gravel route also to the left. Road 58 leads to the well marked trailhead. A gravel pull-out accommodates six cars.

🥾🥾🥾🥾🥾

The quiet, remote and minuscule (6000 acres) Trapper Creek Wilderness Area, an easy drive from Portland, is equidistant between Mount Hood, Mount Adams and Mount Saint Helens. The best vantage point from which to take in its surrounding magnificence is the top of Observation Peak, highest in the Wilderness at 4207 feet.

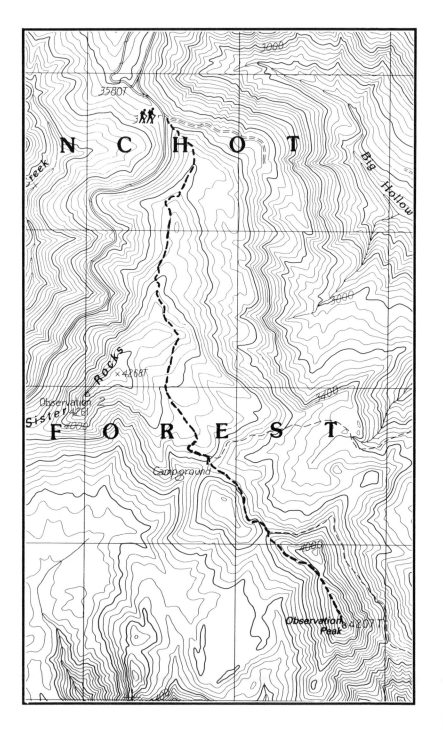

Observation Peak

Although the name "Observation Peak," may not seem very original on the surface, I like its philosophical implications. Unlike similar names such as Vista Ridge and Lookout Mountain (Chapters 24 and 29), "observation" implies not only that you look, but that you look carefully and draw some sort of conclusion.

Here are some observations regarding Observation Peak:

The Trapper Creek Wilderness has three main entry points, all interconnected by trails. Both the Observation Trail, described in this chapter, and the Soda Peaks Lake Trail (Chapter 56), may be reached via the Trapper Creek Trail (Chapter 55), from the Government Mineral Springs trailhead. It's six miles farther to Observation Peak via the Trapper Creek Trail than via the Observation Peak trailhead.

Like other paths in the Trapper Creek and Indian Heaven Wilderness Areas, the Observation Trail runs through magnificent old growth, thinned by altitude and sprinkled with lodgepole pine.

Like those other paths, it is rife with huckleberry. In fact, it is a prime huckleberry gathering site. A close relative of blueberries, huckleberries are smaller and tangier. Evergreen huckleberries are darkest and sweetest while red huckleberries are quite sour (although many people like them). Whortleberries are smaller but just as tasty.

From the trailhead, it's three miles up the Observation Trail, rising 400 feet then dropping 200, to a small saddle. At the saddle, the Observation Peak Trail takes off left. If you continue straight, you'll end up at Government Mineral Springs.

The half-mile summit spur rises 400 feet to the site of an old fire lookout. Look for Mount Adams, Mount Saint Helens and Mount Rainier, with the sweep of the Trapper Creek basin directly below, culminating at Government Mineral Springs and the Carson Fish Hatchery.

58.

Blue Lake

(Indian Heaven Wilderness Area)

Length:	31/4 miles
Difficulty:	Moderate (due to trail conditions)
Elevation:	4250 to 4600 feet
Season:	June through October
Water:	At lakes
Location:	T6N-R8E-Sec. 17
USGS 7.5" topo:	Gifford Peak, Lone Butte
Ownership:	Gifford Pinchot NF
Phone:	(509) 395-2501
Camping:	Falls Creek Horse Camp
Use intensity:	Heavy

Directions*: From Portland, follow I-84 east to Bridge of the Gods (75¢ toll), then cross the Columbia River into Washington. Turn right and follow Highway 14 to the Wind River Road. Proceed up the Wind River to road 65, the Panther Creek Campground turnoff. Head right on the mostly paved road 65 and proceed to the well marked trailhead, which consists of a gravel pullout with room for 12 cars.*

Road 65 is closed (as of October, 1993), between the Blue Lake/Thomas Lake trailhead and the Placid Lake trailhead (Chapter 63).

🚶🚶 🚶🚶 🚶🚶

Oh, what a lot of lakes! At least a dozen pristine pools, plus numerous ponds, are visited by this pathway to the heart of the 20,000 acre Indian Heaven Wilderness. Of course, with 150 lakes in the Wilderness, you needn't travel far on any trail

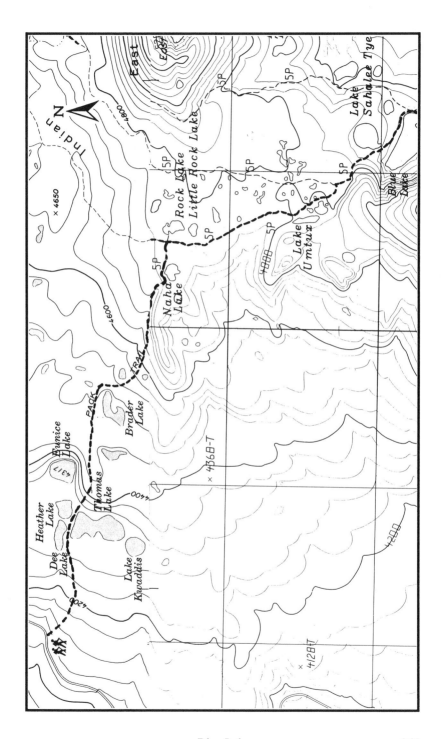

Blue Lake   265

to run into one. This particular route takes you from the Thomas Lake basin, near the trailhead, over a low divide into the Blue Lake basin.

The Blue Lake Trail is rated "moderate" rather than "easy" because of its poor condition in some areas. It is scheduled for maintenance and there should be no difficulty following it.

This main west side access to the Indian Heaven begins by traveling through clearcut and select cut harvest blocks between the trailhead and Wilderness boundary. Many of these areas have regenerated to young, open stands of hemlock and silver fir, with the usual brushy understory of huckleberry and beargrass. Inside the Wilderness, the forest becomes more dense, with larger trees.

I noticed several members of the Wintergreen family early on the trail, with pinedrops especially thick on the more light starved sites. Forests, however, are incidental to this hike. Of far greater interest are the lakes and meadows.

On entering the Wilderness, hikers are greeted by Dee, Heather and Thomas Lakes. Eunice Lake lies a brief walk east, with all lakes accessed by spur trails.

Heather Thomas, in case you've forgotten, was one of the stars of the old TV show, *The Fall Guy.* I presume she had nothing whatsoever to do with the naming of Heather and Thomas Lakes.

For you fisherpeople, Dee Lake covers 21/2 acres and reaches a depth of six feet, Heather Lake encompasses three acres with a depth of seven feet, Thomas Lake takes in 101/2 acres with no depth listed (although it must have one or it wouldn't be a lake), and Eunice Lake surrounds 61/2 acres, with a depth of 22 feet. All lakes are stocked with Twin Lakes cutthroat trout, except Thomas Lake, which also contains rainbow trout.

Beyond Eunice Lake, the trail begins a more significant climb as it works its way up and out of the Thomas Lake basin. It soon enters a spooky forest, draped in shawls of lichen and inhabited by leprechauns. The path emerges in a series of high meadows, giving a feel for the open plateau you are walking on.

Continuing through the meadow, the route meets the Brader Lake Trail, then climbs a braided, poorly maintained route towards Naha Lake. It passes an interesting area of blown over trees here. Based on varying states of decomposition, trees have been falling in this site for years. Yet the forests on both sides have far less windthrow. It's either a wind funnel or a pocket of extremely poor soil.

Further along, the trail parallels a boulder outcrop of volcanic rock as it passes over a saddle.

After dropping to Naha Lake, the trail flattens out in a large meadow dotted with lakes and ponds. At Rock and Little Rock Lakes (obviously named by someone from Arkansas), the path hits a junction. Hang a left for Bear Lake (Chapter 60), three miles away. For Blue Lake, two miles distant, turn right.

Naha, Rock and Little Rock Lakes are all shallow, cover less than an acre and are stocked with cutthroat trout.

South of the junction, the route continues through beautiful subalpine meadows dotted with small ponds. The trail here appears less used than previously, indicating that many hikers wind up at Bear Lake. Beyond Umtux Lake (six acres, cutthroat trout), the trail drops in elevation through a thick forest stand, to Lake Sahalee Tyee (Seven acres, twenty five feet deep, cutthroat trout).

The beautiful, circular Lake Sahalee Tyee appears deep and blue between the trees. Its steep, even shore suggests that it occupies a volcanic crater. The name Sahalee Tyee loosely translates to "Indian Heaven."

A few hundred feet beyond Sahalee Tyee, Blue Lake dominates the scene. Unlike other area lakes, Blue Lake sits directly against a huge basalt wall with rock debris raveling down to its shore. Blue Lake is much bluer than other lakes in the Indian Heaven. At 46 feet dep, it is the deepest among the Wilderness Area's 150 lakes. Blue Lake covers 12 acres and is stocked with cutthroat trout.

The Blue Lake basin (and Thomas Lake basin, and every other natural lake basin in the Northwest), was carved by glacial action. The headwall above Blue Lake marks the glacier's point of origin while other lakes in the basin (except for Sahalee Tyee), are either remnants of a once larger Blue Lake or tarn lakes. Tarns are are depressions caused by detached ice chunks.

The Pacific Crest Trail meets the Blue Lake Trail at the east end of Blue Lake, heading north to Junction Lake and south to Mexico.

59.

Junction Lake

(Indian Heaven Wilderness Area)

Length:	21/2 miles
Difficulty:	Easy to moderate
Elevation:	4036 to 4730 feet
Season:	June through October
Water:	Aplenty
Location:	T6N-R8E-Sec. 26
USGS 7.5" topo:	Lone Butte, Gifford Peak
Ownership:	Gifford Pinchot NF
Phone:	(509) 395-2501
Camping:	Forlorn Lakes, Goose Lake
Use intensity:	Moderately heavy

Directions: From Portland, follow I-84 east to Bridge of the Gods (75¢ toll) and cross the Columbia River. Turn right and follow Highway 14 to the paved Wind River Road. Take the Wind River Road to Forest Road 60. Head right on 60, which is mostly paved, and follow it past Crest Horse Camp, Big Lava Bed (Chapter 63) and Goose Lake, to road 6035 (dirt). Turn north (left) on 6035 and proceed past Forlorn Lakes to the East Crater trailhead, a small parking turnout with room for six cars. The trailhead is signed but not terribly apparent.

Alternatively, take the Wind River Road to the Panther Creek Campground turnoff (right). Continue past the campground on road 65 to the junction with road 60. Turn right onto 60 and proceed to 6035 and the trailhead.

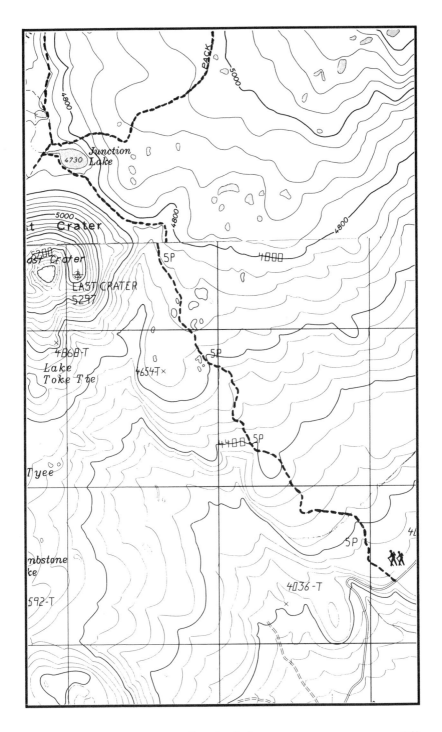

Junction Lake   269

This highly scenic route accesses the lake-laden, 20,000 acre Indian Heaven Wilderness Area from the southeast to join the Pacific Crest Trail. *En route*, it passes dense forests, meadows, ponds, creeks and a large volcanic crater before emerging at Junction Lake.

Unlike other areas adjacent to the Indian Heaven Wilderness, which by and large have been clearcut, the trailhead is situated in a lovely old growth stand. The path's first mile winds among some spectacular Douglas-firs which tower above the usual carpet of beargrass and huckleberry.

It had been moist for several days prior to my visit and I found the local mushroom population positively exploding. While I didn't key them out, I noted considerable diversity, from huge, white things with long, flowing gills to tiny orange buttons.

As the trail makes its way up the 700 feet of elevation gain to Junction Lake, it crosses and recrosses Dry Creek, which appears to be carved from bedrock. I wonder if the creek gets its name because the rocky bed has such little absorption that it quickly empties itself of water. Regardless, it is an interesting drainage which must contain a fair amount of runoff at certain times of year, based on the many log bridges spanning it. Continuing to climb, the character of the forest changes to a more columnar and narrow subalpine look. The terrain here tends to undulate, giving the feeling of waves moving across an ocean suspended in time. Meadows are dotted with small lakes and ponds both east and west of the trail.

The only sounds I heard were the wind and a single raven which loudly announced my position. Since I visited on a day of extreme fog, whenever I passed under the dense forest canopy, droplets of condensed fog showered down on me. I came home drenched as though it had been raining.

Two miles up, the trail crosses, then parallels the meadows around the Dry Creek headwaters. The tread continues on the meadow's west side, skirting the northeast base of East Crater. East Crater rises an abrupt 600 feet before plunging 375 feet into a central volcanic pit.

I was astonished by the color and beauty of the meadow as I approached Junction Lake. The yellow-greens of the grasses, beside the deep greens of evergreen heather, combined with the reds and yellows of the huckleberry, make a magnificent display. All this against a backdrop of deep forest greens and browns.

Junction Lake is irregularly shaped, shallow and, when I visited, shrouded in fog blowing in over the tops of the surrounding trees. It covers eight acres, reaches a depth of 25 feet and is stocked with cutthroat trout.

As I sat by the lake, a raven flew over, calling out periodically. After each call an echo returned. The bird seemed to be navigating through the fog using its call as echolocation, much like bats.

For those wishing to extend the hike, additional trails begin at the west end of Junction Lake, where the path meets the Pacific Crest Trail. Head north on the PCT a mile to Bear Lake and 11/2 miles to Deer Lake. Or follow the side trail right, off the PCT, just after Deer Lake, to make a loop past Clear and Lemei Lakes and back to Junction Lake. The loop covers 31/2 miles and rises to 5100 feet.

Bear Lake is an eight acre pool reaching a depth of 32 feet and containing a population of cutthroat trout. Shallow Deer Lake covers 51/2 acres and is also stocked with cutthroat trout. Clear Lake occupies 13 acres, with a depth of 30 feet. The usual gang of cutthroats lurk in its waters. Lemei Lake is not listed on the Indian Heaven lake list, possibly because it is unstocked. The shallow lake covers seven acres near Lemei Rock, highest point in the Wilderness at 5825 feet.

On the way back to the trailhead, I happened upon a newly deposited pile of bear scat. What caught my interest was that it was composed almost entirely green grass. I have seen early spring bear scat made of semi-decayed grass which the animal uses to keep hunger pangs under control while it hibernates. In Autumn, bears load up with grasses which do not readily digest and remain in the animal until spring. It seems the grasses may also "scour" out their intestines, further preparing the animal for winter.

60.

Deep Lake

(Indian Heaven Wilderness Area)

Length:	21/4 miles
Difficulty:	Moderate
Elevation:	4000 to 5087 feet
Season:	July through October
Water:	At lakes
Location:	T7N-R9E-Sec. 36
USGS 7.5" topo:	Lone Butte
Ownership:	Gifford Pinchot NF
Phone:	(509) 395-2501
Camping:	Cultus Creek Campground
Use intensity:	Heavy

__Directions__: From Portland, head east on I-84 to the Bridge of the Gods (75¢), and cross the Columbia River. Proceed east on Highway 14 to the Wind River Road and the Mount Saint Helens sign. Follow the Wind River Road past where it turns left and becomes Road 30. Remain on 30 when the Mount Saint Helens route swings left and 30 proceeds straight. Road 30 is paved and ends at road 24, which is not. Turn south (right) on 24 to Cultus Creek Campground.
Both the Indian Heaven and Cultus Trails begin at the campground's southwest end. Follow the Indian Heaven Trail for Deep Lake and the Cultus Trail for Wood Lake (Chapter 61). Trailheads are well marked and popular, with parking for a dozen cars.

𓀠𓀠𓀠𓀠𓀠

The Indian Heaven Trail to Deep Lake is the main route into the lake laden, 20,000 acre Indian Heaven Wilderness. The

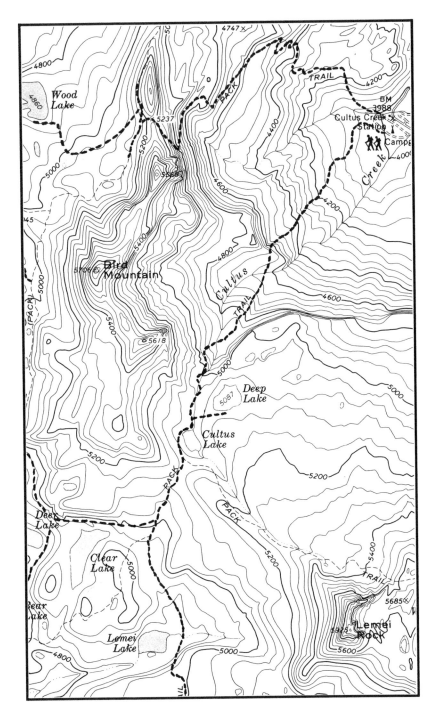

Deep Lake 273

path climbs the Cultus Creek drainage to an outcropping on Bird Mountain, second highest in the Wilderness, before dropping to the Deep Lake/Cultus Lake basin. Lemei Rock, the Wilderness Area's main mountain at 5925 feet, is visible to the southeast.

From the trailhead, the path ascends moderately for a quarter-mile, then steepens as it travels through spectacular timber stands which periodically open up to provide views of the basalt outcroppings above. The trail gains 1200 feet as it rises through multi-aged forests of Pacific silver fir and mountain hemlock, with an occasional red alder.

Look for gooseberry (Ribes spp.) near the beginning of the trail, along with the ever present huckleberry. The Wilderness was and is a favorite Native American huckleberry gathering area. Tribes converged from all over the Northwest to collect berries.

Huckleberries are nearly identical to blueberries and belong to the same genus, except they're smaller and a little tangier. They ripen late, in September mostly. If you've never eaten huckleberry pie, you're missing one of life's great delicacies.

For serious berry gatherers, permits are available, with some areas restricted to use by Native Americans. I know of no law prohibiting human browsing, however. Judging from the animal scat, humans aren't the only ones with an affinity for these delectable morsels.

Gooseberry, a member of the Currant family, has been largely eradicated from many forests because of its role as an alternate host for white pine blister rust, a fungus which kills young white and sugar pines.

Halfway up the trail, a mile from the trailhead, the path ascends a short, very steep upgrade amid rock outcroppings and rubble openings. It continues at a steep grade, making its way along the top of the Bird Mountain ridge for half a mile. The route then eases off, while continuing to rise.

Trees here are draped in lichen, which people from the Southeast call "Spanish moss." Lichen grows on rocks as well as trees and is a symbiotic association between algae and fungi. The fungi form the support structure in which the algae grow.

The reason they "grow" on rock faces is that they derive their nutrition from the air around them. Not surprisingly, lichens are among the first casualties of air pollution. Their abundance in the Indian Heaven Wilderness indicates good air quality.

The trail's high end periodically flattens out as it passes several meadows. The tread then zig-zags into a much denser stand of forest as it heads past a rock wall into the Cultus Lake/Deep Lake basin.

Cultus Lake comes first, although the Deep Lake Trail breaks off just before Cultus Lake. The wooded Cultus Lake covers four acres, reaches a depth of twelve feet and is stocked with cutthroat trout.

The short hike to Deep Lake is well worth the walk. Somewhat larger than Cultus at six acres, Deep Lake is a dark green color and is stunning, in autumn, against the bright yellows and reds of the deciduous shrubs which share the shore with the evergreen conifers. One of the higher lakes in the Wilderness at 5087 feet, Deep Lake is only moderately deep at 26 feet. It contains cutthroat and rainbow trout. Many spur trails lead around the lake, providing ample opportunity for exploration and solitude.

For a more challenging, eight-mile loop, return to Cultus Lake and continue south for a mile, to Clear and Deer Lakes. Then head north on the Pacific Crest Trail to the Cultus Trail. The Wood Lake Trail meets the PCT a little north of the Cultus Trail junction. It's 3/4 mile west (left), on the Wood Lake Trail to Wood Lake and a downhill two miles east, on the Cultus Trail, back to the Cultus Creek Campground.

Do not try this loop in the opposite direction because the final leg, from the saddle above Wood Lake to the Cultus Creek trailhead, is extremely steep.

61.

Wood Lake

(Indian Heaven Wilderness Area)

Length:	21/2 Miles
Difficulty:	Moderately difficult
Elevation:	4000 to 5200 to 4860 feet
Season:	July through October
Water:	Plenty
Location:	T7N-R9E-Sec. 36
USGS 7.5" topo:	Lone Butte
Ownership:	Gifford Pinchot NF
Phone:	(509) 395-2501
Camping:	Cultus Creek Campground
Use intensity:	Moderate to heavy

Directions: From Portland, take I-84 to the Bridge of the Gods (75¢ toll), and cross the Columbia River. Proceed east on Highway 14 to road 30, the Wind River Road to Mount Saint Helens. Remain on the Wind River Road where it turns right and becomes Road 30. Continue on 30 where the Mount Saint Helens route turns left and Road 30 goes straight. Road 30 is paved and ends at Road 24. Turn south (right) on 24 to Cultus Creek Campground.

Both the Cultus and Indian Heaven Trails begin at the campground's southwest end. Follow the Cultus Trail for Wood Lake and the Indian Heaven Trail for Deep Lake (Chapter 60). The Trailhead is well marked and popular, with plenty of parking.

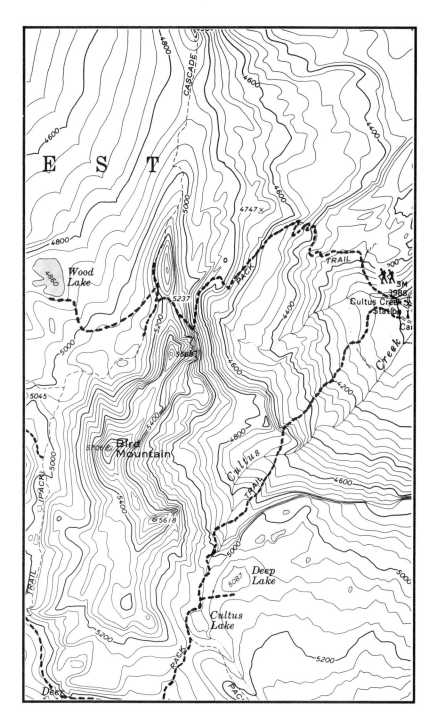

Wood Lake   277

𝕩𝕩 𝕩𝕩 𝕩𝕩

The hike to Wood Lake involves three trails in the Indian Heaven Wilderness. From the Cultus Creek Campground, the Cultus Trail ascends the east side of 5706 foot Bird Mountain, crossing at a saddle amid outstanding vistas. After a brief stint on the Pacific Crest Trail, the Wood Lake Trail follows a series of meadows to the lake.

From the trailhead, the path chugs steeply uphill through a forest stand recuperating from harvest. I spotted a small flock of golden-crowned kinglets near the trailhead, working their way through the shrubbery. Their distinct yellow heads, black eyebrows and black wings with white wing bars, along with their high pitched tweets, are unmistakable.

I also noticed some coyote scat composed of solid huckleberry, a fruit closely related to blueberry and for which the Indian Heaven is famous. One wonders how much nutrition coyotes get from the fruit, as it seems to pass through them undigested.

(Note: Coyote droppings are smaller than bear droppings and larger than squirrel droppings.)

The forest here consists of Pacific silver fir, mountain hemlock, Western white pine and a few very large Douglas-firs. Beargrass, and the ever present huckleberry, inhabit the understory. In open areas, look for corn lily and various daisy-esque members of the Sunflower family, including yarrow. There are also small stands of alder and elderberry. Kinnikinnick forms dense mats in open, upper elevation sites.

Approaching a large boulder outcrop, the trail parallels the slope through an expanse of purple lupine, intermixed with some bright orange paintbrush flowers, probably bristly paintbrush. Lupine belongs to the Pea family while paintbrush is a member of the Snapdragon family. They make an impressive combination.

This strenuous hike continues along the basalt rock outcrop, then steepens even more as it approaches the saddle. The 5200 foot saddle, 11/2 miles from and 1200 feet above the trailhead, marks the top of a north-south ridge on Bird Mountain, second highest in the Indian Heaven Wilderness at 5706 feet. Bird Mountain crests a mile south of the saddle.

The view from the saddle well justifies the effort. Mount Adams can be seen in the distance, along with Mount Rainier and much of the Indian Heaven Wilderness. At the saddle, a short way trail leads north to a rock outcrop with an even better view.

Hikers should bring plenty of water since unlike other trails in the area, this one is very demanding and lacks water. Judging from the corn lily in the small meadows, however, there must be plenty of moisture around.

Beyond the saddle, the trail drops through the woods to intersect the Pacific Crest Trail. Jog north on the PCT a brief distance for the Wood Lake Trail. The 3/4 mile path descends 300 feet as it wanders through a variety of meadows and past a couple small ponds. The eight acre lake appears green in color and quite deep. While not on the list of stocked lakes for the Indian Heaven Wilderness, there is a naturally reproducing cutthroat trout population.

I'd like to think the lake was named because as you look at the water, the surrounding trees seem to fill it with their reflection. More likely, it was named for a Mister (or Mrs.) Wood.

62.

Placid/Chenamus Lakes

(Indian Heaven Wilderness Area)

Length:	2 miles
Difficulty:	Easy
Elevation:	4100 to 4245 feet
Season:	June through November
Water:	At lakes
USGS 7.5" topo:	Lone Butte
Location:	T7N-R8E-Sec. 34
Ownership:	Gifford Pinchot NF
Phone:	(509) 395-2501
Camping:	Upper Wind River Campground
Use intensity:	Moderate

Directions: *From Portland, take I-84 to the Bridge of the Gods (75¢ toll), cross the Columbia River, and turn right on Highway 14. Head east to the paved Wind River Road and follow it beyond where it turns right and becomes road 30. Continue straight on 30 where the Mount Saint Helens signs route you left. Proceed to road 420, which is dirt and a little rough, and follow it a mile to the well marked trailhead. There is room for 24 cars in the gravel parking lot across from the trailhead.*

🚶🚶🚶🚶🚶

Placid Lake, measuring about 19 acres, is the largest in the 20,000 acre Indian Heaven Wilderness, that contains 148 lakes in addition to the two (Placid and Chenamus) visited in this chapter. Lake Placid, New York, lies 3200 miles east of Placid Lake.

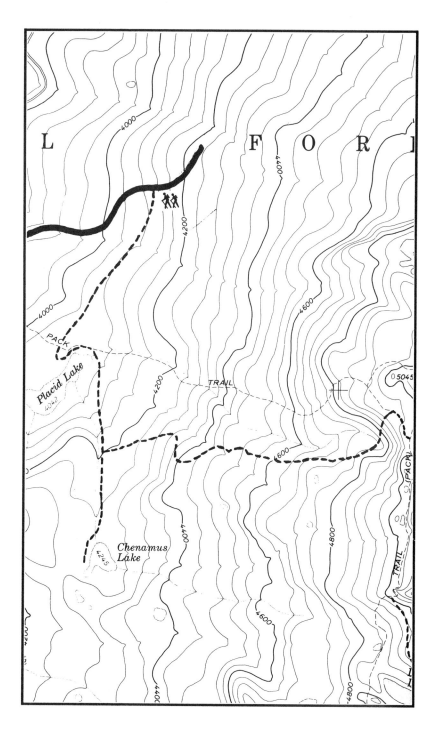

Placid/Chenamus Lakes

The Placid Lake Trail begins in a placid stand of mature Pacific silver fir, mountain hemlock and Western white pine, with beargrass and huckleberry dominating the understory. Initially, the path is quite wide, suggesting that it might be an old jeep road. It narrows at the Wilderness boundary.

After a nearly level, densely forested 3/4 mile, which actually drops a few feet, the trail passes the wooded north shore of Placid Lake. Several side trails lead around the oval pool, which reaches a maximum depth of 15 feet and is stocked with cutthroat trout.

Beyond Placid Lake, the trail begins a gentle climb through dense forest stands. From the look of the tread, it appears that most visitors do not venture beyond Placid Lake.

Soon after leaving the lake, I encountered a bright golden-orange club fungus pushing up from beneath the decaying forest debris. I'm told these conifer loving fungi are sweet and delicious, if picked at the proper time and lightly sauteed. Never eat any mushroom, however, unless you've identified it to an absolute certainty. A permit is required to remove mushrooms from Wilderness Areas.

Also to be found along the trail are small pools of water, stained brown from fallen leaves. I noted a log in one, with several frogs sitting on it. When I approached, all but one dove into the black-tea pond.

After 11/4 miles, the path arrives at a junction where the Placid Lake Trail swings left (east), and the Chenamus Lake Trail continues south (right). If you remain on the Placid Lake Trail, you'll meet the Pacific Crest Trail after 21/2 miles and a rise of 800 feet. It's 11/2 miles south on the PCT to Deer Lake (Chapter 59) and the same distance north on the PCT to Wood Lake (Chapter 60). Wood and Deer Lakes lie five miles from the Placid Lake trailhead.

The less traveled Chenamus Lake Trail winds up at Chenamus Lake, 3/4 mile beyond the junction and two miles from the trailhead. Approaching the lake, the path opens into a meadow area, although the lake is lined with both trees and meadow. The shallow lake covers four acres and is stocked with cutthroat trout.

63.

Big Lava Bed/
Little Huckleberry Mt.

Length:	21/2 miles
Difficulty:	Difficult
Elevation:	3000 to 4781 feet
Season:	June through October
Location:	T5N-R9E-Sec. 20
Water:	A little
USGS 7.5" Topo:	Little Huckleberry Mountain
Ownership:	Gifford Pinchot NF
Phone:	(206) 395-2501
Camping:	Goose Lake
Use intensity:	Light

__Directions__: Take I-84 to Bridge of the Gods (75¢ toll). Across the bridge, follow Highway 14 east to County Road 7/Forest Road 86, just past Cook, Washington. Take this north to Willard. Through Willard, road 66 breaks off left. Continue on 66, which is paved then gravel, along the east edge of Big Lava Bed to the Little Huckleberry trailhead, just before South Prairie. The trailhead is well marked, with room for six cars.

🚶🚶 🚶🚶🚶

Big Lava Bed, covering 12,500 acres, ranks among the major landmarks of southwest Washington. If Mount Saint Helens and Mount Adams weren't nearby, it could be the major landmark.

Unfortunately, no trails penetrate Big Lava Bed's tortured jumble of jagged rock. For those not up to bushwhacking across this impenetrable, nine mile by five mile mass, a marvelous over-

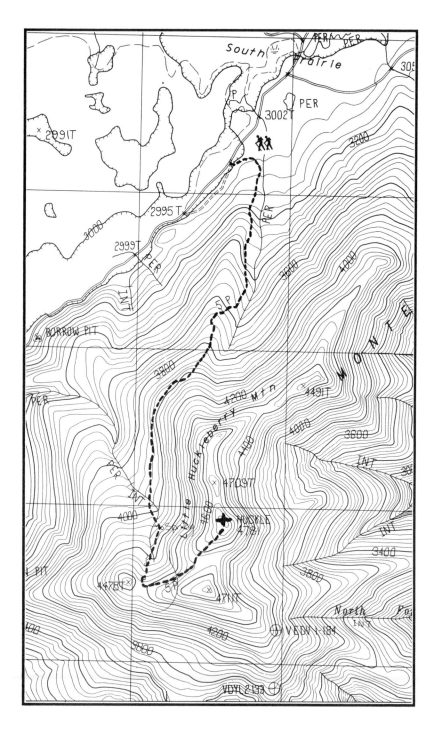

Little Huckleberry Mt.

view can be had from the summit of Little Huckleberry Mountain, rising 1800 feet above the lave field's eastern edge.

Before describing the trail to the top of Little Huckleberry, let me elaborate on Big Lava Bed. The giant flow of slow moving, blocky lava (known as "aa" lava), originally spewed from a prominent cinder cone in the center of the bed's north half. The cratered cone towers 800 feet above the lava bed and is clearly visible from Little Huckleberry Mountain.

Although Big Lava Bed is shown on USGS topo maps as forested, vegetation mostly consists mostly of small, scattered lodgepole pines, a tree which thrives under harsh conditions. There are pockets of Douglas-fir in moister sites.

For the truly adventurous, I'm told the cinder cone is quite a hike, over no less than two miles. There is neither trail nor water and the going is extremely difficult, crossing loose rock piles, crevasses, short caves, etc.

The cinder cone rises to an elevation of 4195 feet while the bulk of the lava field averages 3000 feet. The rim of the cone's cratered summit offers an outstanding panorama. A small meadow inside the crater bursts with wildflowers each spring.

Outside the lava beds, across the road, the Little Huckleberry Trail offers much easier going and even better vistas, although it too has its exhausting moments. From the trailhead, the path makes its way up a ridge densely forested with Douglas-fir and hemlock, gaining a whopping 1000 feet in its first mile.

This initial mile follows a small creek canyon up a ridge facing away from the lava fields. While it is a pretty little creek, the trail runs well up the hillside and catches only glimpses of it.

After a mile, the path levels for 3/4 mile, contouring around a slope directly above the lava beds. While there are no great vistas here, occasional views do pop up.

Toward the end of mile two, the path steepens for a short distance, passing several springs as it climbs a narrow draw. The springs once provided water for the lookout, a half-mile away.

You know you're on the final leg when the trail hits a wooded saddle, then makes a sharp switchback left. Soon after, it breaks into the open and begins its final push up the rocky slopes to the summit. The open area is a sea of huckleberry brush. There is also abundant huckleberry back in the woods.

Southwest Washington, of course, is famous for its huckleberries. At least 10 species of this miniature blueberry are found in the region. While the huckleberries on Little Huckleberry Mountain are indeed little, they're no smaller than huckleberries elsewhere, including those on Big Huckleberry Mountain.

Big Huckleberry, little Huckleberry's sister peak, lies five miles to the southwest, on the other side of the lava beds. Oddly enough, it is 500 feet lower than Little Huckleberry. The forested peak is easily visible from the Little Huckleberry summit.

That's not all there is to see from Little Huckleberry's rocky crest, which was blasted level years ago to accommodate a now dismantled lookout. In addition to Big Lava Bed and Big Huckleberry Mountain, look for South Prairie, Goose Lake and the ever present trio of Mounts Adams, Rainier and Saint Helens, plus endless forested valleys receding to the horizon.

64.

Takhlakh Lake

Length: 2 mile loop
Difficulty: Easy
Elevation: 4400 to 4700 feet
Season: June through October
Water: At lake
Location: T9N-R10E-Sec. 8
USGS 7.5" topo: Green Mountain
Ownership: Gifford Pinchot NF
Phone: (509) 395-2501
Camping: Takhlakh Lake CG
Use intensity: Moderate

Directions: *From Portland, take I-5 north to Highway 503 at Woodland. Proceed east on 503, which becomes Forest Road 90. Both roads are paved and follow the Lewis River. Past Twin Falls Campground, take a left onto road 23, which is gravel, then a right onto road 2329, which is also gravel.*

Proceed past the Takhlakh Lake turnoff to the Takh Takh Meadow Loop Trail. The signed (minimally) trailhead is at the loop trail's second crossing of road 2329. The first crossing is unsigned. There is parking on the shoulder for six cars at the second crossing.

🚶🚶 🚶🚶 🚶🚶

This easy and exquisite path explores Takh Takh Meadow, Takhlakh Lake and a large lava flow, all within view of Mount Adams, Washington's second highest mountain at 12,326 feet. While this short, double loop wanders precariously close to road 2329, crossing it twice, it boasts abundant vistas and some unusual wildlife. Takhlakh Lake is not visible from road 2329.

Paddling in the Takhlakh Lake.

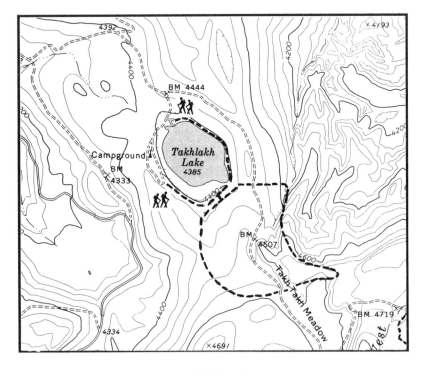

Takhlakh Lake

I began at the marked trailhead in Takh Takh Meadow, the route's second crossing of road 2329. The loop can also be accessed from either end of the campground at Takhlakh Lake or from an unmarked trailhead a half-mile back down road 2329, towards the lake.

Actually, there are two loop trails, one around Takhlakh Lake and one ringing the meadow. They form a figure eight, with the loops meeting at the lake's southeast shore. I proceeded clockwise from the trailhead, hitting the lake, circling it, crossing the road a second time, then visiting the meadow and lava flow before returning to my starting point.

From the trailhead, I headed downhill through a forest of Pacific silver fir, Douglas-fir and mountain hemlock. Despite many openings and vistas, the trail pretty much remains in the woods, even near the meadow and lava flow.

The path soon hit the junction at the center of the figure eight, where the meadow loop meets the lake loop. To visit the lake, follow the lake loop in either direction. For a great view of Mount Adams framed by the lake, make your way left on the lake loop, around to the south shore.

Takhlakh Lake occupies what looks like a large volcanic crater, as suggested by its circular shape and steep bluffs ringing the water. It covers 35 1/2 acres and is stocked with Eastern brook and cutthroat trout.

After completing the lake loop, I continued clockwise on the meadow loop, crossing the road and heading uphill towards the lava flow. During my encirclement of Talk Takh Meadow, I ran across what I believe was a sharp-shinned hawk; based on its size, somewhat rounded tail, and the fact that it was flying through a dense forest.

I also encountered a marten (sable). Martens belong to the same family as weasels and skunks. The large brown mammals are about 16 inches long, not including the tail. The one I saw was on the ground when I approached, but quickly scurried up a tree. While it climbed very well, it made much more noise than a squirrel would. It stopped on a small branch 15 feet up and watched as I passed by.

Martens inhabit coniferous forests but are rarely seen. Not being hibernators, they spend the majority of their summers in the trees and their winters foraging on the ground.

North of the meadow, the trail climbs sharply to the base of a remarkably abrupt lava flow. Talk about rock piles! It appears as though a gargantuan bulldozer has formed the massive heap of basalt boulders into a giant wall.

The meadow trail splits at one point, with one leg climbing the boulder wall and the other making its way along the bottom. They rejoin back at the edge of the meadow. Several paths among the boulders offer an opportunity to explore, climb and enjoy vistas of Mount Adams. After that, it is back downhill across the meadow to your car.

65.

Divide Camp Trail

(Mount Adams Wilderness Area)

Length:	2 3/4 miles
Difficulty:	Moderate
Elevation:	4700 to 6000 feet
Season:	July through October
Water:	Much
USGS 7.5" topo:	Green Mountain, Mount Adams West
Location:	T9N-R10E-Sec. 16
Ownership:	Gifford Pinchot NF
Phone:	(509) 395-2501
Camping:	Takhlakh Lake
Use intensity:	Moderately heavy

**Directions**: From Portland, take I-5 north to Highway 503 at Woodland. Proceed east on 503, which becomes Forest Road 90. Both roads are paved and follow the Lewis River. Where 90 ends, take a left onto road 23, which is mostly gravel, then a right onto road 2329, which is also gravel. Watch for road construction.

Proceed past Takhlakh Lake (Chapter 64), to the well marked Divide Camp turnoff. A short side road leads to the trailhead, which has parking for eight cars. It also has a couple campsites and turnaround room.

🚶🚶 🚶🚶 🚶🚶

The highlight of this moderate outing along the Divide Camp Trail is a spectacular alpine meadow on the upper flank of Mount Adams, Washington's second highest peak at 12,326 feet. The meadow offers closeup views of the massive Adams Glacier while

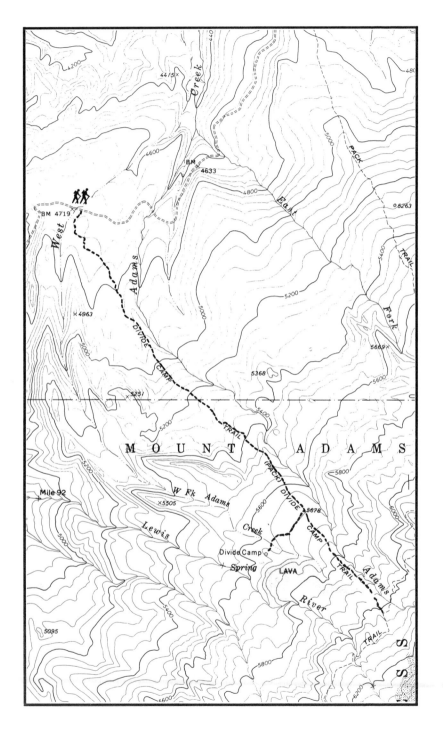

a short side hike into Divide Camp visits a spring marking the headwaters of the Lewis River.

The trail is named for the ridge separating Adams Creek from the Lewis River system. Slopes east of the trail contribute to Adams Creek while those to the west flow into the Lewis.

From the trailhead, the route climbs gradually through conifer stands intermingled with beargrass, huckleberry and lupine. Conifers include Pacific silver fir, noble fir, mountain hemlock and lodgepole pine. In autumn, many of the deciduous shrubs, particularly vine maple, turn a deep red and yellow, adding color to the browns and greens of the forest. Every now and then, Mount Adams pokes its head out as the path works its way up the ridge via a series of level benches and short switchbacks.

For the trail's initial 1 1/2 miles, several spurs lead down to Adams Creek, which is pretty enough in its own right to justify the hike.

At mile two, I was joined by a couple gray jays who decided to hike along with me. Gray jays share habitat in parts of their range with Clark's nutcrackers, to whom they are related and for whom they are often mistaken. Jays are smaller and have a more rounded head. Their coloration makes them appear as large chickadees. Chickadees are best described as looking like small gray jays.

I also encountered a horse packer upgrading signs for the Forest Service. There has been a much debate over sign policy in Wilderness Areas. Purists contend that signs, as indicators of human intrusion, are inappropriate. Some would also do away with designated campsites, bridges, trails and all regulation. Due to heavy use, however, many areas within designated Wildernesses are only semi-wild. Concessions must be made if people are to be allowed in. It is Forest Service policy not to post distances on Wilderness trail signs.

Two miles up the trail, at elevation 5678 feet, a half-mile side spur cuts west and slightly downhill, leading to Divide Camp and a spring which is the headwaters of the Lewis River. The spring emerges from the snout of a lava flow.

Beyond the Divide Camp junction, the main trail continues for a final half-mile. It steepens at first, then levels off as it enters a high alpine meadow with the north side of Mount Adams clearly in view. From here, it is less than a mile to the Adams Glacier, a system of ice flows on the peak's northwest flank. The glacier begins in an eroded summit crater, tumbles steeply down the mountain in a massive series of ice falls, then levels off as it approaches the meadow.

Note the snow depth gauge in the center of the meadow. From the hash marks on the pole, it appears that snow depths of 15 and 20 feet are common.

The Divide Camp Trail ends in the meadow, at the junction with the Pacific Crest Trail. By heading north (left), through the meadow along the PCT, you get a look at the Lava Glacier, one glacier north of the Adams Glacier. A hike south (right), on the PCT, leads to a huge lava flow after 3/4 mile.

Divide Trail. Adams Glacier. Mount Adams.

66

Stagman Ridge

(Mount Adams Wilderness Area)

Length:	2 to 4 1/2 miles
Difficulty:	Moderate
Elevation:	4200 to 5700 feet
Season:	July through October
Water:	None
Location:	T8N-R10E-Sec. 31
USGS 7.5" topo:	Mount Adams West
Ownership:	Gifford Pinchot NF
Phone:	(509) 395-2501
Camping:	Trout Lake
Use intensity:	Moderate

Directions*: From Portland, head east on I-84 to Hood River, cross the Columbia into Washington and turn right (east) on Highway 14. From 14, follow Highway 141 up the White Salmon River to Trout Lake. Turn right on County Road 17, which becomes Forest Road 23, which is paved. Continue to gravel road 8031, on the right. Proceed to road 070 after a quarter-mile, and follow it to road 120.*

Roads to the trailhead are either blacktop or gravel and easily driven in a normal automobile. The route is well signed from road 23. The trailhead is located in a former logging landing. Although the parking area is a little rough, it holds a dozen cars.

粆粆粆粆粆

    The Stagman Ridge Trail begins in an inauspicious logging landing, climbs through dense old growth and ends in a high

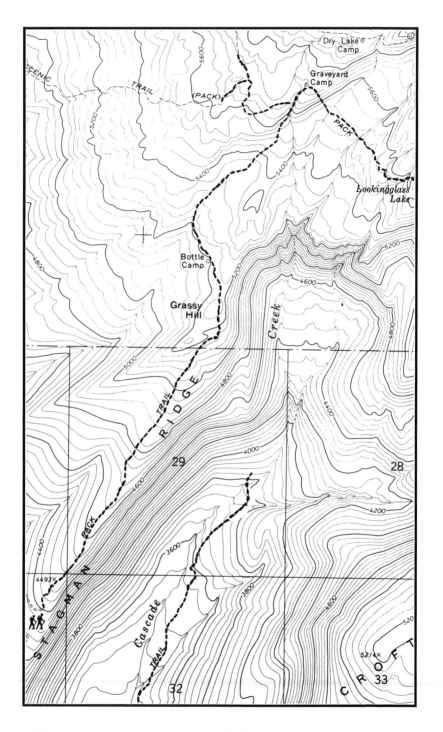

Stagman Ridge

meadow on the side of Mount Adams, Washington's number two peak after Mount Rainier. At 12,326 feet, Mount Adams beats Mount Hood, Oregon's highest summit, by 1100 feet.

The path begins as a remnant logging road through a former clearcut which has regenerated into a dense stand of small conifers. Dominant species include Douglas-fir, Pacific silver fir and Western white pine, with an understory of thimbleberry and huckleberry.

The route becomes a true trail at the Wilderness boundary, a half-mile from the trailhead. The forest changes dramatically here, into a beautiful old growth stand. Entering this light starved universe, the temperature drops, the air smells moist and the understory evolves to much more shade tolerant species such as trillium and Western prince's pine.

For the next two miles, the path winds through the forest in a moderate but continuous climb along a wide ridgetop. Fairly steep at first, the grade levels off for a mile, then picks up again as Grassy Hill is approached. Were it not for the trees, hikers would be treated to views of the Cascade Creek basin, with its beaver ponds, paralleling a half-mile downhill (Chapter 67).

The only birds I observed were sparrows, juncos and gray jays. The latter, often called "camp robbers," are very intelligent and curious. They often hang out near clearings adjacent to conifer forests and sometimes accompany hikers for a considerable distance, sailing from tree to tree. They are not above stealing your lunch right out of your hand. Particular favorites of theirs are granola, apple slices and cookies.

I noted much evidence of deer browsing, especially in the brushier areas. Look for branches stripped on the bottom only, since deer have no upper incisors.

Farther up the trail, a grouse suddenly flushed from the understory. These birds love to wait until you're three feet away, then blast out of hiding. The closest I've ever come to a heart attack resulted from being startled by grouse.

Towards the trail's upper end, the grade steepens and the forest changes, with trees no longer attaining the great size they did earlier. Lodgepole pine, noble fir and mountain hemlock begin to creep into the picture. The understory here is predominantly beargrass, a member of the Lily family which blooms early in the year with a gorgeous, club-shaped spike of white flowers.

Periodic breaks in the forest canopy, in these upper reaches, reveal glimpses of Mount Adams. Also visible is the White Salmon Glacier, laying above the Avalanche Glacier on the Adams's southwest flank. Huge rock walls surround the upper edges of the glaciers.

Approaching the 5000 foot level, the diversity of wildflowers increases. Look for several members of the Sunflower family, all either daisies or daisy-like. Many are still in bloom in mid-October. Lupine is also a late bloomer.

The effect of slope direction on species composition is evident on this ridgetop route. South facing slopes, which receive more sunshine than north slopes in the Northern Hemisphere, are dusty and hot. North slopes tend to be cooler and more moist. Thus, the south facing ridge above Cascade Creek has many grass and brush openings and a high percentage of pines. The north slope contains larger trees, with more silver and noble fir.

After two miles, the trail arrives at a beautiful mountaintop meadow known as Grassy Hill. From there, Mount Adams and the White Salmon Glacier can be seen in their full splendor. Beyond the meadow, the trail continues in a northeast direction, levelling off for a mile before embarking on a short, strenuous ascent to the 5700 foot level. The path ends at a junction near Graveyard Camp. A quarter-mile spur left leads to the Pacific Crest Trail, 31/2 miles from the trailhead.

If you head south on the PCT for a mile, you'll end up at Lookinglass Lake. This one acre gem of a lake is amazingly productive for its size, with a naturally reproducing population of cutthroat trout.

67.

Salt Creek

(Mount Adams Wilderness Area)

Length:	3 miles
Difficulty:	Easy
Elevation:	3300 to 3750 feet
Season:	June through November
Water:	Yes
USGA 7.5" topo:	Mount Adams West, Trout Lake
Location:	T8N-R10E-Sec. 6
Ownership:	Gifford Pinchot NF
Phone:	(509) 395-2501
Camping:	Trout Lake
Use intensity:	Light

__Directions__: From Portland, head east on I-84 to Hood River, cross the Columbia River into Washington and turn right (east) on Highway 14. Leave 14 at Highway 141 and proceed up the White Salmon River to Trout Lake. There, turn right on County Road 17, which becomes Forest Road 23. Both are paved. Continue to gravel road 8031, coming in on the right. Proceed to road 060 (left), which leads to the trail-head. Although road 060 is rough, it can be driven in a regular car. Otherwise, park and walk a mile to the road-end trailhead, which accomodates five cars.

🚶🚶🚶

    While this route into Mount Adams Wilderness Area lacks vistas of the mountain, the quiet, little used path offers one of the better wilderness experiences. Aside from woods and meadows, it visits numerous beaver ponds and is among the few areas within the scope of this book where Western larch is encountered.

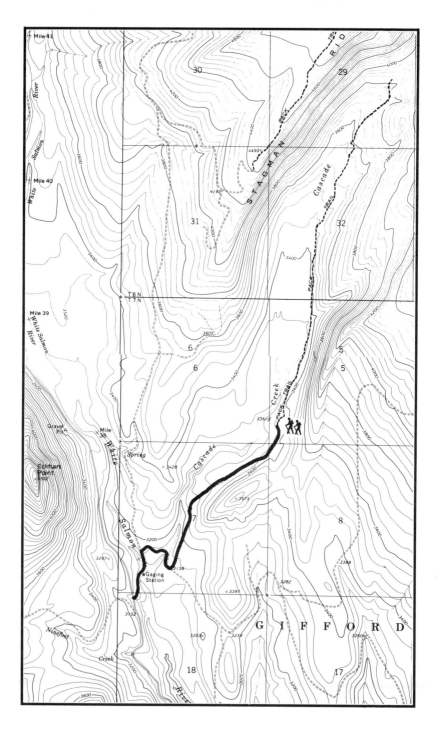

Salt Creek

Traveling north from the trailhead on the sometimes faint path, through the forests adjacent to Cascade Creek, the route quickly crosses the Wilderness boundary. The open, airy forest is a mix of conifer and deciduous trees. Pacific silver fir, Douglas-fir, Western white pine and Western larch intermingle with much red alder and black cottonwood.

Western Larch, unlike other cone-bearing trees, loses its needles each autumn in a spectacular color display, heightened by the yellow of the cottonwoods. Larch is much more common in the mountains of eastern Oregon and Washington, and the northern Washington Cascades, than in the Oregon or southern Washington Cascades.

Cottonwood, a main riverbank species in low elevation areas, is somewhat unusual at these altitudes.

On the forest floor, look for abundant dwarf Oregongrape, along with several Wintergreen family members, including Western princess pine, white-veined wintergreen and bog wintergreen. This is also a popular mushroom gathering area.

A mile from the trailhead, vast ponds begin to inundate the stands of cottonwood and alder. These backwaters are created by *Castor canadensis*, the Oregon beaver. The size of the ponds indicates a considerable beaver population.

Looking around, you can see where water has flooded into the willows, a favorite beaver delicacy. Evidence of chewing is apparent. Willow bark is a natural source of salicylate, the main ingredient of aspirin. Salicylate, in fact, is named for Salix, willow's scientific name.

Beavers get very few headaches!

Beyond the beaver ponds, which extend for quite a ways, the trail begins to climb more steeply through a forest which now also includes Alaska cedar. The path crosses some small side drainages in the upper portions of Cascade Creek.

The route continues to gain elevation as it proceeds towards the confluence of Salt Creek and the now aptly named Cascade Creek. As you walk the upper portion of the trail, cascading creeks fill the air with the sound of rushing water, a distinct contrast from the quiet calm of the beaver ponds. The path fades out just past the Salt Creek confluence.

Writing up this chapter, I stumbled across, in my files, a 1972 map of the Mount Adams Wilderness. On the back, a paragraph about Salt Creek noted that at certain times, the water was distinctly briny. There was a photo of a salt encrusted tree seedling.

I noticed nothing of this nature on my visit. Nor could the Mount Adams Ranger District locate anyone familiar with this phenomenon.

68.

Blue Lake

Length:	3 miles
Difficulty:	Moderate
Elevation:	1994 to 4058
Water:	At the lake
Season:	July through October
Location:	T11N-R9E-Sec. 30
USGS 7.5" Topo:	Blue Lake
Ownership:	Gifford Pinchot NF
Phone:	(509) 395-2501
Camping:	Blue Lake Creek CG
Use intensity:	Moderate to heavy

__Directions__: Take I-5 to US-12, the Cowlitz River Road, and head east. At Randle, turn south on road 23 and continue a half-mile past the Blue Lake Creek Campground to the well marked trailhead. There is a highly developed parking area both adjacent to road 23 and up a short access road. The one adjacent to road 23 is huge. The one up the access road holds ten cars.

🚶🚶🚶

This locally popular trail is not for everyone due to active logging and all-terrain vehicle use. Nevertheless, it is challenging, pleasant and educational. Blue Lake, one of the largest natural lakes in the Gifford Pinchot National Forest.

Signs near the trailhead indicate some of the problems which lie ahead. As of fall, 1993, the trail is closed from 5 AM to 5 PM weekdays, due to logging operations.

The path itself has a wide tread to accommodate all terrain vehicles. While you may not encounter such traffic, track marks

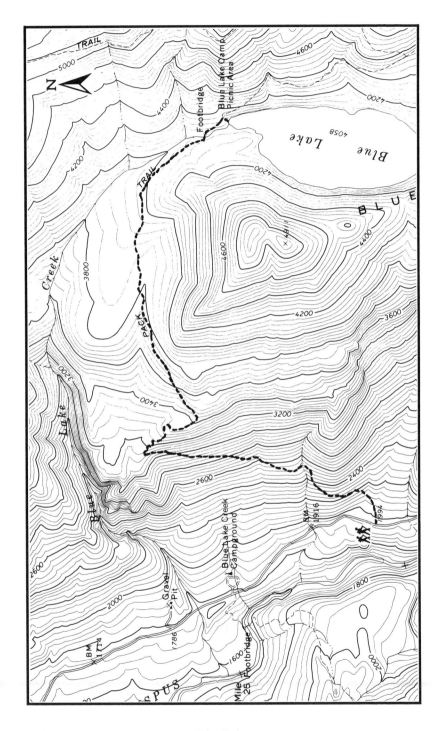

make their presence all too obvious. At present, ATV use is feasible only on lower trail areas. They are considering widening the tread all the way to the lake, however.

From the trailhead, the path sidehills steeply upward, through clearcuts and across logging roads, with old growth remnants in between. The active timber harvest, a mile from the trailhead, is a select cut operation. The largest trees have been removed and the smaller ones thinned out, leaving a healthy replacement stand. The practice of timber fallers carving their names on the largest stumps may be a turn-off to some hikers.

This harvest unit is a prime example of why old growth does not always offer the best timber. The largest trees here are clearly overmature, as evidenced by conk fungi and heart rot in the felled and decked logs. Many trees shattered when they hit the ground and most in the decks are hollow. From a silvicultural perspective, the stand clearly needed thinning. The younger, more vigorous trees are now free to grow.

Beyond the logging show, the trail makes a large switchback, then some smaller ones, as it enters the dense canopy of a spectacular stand of old growth Douglas-fir, red alder and bigleaf maple. The understory is lush and diverse. I noted some beautiful orange tiger lilies and even a couple lady slippers. The latter is an extremely shy and delicate member of the Orchid family.

The path levels somewhat over the last two miles to the lake, with dynamic vistas of the valley below. The forest is a prime habitat for gray jays, juncos and thrushes.

Shortly after crossing the footbridge over Blue Lake Creek, the immense and often busy lake appears. It covers 128 acres and is stocked with rainbow and Eastern brook trout. Like several other Blue Lakes in the region (Chapter 58), the water is particularly blue.

Beyond the lake, the trail continues for nine more miles along Blue Lake Ridge and past Mouse Lake, to road 21.

69

Berry Patch/Goat Ridge Trail

(Goat Rock Wilderness)

Length:	5 mile loop
Difficulty:	Difficult
Elevation:	4600 to 6200 feet
Season:	June through October
Location:	T11N-R10E-Sec. 1
Water:	None
USGS 7.5" Topo:	Hamilton Buttes
Ownership:	Gifford Pinchot NF
Phone:	(206) 494-5515
Camping:	Chambers Lake Campgroud
Use intensity:	Light

Directions: *Take I-5 to Exit 60 and follow US-12, the Cowlitz River Road, east past Randle. Turn south on road 21, following signs to Chambers Lake. For Chambers Lake and the Berry Patch and Snowgrass Flat (Chapter 70) trailheads, turn left onto road 2150, then onto road 040, both gravel. The well marked Berry Patch trailhead comes shortly after the Snowgrass trailhead. There is parking for ten cars in a clearing alongside the road.*

𝕩𝕩𝕩𝕩𝕩

For a breathtaking overview of the spectacular and sprawling Goat Rocks Wilderness, between Mount Adams and Mount Rainier, the Berry Patch Loop Trail, encircling the 6240 foot summit of Goat Ridge, is ideal. Don't be fooled by its short length and the fact that it does not penetrate very far into the Wilderness. The trail rises an exhausting 1400 feet in two miles, transitioning from jungle to a barren mountaintop aerie with a commanding panorama.

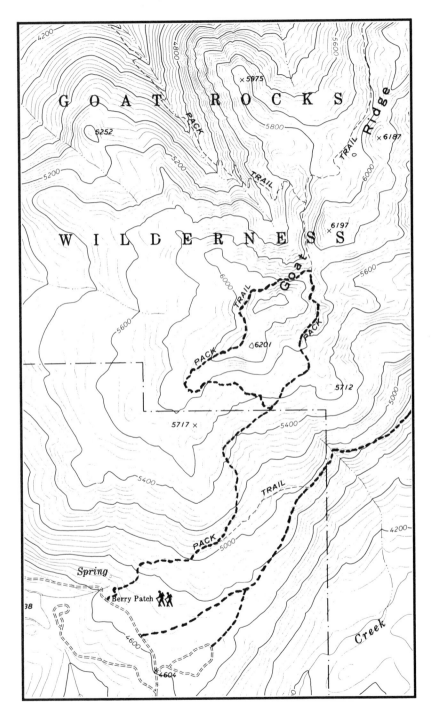

Berry Patch/Goat Ridge Trail   307

Both the Barry Patch Trail, and the adjacent Snowgrass Flat Trail, lie somewhat outside this book's 100 mile radius. Since it would be criminal to omit the Goat Rocks from a list of the region's scenic wonders, both trails were included.

Before describing the trail, I should clear up a few things. First, Goat Ridge is not the same as the Goat Rocks, for which the Wilderness is named. The Goat Rocks lie five miles away, on the other side of, you guessed it, Goat Creek, which flows out of... Goat Lake. It seems every time the area's namers spotted a mountain goat, they named the landmark for it.

Also, this is not the same peak as Goat Mountain, near Mount Saint Helens, described in Chapter 49. It messed my computer up terribly when I inadvertently attempted to name both the Saint Helens file and this one, "GOAT."

From the trailhead, the path immediately crosses the Wilderness boundary. Forests are lush and well developed, consisting mostly of Pacific Silver fir and Mountain hemlock. It's 11/2 miles through the woods, with a 1000 foot rise, to the junction with the one mile Goat Ridge Loop Trail. Turn left for Goat Ridge or continue straight for the loop's far end, the Jordan Basin and Goat Lake (six miles from the trailhead). It doesn't matter which way you hike the loop.

Decaying woody debris in these old growth stands is fascinating. Often, all that remains of a decomposing log is a raised berm. The coarse material therein plays an important role in the survival of many insect and animal species. Because of its spongy composition, it holds much more water than the rest of the forest floor. The amount of nitrogen released into the ecosystem by a decomposing tree can be as much as four times the amount contained within the tree itself.

The population of varied thrushes along the trail is impressive. Look for these robin-like birds moving around in the trees and shrubs. You can recognize them by their orange breasts and black eye lines.

I also spotted one of the region's most spectacular song birds, the hermit thrush. Although this fellow does not sing often, its flute-like melody is not easily forgotten. Hermit thrushes migrate long distances, some from as far away as Mexico. Look also for chickadees and juncos in the canopy.

Climbing steeply, the Goat Ridge Loop leaves the forest cover and doubles back west, hitting the ridgetop. It follows along the open, vista rich, rocky crest, passing a short side trail to the old lookout site which is the route's culmination.

The 6200 foot elevation lookout site offers views of Mount Rainier, Mount Adams and the sheer, glaciated, 1800 foot wall of the Goat Rocks. And yes, it is sensational and worth the long drive and steep hike.

But no, the lookout site is not the highest point on Goat Ridge. That lies a little to the northeast. Give it a shot, if you like, although it is quite rocky and forbidding. Beyond the main summit, the path drops back down to the Berry Patch Trail, a mile from where it left it.

Stagman Ridge. White Salmon Glacier. Mt. Adams.

70.

Snowgrass Flat

(Goat Rock Wilderness)

Length:	21/2 to 4 miles
Difficulty:	Moderate
Elevation:	4700 to 5800 feet
Season:	June through October
Location:	T11N-R10E-Sec. 1
Water:	None
USGS 7.5" Topo:	Hamilton Buttes, Walupt Lake, Old Snowy Mountain
Ownership:	Bronson Pinchot NF
Phone:	(206) 494-5515
Camping:	Chambers Lake Campground
Use intensity:	Moderate

__Directions__: Take I-5 to Exit 60 and follow US-12, the Cowlitz River Road, east past Randle. Turn south on road 21, following signs to Chambers Lake. For Chambers Lake and the Berry Patch (Chapter 69) and Snowgrass Flat trailheads, turn onto road 2150, then road 040, both gravel. There is parking for ten cars at the well-marked hiker's trailhead. A short loop road, just before the hiker's trailhead, leads to the horse trailhead. Paths from the two trailheads connect after a quarter-mile.

🚶🚶🚶

Although the Goat Rock Wilderness lies somewhat outside this book's 100 mile radius, spectacular vistas of Mount Adams and Mount Rainier, plus outstanding high mountain scenery in its own right, places it among our region's scenic blockbusters. At 106,000 acres, the sprawling Wilderness reaches a height of

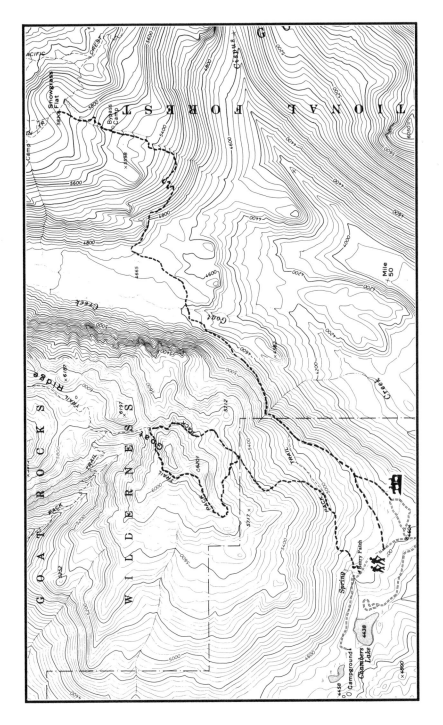

Snowgrass Flat   311

8200 feet at Gilbert Peak, not far from the Snowgrass Flat Trail's upper terminus.

Despite the rugged topography, the route offers an easy hike, for the first 21/2 miles at least, through lush forest and later, floral alpine meadows. The Berry Patch Trail, from a trailhead a quarter-mile down the road, offers a shorter, more challenging trek to the 6200 foot summit of Goat Ridge.

Just past the Snowgrass Flat trailhead, the path enters the Goat Rock Wilderness. The gradual altitude gain make this an easy hike, with frequent spectacular vistas. The denseness of the forest is amazing, especially in contrast to the intensive logging on the trailhead drive. A mile into the hike, the path crosses a small creek via a wooden footbridge.

As one walks the pathway, the sounds of ravens and flickers fill the air. Along the trail's edge grows an abundance of wildflowers. In the clearings, look for thistle, vetch and Indian paintbrush. Moister areas are home to the showy corn lily. Several berry species inhabit the moist draw areas, including gooseberry, thimbleberry and huckleberry, each of which belongs to a different family (Currant, Rose and Heath).

In the shaded understory, you'll find two members of the Wintergreen family; Western princess pine and pinedrops up to three feet high. Pinedrop is a saprophyte (lacking green chlorophyll), which lives at the base of Douglas-fir trees in dry, mature conifer forests of the Pacific Northwest.

Note the severely and uniformly curved bases of the trees in some stands. Referred to as "pistol butt," this indicates soil instability. As soil creeps slowly down the slope, trees are gradually pushed over, constantly straightening themselves to develop this characteristic curve. The condition impedes vertical growth and degrades the log's market value. To loggers, pistol butt trees are highly undesirable (except, I suppose, for making skis or sled runners).

A mile into the hike, one begins to understand why this is called the Goat Rock Wilderness. Outstanding high altitude outcroppings of rim rock, visible through thin spots and breaks in the forest, surround the area. To the east lies the main Goat Rocks ridge, with its sheer, 1800 foot wall, craggy summits and miniglaciers. Mount Rainier, high point of both Washington and the Pacific Northwest at 14,470 feet, decorates the northeast horizon.

As one walks, the habitat evolves from old growth with large diameter trees to open meadows, with an ever changing mosaic of plants and animals. After two miles, a bridge crosses Goat Creek, one of the principal streams in the Wilderness. The creek boasts several small, cascading waterfalls and many clear, swimmable pools. Goat Creek runs along the western edge of a level, half-mile wide valley of forest, marsh and meadow.

As noted, the trail's first 21/2 miles climb only minimally. A half-mile beyond Goat Creek, the gradient takes off like a jetliner, climbing 600 feet in a mile before even thinking of levelling off. The path inscribes a series of long switchbacks, then follows a rushing creek uphill through the woods to Bypass Camp and Snowgrass Flat.

At Snowgrass Flat, 41/2 miles from the trailhead at an elevation of 5800 feet, the path breaks out onto a large meadow, then hits a junction. Go right a steep half-mile for the Pacific Crest Trail.

If you follow the PCT north a mile or so, you'll skirt the top of the Packwood Glacier. Head south three miles on the PCT, to Cispus Pass, and you'll be in the very heart of the Goat Rocks high country, not far from the towering and tortured crags of Gilbert Peak, height of the Wilderness at 8184 feet. Gilbert Peak is heavily glaciated on the eastern side and nearly vertical on the west.

As I hiked out, I heard the call of a golden eagle. By moving off the trail into a nearby clearing, I was able to watch the bird as it circled above me, until it slowly disappeared from view.

Hiker rests at Cooper Spur Trail. View of Mt. Hood.

Snowgrass Flat

Index of trails, locations and places:

Other Titles from Mountain N' Air Books

ADVENTURE GUIDES

Cross Country NORTHEAST
John R. Fitzgerald Jr.
ISBN: 1-879415-07-0 $12.00

Cross Country Skiing in Southern California
Eugene Mezereny
ISBN: 1-879415-08-9 $14.00

Great Rock Hits of Hueco Tanks
Paul Piana
ISBN: 1-879415-03-8 $6.95

Mountain Bike Adventures...Moab Utah
Bob Ward
ISBN: 1-879415-11-9 $15.00

The Rogue River Guide
Kevin Keith Tice
ISBN: 1-879415-12-7 $15.00

ADVENTURES, LITERATURE

High Endeavors
Pat Ament
ISBN: 1-879415-00-3 $12.95

A Night on the Ground, A Day in the Open
Doug Robinson
ISBN: 1-879415-14-3 $19.00

On Mountain and Mountaineers
Mikel Vause
ISBN: 1-879415-06-2 $12.95

Rock and Roses
Mikel Vaus, editor
ISBN: 1-879415-01-1 $11.95

The View from the Edge: Life and Landscapes of Beverly Johnson
Gabriela Zim
ISBN: 1-879415-16-X $17.00

COOKING
(Bearly Cooking)

Cooking with Strawberries
Margaret and Virginia Clark
ISBN: 1-879415-26-7 $10.95

HIKING AND HIKING GUIDES

Backpacking Primer
Lori Saldaña
ISBN: 1-879415-13-5 $12.00

Best Hikes of the Marble Mountain and Russian Wilderness Areas, California
Art Bernstein
ISBN: 1-879415-18-6 $16.00

Best Day Hikes of the California Northwest
Art Bernstein
ISBN: 1-879415-02-X $13.50

Best Hikes of Trinity Alps
Art Bernstein
ISBN: 1-879415-05-4 $17.00

Portland Hikes
Art Bernstein and Andrew Jackman
ISBN: 1-879415-22-4 $18.00

So... How does the Rope Get Up There, Anyway?
Kathy Myers and Mark Blanchard
ISBN: 1-879415-17-8 $10.00

RESTAURANT GUIDE

The Nose Knows
Lloyd McAteer Battista
ISBN: 1-879415-23-2 $13.00